THE MODERNISER'S DILEMMA
Radical Politics in the Age of Blair

Edited by
Anne Coddington and Mark Perryman

Lawrence & Wishart
LONDON
In association with Signs of the Times

Lawrence & Wishart Limited
99a Wallis Road
London E9 5LN

First published 1998

British Library Cataloguing in Publication data.
A catalogue record for this book is available from the
British Library.

ISBN 0 85315 874 6

Photoset in North Wales by
Derek Doyle & Associates, Mold, Flintshire.
Printed and bound in Great Britain by
Redwood Books Limited, Trowbridge.

Contents

Acknowledgements

The essays in this collection were mainly, though not exclusively, given as papers and talks to discussions organised by the London-based group *Signs of the Times* (for further details of publications and events see page viii). The seminars were held as two series, the first in Autumn 1996 on the theme 'The Blair Necessities: Seminars of Critique'; the second in Spring 1997 under the theme 'Great Expectations: Seminars of the New Governance'. In addition in March 1997 a residential weekend 'Agency for a Change' was held and in June 1997 a major post-election conference, 'Critical Masses: Popular Politics and New Labour'. The 'Critical Masses' conference was generously supported by the Barry Amiel and Norman Melburn Trust, while sponsorship was provided by the magazine the *New Statesman*, the journal *Soundings* and our publishers, *Lawrence & Wishart*.

The Moderniser's Dilemma as a book is very much part of a continuing programme of initiatives from *Signs of the Times*. Together, they seek to contribute to a generalised remaking of a public intellectual culture while seeking the specific recreation of an academy of dissent. In seeking to create an open, pleasurable, space of radical, dissenting dialogue we are grateful not only to those who have contributed chapters to this volume but also those who help to plan and organise our programme of activities. In particular, Stefan Howald, Francis James, Herbert Pimlott, Jonathan Rutherford and Paula Smith. We are indebted too to our designer, Jan Brown, for continuing to provide such a vivid visual image for the group's work.

Until Spring 1997 our seminars were held in the highly unusual surroundings of London's premier Swedish restaurant, *Anna's Place*, on Newington Green. The kindness of the then proprietor, Anna Hegarty, to allow us to use such a splendid venue for free was considerable and without her help the group would have certainly struggled in its early days. On her retirement we were extremely fortunate in finding a new and equally splendid venue for our seminars. *Signs of the Times* now meets in the East London photography gallery *Camerawork*. Scenes of Swedish scenery and assorted stuffed animals have been replaced by cutting edge art, computer screens and brightly-lit white walls. The encouragement and co-operation of our successive *Camerawork* hosts Sandi Weiland, Geoff Cox and Philip Sanderson is hugely appreciated.

This is the third *Signs of the Times* book to be published by Lawrence & Wishart. In these times where all and sundry are so desperate to locate a position 'beyond left and right' it is refreshing to find a publisher neither ashamed of its history nor unafraid of its future. Dedication and commitment might not make Lawrence & Wishart rich, but it doesn't make them wrong either. A pleasure to work with, they understand what it means to be independent and radical. For this authors have a lot to be grateful for.

Anne Coddington and Mark Perryman, September 1998.

Notes on Contributors

Geoff Andrews is Senior Lecturer in Politics at the University of Hertfordshire. An occasional contributor to magazines and journals ranging from *Renewal* to the *Times Higher Education Supplement,* he also co-edited the collection *Opening the Books: Essays on the Social and Cultural History of the British Communist Party.*

Nicola Baird in 1995 won the prestigious *Financial Times* David Thomas award for her essay on the ecological impact of development policies. Her book *The Estate We're in: Who's Driving Car Culture?* was published by Indigo in June 1998.

Timothy Bewes teaches English and Critical Theory at the University of North London, and Cultural Theory at Coventry University. He is the author of *Cynicism and Postmodernity,* published by Verso in 1997.

Andrew Blake is Professor of Cultural Studies at King Alfred's College, Winchester. His two most recent books are *The Land Without Music: Music in Twentieth Century Britain,* published by Manchester University Press, and *Body Language: The Meaning of Modern Sport,* published by Lawrence and Wishart.

Anne Coddington works as a freelance journalist and writer. She contributes to a wide range of publications including the *Guardian,* the *New Statesman* and *When Saturday Comes.* Formerly Editor of the Democratic Left fortnightly newspaper *New Times,* her book *One of the Lads: Women Who Follow Football* was published by Harper Collins in October 1997.

Kevin Davey writes a column for *New Times.* A former chair of both the Socialist Society and the Socialist Movement, in 1998 he was closely involved in 'The People's Europe' initiative. His book *English Imaginaries: Six Studies in Anglo-British Whiteness* is published by Lawrence and Wishart in late autumn 1998.

Nina Fishman helped found the Voting Reform Group and is a Council member of The Electoral Reform Society. A Labour historian, she is presently working on a biography of the Welsh communist and miners' leader, Arthur Horner, with fellow historian Hywel Francis.

Andrew Gamble is Professor of Politics at Sheffield University. One of the pioneers of an analysis of Thatcherism, latterly his work has been more concerned with the politics of ownership. The co-editor of a collection of essays *Stakeholder Capitalism*, published by Macmillan, Andrew has contributed pieces on this subject to *New Left Review*, the *New Statesman* and *Renewal*.

Jeremy Gilbert researches cultural and political theory and contemporary popular culture as part of a PHD he is currently completing at Sussex University. A member of the editorial board of, and contributor to, the cultural politics journal *New Formations*, he is also the co-author, with Ewan Pearson, of *Discographies: Dance/Music/Culture and the Politics of Sound* which will be published by Routledge in 1999.

Michael Gove wrote the authorised biography of Michael Portillo, *Michael Portillo: The Future of the Right*, published by Fourth Estate. In 1997 he was the winner of the Charles Douglas Home Award for Political Writing. He has recently been appointed the Op-Ed Editor of *The Times*.

Gerry Hassan is Director of the Centre for Scottish Public Policy. The organiser of the Scottish Nexus group – a network for new policy ideas – he has written widely in Scottish and British publications including the *New Statesman, Tribune, Renewal* and *New Times*. In 1999 Lawrence and Wishart will publish his book on the history of Scottish Labour and Home Rule.

Rupa Huq is completing a PHD on youth culture at the University of East London. Her writing on race, popular culture and politics has appeared in *Red Pepper* and *Soundings,* and the Zed Press collection *Dis-Orienting Rhythms: The Politics of the New Asian Dance Music.*

Mark Perryman edited two previous *Signs of the Times* collections, *Altered States: Postmodernism, Politics and Culture* and *The Blair Agenda*. He also writes extensively on football. One of the partners who set up 'Philosophy Football', a T-shirt company that styles itself 'Sporting Outfitters of Intellectual Distinction', his book *Philosophy Football: Eleven Great Thinkers Play it Deep* was published by Penguin in November 1997.

Paul Richards serves on the Fabian Society National Executive and was the Labour Party's parliamentary candidate for Billericay in the 1997 General Election. His book *Be Your Own Spin-Doctor* was published in 1998 by Take That Ltd.

Anne Showstack Sassoon is Professor of Politics at Kingston University. A long-term theorist of Gramscian Politics, her book *Gramsci's Politics* and the edited collection, *Approaches to Gramsci,* are two of the main texts in the study of the legacy of this key thinker of the twentieth-century left.

Stephen Twigg was one of the stars of the early hours of 2 May 1997 when his victory over Michael Portillo in Enfield Southgate was famously announced. Stephen currently combines his work as an active constituency MP with other responsibilities including membership of the Modernisation of the House Select Committee and chairing the Labour Campaign for Electoral Reform.

Wendy Wheeler is Reader in English Literature and Critical Theory at the University of North London. A member of the editorial board of, and contributor to, the cultural politics journal *New Formations,* she also writes for *Soundings* and *New Times*. Her book *A New Modernity? Reason and Passion at the Century's End* is due to be published by Lawrence and Wishart in 1999.

ABOUT SIGNS OF THE TIMES

Signs of the Times is an independent and open discussion group whose principal activities are organising two series of seminars each year.

Two previous *Signs of the Times* books are still available. Both are published by Lawrence & Wishart.

For details of *Signs of the Times* seminars, conferences and occasional discussion papers please contact: Signs of the Times, PO Box 10684, London N15 6XA. Tel: (0181) 809 7336.

INTRODUCTION:
A DEEPER SHADE OF
POLITICS

Anne Coddington and Mark Perryman

The collapse of political certainty, and our immersion in the impermanence of the contingent, is in one sense liberating.[1] In such a situation
it is to be welcomed that radical thought is freed from the restrictions
of dogma, the narrow discipline of the party line and the overbearing
orthodoxies of political theory. Thus it is a valuable asset of the Blair
project that it enjoys a looseness that enables freedom of thought to
flourish: 'Modernisation is a political method – a broad strategic
approach rather than a rigid set of beliefs.'[2] The new organisational
forms, from networks to focus groups and on-line conferencing, reflect
the cultural imperatives of these new ways of operating politically.
Power tends to operate on a horizontal plane rather than vertically.

The experience of nearly two decades of defeat and decline has
undoubtedly led to an erosion of confidence in the ideology which
once was comfortable with the label 'left' – and had a strong sense of
its meaning; and this loss of confidence often hinders the left in its
necessary task of rethinking. The left shares this sense of a loss of
meaning and belief with other traditions that can claim descent from
the Enlightenment.[3] At the end of the millennium, society more
broadly is experiencing a faltering of faith in reason and progress. And
this produces a sense of loss, which can result in a revulsion against
cynical and calculating coldness and a 'deep yearning for decency,
compassion and a liberal ethical community.'[4] But this desire for the
pure, often manifested in an intense fascination with the moral standards of our politicians, is in effect a retreat from politics. Moralising,
when taken out of the context which produced all the wrongdoing and
hypocrisy, leads to flights of ideological fancy divorced from a politics
of change. The present reigns supreme, vision is eclipsed and idealism
stays on permanent standby. Politics has more than its fair share of

1

sinners, and plenty of would-be saints too, but neither matter nearly as much as we like to lead ourselves to believe. The more we delude ourselves that they do matter, the faster the process of emotional privatisation will become.

A WIDER SENSE OF POLITICS

Thirty years after that extraordinary year 1968, Tariq Ali is still writing of the passion that takes politics out of the cosy confines of the cloisters and committees that seek to constrict it and finally kill it off: 'We were happy because we carried within our collective self a vision of a better future. Not for ourselves, but for the oppressed throughout the world: for everyone. Ours was not just a soft happiness or rapture but one that was linked to taking risks, to danger, to sacrificing one's own life if it would help to further the cause of humanity.'[5] Only when politics is thought of in this way does it connect with an active minority that alone can make movements of ideas effective. It requires a direct engagement, and a prefigurative practice that most powerfully belongs to the 1960s; and that time seems far removed – notwithstanding attempts to get Britain swinging again courtesy of Oasis, Blur and their musical acolytes.

And while debate rages on, and on, about Tony Blair's 'third way',[6] there seems a blissful historical ignorance of an earlier search for a 'third way', which was prompted by a different, and wider, conception of politics. The earlier search for a third way was concerned to find a way that could connect the radical commitment and passion of the far left with the narrower paths of the Labour Party, and could steer itself between the errors of Leninism and the inadequacies of Labourism. Since 1956 and the birth of the First New Left[7] there have been a whole series of attempts to work out a politics that rejected the shared statism of Labourites and Leninists, and their shared unthinking acceptance of the homogeneities of class politics, together with a refusal of the all too easy descent from direct democracy to centralisation. These earlier third-wayers battled against a set of dilemmas that still bedevil us today, but with a set of answers that few would validate within the terms of today's much narrower 'third way'. These answers included a move towards a cultural politics, a deep investment in civil society, and a vastly expanded definition of what we have come to understand as power relations. How do these problematics figure within a project that finds the maxims of social democracy a mite too radical?

Stuart Hall was the most significant proponent of the earlier third-wayers' radical relocation of the political. Citing the legacy of the Italian Marxist Antonio Gramsci, he powerfully argued, 'We cannot go back to the notion of mistaking electoral politics or party politics in a narrow sense, or even the occupancy of state power, as constituting the ground of modern politics itself. Gramsci understands that politics is a much expanded field; that especially in societies of our kind, the sites on which power is constituted will be enormously varied.'[8] It is this voice, for the radical remaking of politics, that is so startlingly absent today. Its illegitimate representatives prefer instead to use the apologia of globalisation to excuse away any prospects for meaningful change.[9] The definitions that Stuart Hall[10] and others have offered us remain indicative of a 'third way' that is irresistibly different from the 'new' social democrats, those who have turned their back on social democracy in the cause of modernisation.

Jeremy Gilbert identifies the unifying ideals of new Labour as yet another British attempt at conservative modernisation. He argues that, for new Labour, to modernise is to 'become more efficient and more successful under circumstances and criteria which are not only not of one's own choosing, but in which there is no imagined possibility of changing.'[11] New Labour is intent on adapting to what already exists, which it defines as the modern; it still lacks an imaginative commitment to reshaping modernity. The new oppositional movements also lack a strong sense of what is politically possible – although their problem stems from a different cause. The imagination of the possible is hindered by an overwhelming emphasis on the immediacy of direct action, which produces a form that is inaccessible, and therefore unimaginable, to all but the most committed. In the welcome glow of courage and commitment of the direct action movements this is an unspoken home truth that few of the supporters of the new oppositional politics are prepared to utter.

POLITICAL AGENCY

Geoff Andrews cites 1968 as a key instance where intellectual pluralism was allowed to flourish within the left.[12] It forced a re-evaluation of what have more recently been described as grand narratives, whilst producing a de-centring that didn't rule out the potential for wholesale societal change. *The May Day Manifesto 1968*, written principally by

Stuart Hall, E P Thompson and Raymond Williams, is a sustained case for just this kind of de-centring: 'Association and co-operation have to be open and equal. Nobody can narrow his eyes and calculate, count recruits. Or rather, anybody can do this, but he will get nowhere; the mood to co-operate is not in that style.'[13] Crucially, the authors put forward the alternative of a prefigurative politics: 'The institutions we want must be prefigured in the institutions we create to fight for them; or we shall not be there at all.'[14] Against centralism yet for co-operation, the priority given to opening up channels of communication to the widest possible debate, whilst privileging the autonomy of the groups and individuals who participate, such was the basis of this late 1960s 'third way'. It built on the work of those who had coalesced around a similar challenge in 1956, and remained, like those previous pioneers, as implacably opposed to Leninism as it was to Labourism. The failure of this new left to break out of the confines of an intellectual coterie, however influential, was founded on the intricacies of this final distinguishing characteristic, the commitment to autonomy. How does one retain the momentum that radicalism demands while balancing the need for autonomy with a sufficiently shared sense of purpose? Without some kind of sense of agency, organisation becomes so fragmented that it loses any sense or semblance of existence.

The 'massive but passive' new Labour plebiscite membership is one consequence of the need for the left to find ways of re-connecting with society. It is inadequate certainly, but then so has been the experience of most, if not all, of the groups to the left of Labour that have sought to challenge its hold on that much-contested – until now – property, 'the left'. The left has yet to come up with a form of agency that can offer ties that bind without falling into the excesses of old-style party discipline.

THE OUTSIDE LEFT

The playwright Trevor Griffiths has chillingly captured the cult of leadership that these old-style leftist groups depend upon:

> The party means discipline. It means self-scrutiny, criticism, responsibility, it means a great many things that run counter to the traditions and values of Western bourgeois intellectuals. It means being bound in by a common purpose. But above all, it means deliberately severing yourself

from the prior claims on your time and moral commitment of personal relationships, career, advancement, reputation and prestige.[15]

Griffiths' fictional character, John Tagg, was famously based on the late, if not lamented, Workers Revolutionary Party's Gerry Healey; but it could just as easily have been Ted Grant, who once led and dominated Labour's Militant Tendency, or the third member of this troika of gurus, the Socialist Worker's Party's (SWP) Tony Cliff.[16] This type of politics demands such a degree of surrender to the organisation that once those ties are loosened it is robbed of any sense of purpose it once had. In the 1990s, and particularly now that there is no Communist Party to speak of, there is a very wide unoccupied space to the left of the Labour Party. This has given the Militant Tendency (in its new guise as The Socialist Party) and the SWP a space for manoeuvre and recruitment that was previously denied to them. Forced to loosen their Leninist ties in this new situation, as the prospects for growth unfolded, they have each in their different ways found it difficult to adapt. The discipline that once made them effective political machines, if deeply unattractive, is on the wane, and the growth in membership has reduced their level of activity rather than increased it. The Socialist Party is responding to the pressures for change by seeking to extend its electoral activity, and any failure to turn votes into seats is bound to affect morale and force further dissipation of its unifying ideals. The SWP, eschewing for the moment any electoral challenge to new Labour, is forced into a whirlwind of activity, to give its now much larger membership the continuing need to belong. But as it goes for growth, the variegation of its membership is such that the unifying revolutionary appeal is being dissipated. The disciplines of Leninist democratic centralism are what give this kind of group its limited effectiveness – and they remain in this sense anything but prefigurative.[17]

PREFIGURATIVE POLITICS: PLURALIST FORMS OF ORGANISATION

The sad fact is that, without the rigid adherence to doctrinal loyalty that Leninism imposes on its followers, looser formations invariably appear to lack a sense of continuing viability once the first flash of initiative has disappeared. The *May Day Manifesto* recognised this likelihood from the outset: 'It follows from our whole analysis and approach that we do not want to set up the kind of centralising organisation which would demand any premature declaration of loyalties. Rather we are interested in promoting a connecting process.'[18] So, while no party or group remained in existence for very long after the manifesto's publication, the on-going impact of its principal authors remained substantial.[19] The contribution of these thinkers, linked to political activity and public spaces where their ideas would be discussed and debated, was rarely uniform, but this was part of their untidy strength. Although the organisational forms thrown up by this third-way tendency have been fragile, its influence has been important. It is a pluralist tradition, which, in another context, is recognised by Anne Showstack Sassoon as a vital feature of the untidy engagements left intellectuals must make with new Labour: 'All are stronger for having to meet the challenge of co-operation between diverse talents. All are weaker without it.'[20]

Coinciding with Thatcher's first general election victory in 1979 *Beyond the Fragments* was a further attempt to formulate a pluralist project of practical radicalism which would have just enough coherence to make it sustainable.[21] Clearly influenced by the work of at least some of the *May Day Manifesto* authors, this new set of writers, all women, drew their principal influence from feminism. The book was founded on an opposition to the way the left – and in particular the Communist Party, the SWP and other far-left groups – reproduced authoritarian and hierarchical structures. In their place a left libertarianism was proposed, founded on a commitment to autonomy, a recognition of the enriching experience of difference, the vital contribution of prefigurative practice, and the important contribution a politics of localism can make. A totality is still sought – hence 'beyond the fragments' – but it is recognised that this must be patiently worked for, not imposed from on high by a Central, or still less a National Executive, Committee.

Several of the contributors to this book write from within a framework which continues this tradition of resistance to centralisation – and new Labour is certainly open to criticism from this standpoint. Rupa Huq charts the implications that race and diaspora have for any attempt at a totalising project,[22] while Gerry Hassan recounts the fractured history of the Scottish nationalist challenge to the totalising tendencies of a politics founded on a unitary British state.[23] Nina Fishman argues that only a democratic modernisation will enable new Labour to create the state institutions that will entrench pluralism; her concern is that, because it is in thrall to the supposed achievements of the Clintonisation of the US political system, this will not happen, and that the consequences of this failure will be severe: 'Popular disillusion and disappointment are the most likely results if new Labour persists in equating modernisation with Americanisation.'[24]

As Thatcher approached her second general election triumph, the part of the left which most clearly identified with the ideas of the political milieu broadly stretching from the *May Day Manifesto* to *Beyond the Fragments*, once more tried to find a project around which they could collaborate. The Socialist Society was the outcome, and it set out in its 1982 founding statement some bold and ambitious intentions: 'To aim to regain the initiative for socialist ideas and help them become the common sense of the age. To help create a forum and common framework for considering fundamental questions of socialist programme and purpose. To bring together intellectual workers and worker intellectuals in the common task of developing the promise of socialism.'[25] The failure of The Socialist Society,[26] to get anywhere close to fulfilling these undoubtedly noble aims explains in some part how new Labour has emerged for many as 'the only game in town' worth playing. The failure of the Socialist Society can be accounted for, to a greater or lesser extent, by a number of factors: the inability of large sections of the left to recognise the depth of the crisis of labourism; a misunderstanding of the factors that fuelled the success of Thatcherism, allied to a refusal to recognise the specificities of Thatcher's brand of Conservatism; a refusal to accept that socialism itself may be problematic; the insistence that socialism alone encompasses the radical project; and, once more, an inability to overcome the organisational weaknesses that have characterised this political territory.

ONLY CONNECT

So how can politics acquire the essential idealism that can give it a future worth thinking about, and working for? Idealism, in the past, has too often been an excuse for rigidity and the refusal to recognise new realities. But without ideals politics is robbed of hope, courage and commitment. Trevor Griffiths, in his play *Occupations*, gives Antonio Gramsci a speech to deliver that sums up brilliantly and poignantly the necessity for political passion:

For many years, the thought that I could be loved seemed an absolute, almost fatal, impossibility. So perhaps I came to the masses with the same mechanical view of them. Use them. Tool them up. Keep them greased. Discard when they wear out. But then I thought, how can a man bind himself to the masses, if he has never loved anyone himself, not even his mother or his father. I thought, how can a man love a collectivity, when he has not profoundly loved single human creatures. And it is then I began to see masses as people, and it was only then that I began to love them, in their particular, detailed, local, individual character. You would be wrong to see this ... love ... as the product of petit-bourgeois idealism. It is the correct, the only true dialectical relationship between leaders and led, vanguard and masses, that can ensure the political health of the new order the revolution seeks to create. Treat masses as expendable, as fodder, during the revolution, you will always treat them like this. If you see masses that way, there can be no revolution worth the blood it spills.[27]

Or, it could be paraphrased, no election worth voting in. Deprived of passion, and its very necessary headiness and other-worldliness, politics becomes barren, empty, devoid of dedication and worth.

NEW TIMES AND THE RELOCATION OF THE POLITICAL

In 1988 a further attempt was made to redefine radical politics. The magazine *Marxism Today*, published by the Communist Party, coined the term 'new times'.[28] These 'new times' were defined through theories including post-fordism, postmodernism, globalisation, and a new politics of identity and citizenship, and at the heart of this way of looking at the world was the insight that party politics, the contest for votes, was of declining political significance: 'Politics is less and less confined to a distant realm of parties, resolutions and elections'.[29] The paradox was clear: most would agree with this observation, but many would also retain a definition of the political confined solely to a notion of the party political. The expansion of the realm of politics to touch every aspect of our lives, the diminishing role of the state, the internationalisation of power, new thinking, social fragmentation, and the new divide between modernisers and traditionalists – together these differing symptoms have failed to deliver an effective remaking of what is commonly understood as the political. Until that process begins politics will remain as alien as it has always been, something not be uttered in polite conversation for fear it might upset the neighbours.[30]

IS 'WEAK POWER' THE ANSWER?

The *New Times* analysis paid particular heed to organisational theory as one solution to the apparent inexorable decline of party politics. Geoff Mulgan, who was to become Director of the independent think-tank Demos, and more recently a key figure in the Number Ten Policy Unit, set out how 'weak power' had a greater inner strength than 'strong power'.[31] Organisations founded on 'strong power' derive their authority from position rather than from knowledge or ability. Formal rules determine how decisions are made and responsibilities allocated. Structures are pyramidical, with vertical lines of authority and accountability. The exercise of control absorbs enormous amounts of time and energy, while communication is always downwards from superiors to their subordinates, rather than lateral, between equals. An explicit identity generates a hierarchical, rigid form of organisation, that seeks predictability out of chaos, and leaves little scope for initiative, imagination and autonomy. And this description fits new Labour as a party entity almost as well as it sums up the now discarded institutions of old Labour.

By contrast, weak power is characterised by decentralisation: there is no single point of leadership. Communication is horizontal, structures are cellular. The individual units of the organisation tend to regulate themselves rather than being governed by rules and commands that flow down from a higher body. Structures thrive on fluidity, change and the creativity that can flow out of chaos. Energies are directed outwards rather than inwards. Unlike strong power, which is founded on an imposed discipline and external authority, weak power depends on a quite different kind of implicit bonding that must flow from the self. It depends on an accumulation of trust and the replacing of explicit controls. Long-term relationships become more important than short-term achievement; co-operation, support networks, the generation of a social milieu, all become more vital than recruitment drives and the issuing of party cards. Relationships are constantly being negotiated and re-negotiated. The analysis suggests that the crisis of socialism is more a crisis of structures than one of values, for co-operation, compassion and the taking of responsibility have always been at the centre of the left's lexicon.

New Labour has enjoyed dynamic membership growth, with the organisation surviving the party's first year in office largely intact. But, with all these new members joining, the question is raised of what the party can offer in return. Labour has almost no other reason to exist except to contest, and win, elections. Its members have a markedly peripheral role in that contest, except to donate funds to finance the campaigns and, in the case of a tiny few, to stand for public office as candidates. Hardly any take part in any meaningful sense in the party's policy-making process, and even for those that do it is unclear what power and influence they are able to wield. The party certainly does not champion exemplary prefigurative models of democracy in practice, nor does it in any meaningful sense seek to emancipate the individual members in a modern version of its previously historic role in working-class communities. There is little emphasis on education, and the voice the party offers, even in its most populist modes, is rarely truly representative of those it seeks to speak for and about. The parties of the old – Leninist and Labourist alike – demanded loyalty, inspired love and devotion, promised delivery from evil, fought battles on behalf of the needy and brought nobility into the drab lives of the many. They were a collective experience, depending on commitment, exacting discipline and expecting great sacrifice in return. Above all the party sought heroic achievement.[32] Today no party of any note would even begin to pretend to share these ambitions – the heroic and the romantic has been almost squeezed out of party politics. (Nicola Baird, however, writes in this volume of a form of protest that still manages to mobilise these feelings.[33]) New Labour needs a modernising strategy for the party which acknowledges the need for passion, and is based in a view of politics that is wider than Westminster.

THIS IS THE MODERN WORLD

Radicals need to engage with modernity: but this engagement should be based on an understanding of how modernity relates to the past, rather than a glorification of the ahistoricism that derives from the ever-growing fixation with all things 'new'. The engagement must be at a number of levels, aiming to unsettle the fixed locations of political power. The self, the locality and civil society are all good enough starting-points, but if the engagement ends here then sectionalism and essentialism will surely follow. Instead the engagement must constantly broaden, to encounter regional, state, continental and global structures of power. At our best we will start to close the gap between personal feelings and political action. The liberatory experience of political action will become as important as the victory it brings, all the more so when opposition can no longer be defined in cosy win or lose summaries of outcome. Direct action as a form of self-expression will be seen as being equally as effective as slavishly abiding by more formal political procedures – if not more effective. Changing cultural attitudes as a goal will be seen as being equally as legitimate as the reform and repeal of laws. Most fundamentally, the idea that there is a single source of power to be undermined or captured will be rejected. This will be a radical cultural politics, refusing to accept the arbitrary division between the cultural and the political which has served to make each so alien and aimless, in almost interchangeable degrees.

Such a project is not 'new' – anything that has to claim that moniker rarely is: 'The cultural revolution is summoning for examination and revaluation everything which mobilises our consciousness. In this parade of objects there are no non-combatants – nor can there be! Plates and cups, things we see daily, several times a day, can do their bit for the organising of consciousness.'[34] This was how the artists and cultural workers of the early Russian Revolution described their task. They ended up as production-line creators, manufacturing socialist realism and prolecult art as the artistic comrades of Stalinism and the Gulag. Their dilemma was solved for them – serve and obey or join the ranks of fellow dissidents on the way to the labour camp. In our worst imagination, failing to buy into Cool Britannia won't ever cost us the loss of our liberty. But dissident positions are needed all the same, standing on the outside, holding on to passion and ideals, romance and revolution. The poverty of politics will be all the greater without that dissidence. The new will die before it gets old, and then we'll all be back where we started from, in the dog-days of a regime that has served its purpose and run out of time. This is not a dilemma, more like a nightmare waiting to happen, if we let it. There will be no single way of preventing this – there will be multi-faceted ways, which will compete against each other, and on occasion – many we must hope – will co-operate too. Such political polycentrism is undoubtedly messy, bordering on ill-definition, but it is creatively preferable to a party-based politics which so often closes down debate. (See Kevin Davey in this volume: 'the problem of parties ... forced to differentiate them-selves from others in a competition for support but ... also increasingly compelled to create unitary voices, closing debate.'[35])

This is the dilemma, how to perform a balancing act between the 'pick n'mix' of a pluralist politics committed to radicalism and a readi-ness to stare reality in the face, between a recognition that practical politics starts from first principles and a willingness to compromise to get them put into practice; how to build a politics which has the capacity to distinguish between strategy and tactics. Dilemmas there will be aplenty – making choices, after all, is what the exercise of power is all about. We just have to learn to accept that power is everywhere and each and everyone one of us has the capacity to use, and abuse, it. The moderniser's dilemma, if you like, is with us night and day. Shun it or deny it, pretend there are easy choices to be made, and the dilemma will become a spectre haunting politics, with just as much capacity to disappoint as the one summoned up by old man Marx more than a century and a half ago.

NOTES

1. It is, for example, an eminently valid reaction to the electoral volatility which Andrew Gamble pinpoints as one of the key characteristics of the current political terrain. See his essay in this collection.

2. Paul Richards in this collection.

3. See Wendy Wheeler, 'Nostalgia isn't Nasty – The Postmodernising of Parliamentary Democracy', in Mark Perryman (ed), *Altered States: Postmodernism, Politics, Culture,* Lawrence & Wishart, London 1994; also Wendy Wheeler, 'Dangerous Business: Remembering Freud and a Poetics of Politics', in Mark Perryman (ed), *The Blair Agenda* , Lawrence & Wishart, London 1996.

4. See Wendy Wheeler in this collection.

5. Tariq Ali and Susan Watkins, *1968 Marching in the Streets*, Bloomsbury, London 1998, pp215-216.

6. For two of the more substantial contributions to the debate on the 'Third Way' see Anthony Giddens, 'After the Left's Paralysis' in *New Statesman*, 1 May 1998, pp 18–21, and Charles Leadbeater, 'A Hole at the Heart of the Third Way' in *New Statesman*, 8 May 1998, pp 32–33. For a trenchant response to the prospects for the kind of way offered by these two authors and others see David Marquand, 'The Blair Paradox' in *Prospect*, May 1998 pp 19–24.

7. For a detailed history of the formation of the 1956 New Left see Michael Kenny, *The First New Left : British Intellectuals after Stalin*, Lawrence & Wishart, London 1995. The best single source of original documents tracing the evolution of the New Left is available in David Widgery (ed), *The Left in Britain 1956-68*, Penguin Books, London 1976.

8. Stuart Hall, 'Gramsci and Us', in Roger Simon, *Gramsci's Political Thought:*

An Introduction, Lawrence & Wishart, London 1991, p123.

9. For an effective rejoinder to a debate that on occasion threatens to surrender itself wholesale to neo-liberalism see David Goldblatt et al ,'Economic Globalisation and the Nation State: The Transformation of Political Power?', *Soundings,* Autumn 1997.

10. See Stuart Hall, *The Hard Road to Renewal: Thatcherism and the Crisis of the Left* , Verso, London 1988.

11. See Jeremy Gilbert in this collection.

12. See Geoff Andrews in this collection.

13. Raymond Williams (ed), *May Day Manifesto 1968,* Penguin Books, London 1968, p184.

14. *Ibid,* p184.

15. Trevor Griffiths, *The Party,* Faber & Faber, London 1974, pp52-53.

16. For a truly bizarre inside account of Gerry Healy's leadership of the Workers Revolutionary Party see Corinna Lotz and Paul Feldman, *Gerry Healy: A Revolutionary Life,* Lupus Books, London 1994. The fact that Ken Livingstone provided a glowing testimonial of Healy's contribution to 'the working class socialist movement' only adds to the intriguing nature of this thankfully obscure book.

17. It is ironic that these Leninists are so different from the those who, finally, proved the most effective challengers of the actually existing stalinist dictatorships of eastern Europe. To quote the 'rules of dialogue' that Czechoslovakia's late 1980s Civic Forum: 'When searching for the truth together, your opponent must not be an enemy. Try to understand the other person. A statement without proof is not an argument. Do not run away from the original subject. Do not try to have the last word in the discussion at all costs. Do not threaten the dignity of your opponent. Do not forget that a dialogue requires discipline.Do not mistake dialogue for monologue.' Quoted in Jon Bloomfield, 'Citizen Power in Prague', in Geoff Andrews (ed), *Citizenship,* Lawrence & Wishart, London 1991.

18. *May Day Manifesto 1968, op.cit.,* p186.

19. For just one example of the political foresight of the principal intellectual identified with the Manifesto see Raymond Williams, *Towards 2000,* Penguin Books, London 1983. Amongst others involved were Michael Barratt Brown, Terry Eagleton, Stuart Hall, Bob Rowthorn, Michael Rustin and Edward Thompson.

20. See Anne Showstack Sassoon in this collection.

21. Sheila Rowbotham, Lynne Segal and Hilary Wainwright, *Beyond the Fragments: Feminism and the Making of Socialism,* Merlin Press, London 1979.

22. Rupa Huq in this collection.

23. Gerry Hassan in this collection.

24. Nina Fishman in this collection.

25. Founding Statement of the Socialist Society, published in the December 1981 issue of the magazine *Marxism Today*.

26. For an outstanding contemporary account of the flawed socialism of The Socialist Society and its principal initiative, the 1987 Chesterfield Conference, see Rosalind Brunt, 'The Left's Hallelujah Chorus', *Marxism Today*, December 1987, pp32-35.

27. Trevor Griffiths, *Occupations*, Faber and Faber, London 1980, p46.

28. See *Stuart Hall and Martin Jacques (eds), New Times : The Changing Face of Politics in the 1990s,* Lawrence and Wishart, London 1989.

29. *Ibid*, p449.

30. Stephen Twigg's account in this collection of his first year in parliament gives a feel of the many and varied ways a constituency – in the widest sense of the word – MP has to grapple with what his or her differing constituents perceive as their MP's political responsibility – the sheer range of means by which this new Labour MP, and many more like him, has to remake himself, over and over again, is nothing less than momentous. But what is it that fuels that process, and to what end?

31. Geoff Mulgan, 'The Power of the Weak', *New Times, op. cit.,* pp 347-364.

32. There is in existence a vast array of autobiographical accounts that pay testimony to this heroic sacrifice. Amongst the best is Wal Hannington, *Unemployed Struggles 1919-1936,* Lawrence and Wishart, London 1979. Undoubtedly partisan and historically flawed, they nevertheless deserve a respectful reading and are in their own way far more reliable than contemporary after-the-event accounts written with the dubious advantage of jaundiced hindsight. For a spectacularly poor example of this unfortunate political genre, see Francis Beckett, *The Enemy Within: The Rise and Fall of The British Communist Party,* John Murray, London 1995.

33. Nicola Baird in this collection.

34. Quoted in the catalogue for the *Art into Production* exhibition of Soviet Textiles, Fashion and Ceramics 1917-1935, The Crafts Council December 1984, London p15.

35. Kevin Davey in this collection.

SECTION ONE:
THE NEW LABOUR SETTLEMENT

AFTER THE WATERSHED,
THE CONSERVATIVE ECLIPSE

Andrew Gamble

Labour won an overwhelming victory in the general election on 1 May 1997. Opinion is divided though as to whether 1997 was a landmark general election, comparable to those of 1906 and 1945, which will shape the future direction of British politics, or whether it was a consolidating election, primarily involving a change of personnel rather than a change of policy.[1] The election campaign which Labour waged seemed deliberately designed not to raise but to lower expectations. Victory produced euphoria and a sudden burst of enthusiasm and hope that a Blair Government might turn out, after all, to be a great reforming administration in the manner of the Liberal government of 1906 or the Labour government of 1945. However, it did not take long for pessimism to re-emerge and for the opinion to form that this would indeed be a government that broadly accepted the agenda it inherited from the Conservatives, and in particular from Margaret Thatcher.

These varied assessments of the Blair government reflect different views of the meaning of new Labour as a political project. Pessimists see new Labour as both product and agent of a new consensus in British politics: a consensus created not by the centre-left but by the radical right, grounded in the neo-liberal doctrines of the Thatcher years. From this perspective Labour won so overwhelmingly in 1997 because it accepted most of the achievements and legacies of Thatcherism and proposed few changes. Former Conservative voters could desert the most unpopular government since 1945 knowing that Labour was a safe alternative.

This view has been rehearsed many times by intellectuals otherwise sympathetic to new Labour. Blair was criticised before the election by Martin Jacques for having a project for the party but not one for the country. It had a clear idea of how it wanted to change its image in order to gain office, but was much less certain about what it wanted to do in government. Many other centre-left intellectuals expressed dismay that the new leadership was so timid in its pronouncements, often seeming ready to abandon core Labour principles (for example on redistribution) if it thought it might enhance its electability. Worse still, in its quest for votes and a new image with the public, new Labour appeared to be embracing not just economic neo-liberalism but social conservatism and moral authoritarianism, particularly in its policies on crime, education, and welfare.

Some of the most creative intellectuals on the left in the 1980s, such as Stuart Hall, had long recognised the need for a far-reaching modernisation of the party if it were ever to regain the political initiative from Thatcherism. For Hall this meant that the left had to learn from Thatcherism not by borrowing Thatcherite policies but by understanding that a political strategy meant: 'a perspective on what is happening to society now, a vision of the future, a capacity to articulate these vividly through a few clearly-enunciated themes or principles, a new conception of politics.'[2] For many supporters of this kind of modernisation new Labour at first promised to deliver but has now proved a cruel disappointment. Instead of challenging Thatcherism it has consolidated and refined it. As a consequence, the electorate now has two Conservative parties to choose between, and in 1997 Labour won because it was much the more attractive, able to make use of the One Nation rhetoric which Conservatives themselves had once deployed so adeptly, but increasingly had abandoned.[3] From this perspective the 1997 election should be classed with 1951 rather than with 1945, because it confirmed the radical change in direction initiated in 1979 rather than signalling a new one.

This chapter takes a different stance. It argues that disillusion with Blair and new Labour is premature. The radical potential of the Government should not be judged simply by its early plans and intentions. What is also important is whether the advent of the Blair government signals a permanent change in some of the long established continuities and certainties of British politics, or whether it is merely another temporary interruption in the long sequence of Conservative governments which have dominated British politics in this century.

The possibility that it is not is worth exploring, and has substantial implications for the future direction of British politics. To assess it the first step is to ask why it was that the Conservatives suffered such a comprehensive and overwhelming defeat in 1997 after being in government for eighteen years.[4]

THE PECULIARITIES OF 1997

One version of the argument that the 1997 election will have no lasting effect on British politics depends on explaining the result as a number of special factors which were operating and which distorted the result. Top of the list is the electoral system. Its bias is notorious and undeniable. Labour's election victory in 1997 was a true landslide, but of a kind familiar in British politics. It won two thirds of the seats with just 44 per cent of the vote, while the Conservatives ended up with 6 per cent fewer seats than they would have obtained if the electoral rules guaranteed that seats and votes were proportional.[5] The vagaries of the British first-past-the-post voting system were again dramatically demonstrated. The British system generally (although not always) produces a government with a clear parliamentary majority. But the relationship of seats won to votes cast changes erratically. The Conservative governments elected in 1979, 1983, 1987, and 1992 had almost identical shares of the vote (43/44 per cent) but the respective majorities were 45, 143, 100, and 25. The difference can be explained partly by the margin in the share of the vote between the winning party and the party in second place, partly by the regional concentration of votes, and partly by factors such as tactical voting and the level of turnout.

The likelihood of a serious mismatch between seats and votes is greatly increased when there is a substantial difference in the share of the vote won by the two leading parties. One of the main reasons for the scale of the Conservative defeat in 1997 was therefore a consequence of the collapse in their share of the vote from 43 to 31 per cent, while Labour's rose from 35 to 44 per cent. This margin approached, although did not quite equal, the gap between Conservatives and Labour in 1983, when Labour's share was 28 per cent and the Conservatives had 43 per cent, with a parliamentary majority of 143.

The British electoral system generally exaggerates the electoral support which the winning party enjoys, and this is particularly true of landslides. 1997 is a classic illustration of this. Labour is not as popular as its parliamentary majority suggests. Its winning share of the vote is less than in 1945 or 1966, although its parliamentary majority is higher. It is a long way from having even 50 per cent support among those who voted and, once the non-voters are added in, the actual number of those voting Labour comprised less than a third of the electorate. The rules of the British electoral system mean that the shift of control from one party to another often appears to be more decisive than it really is. Control can shift back just as suddenly. Nevertheless even in the British system landslides like 1997 do not happen often.

Other special factors said to be operating in 1997 which exaggerated the scale of the Conservative defeat include electoral volatility, the intervention of new parties, tactical voting, and turnout. The volatility of the electorate has clearly increased substantially in the last twenty years. Winning by-elections has become much more difficult for incumbent governments, and huge swings in popularity in the opinion polls have become commonplace. Between 1992 and 1997 the Conservatives lost every by-election they contested including the eight held in constituencies which they had won in 1992. Until their win in Uxbridge in 1997 the Conservatives had not managed to win a by-election since 1988 when William Hague was elected in Richmond. Since 1970 voters have become less attached to the established parties and have been prepared not only to change their vote to one of the other established parties, but also to vote for new ones such as the SDP, the Referendum Party, and the Socialist Labour Party. In 1997 29 per cent of those who had voted Conservative in 1992 (4million voters) defected to other parties. 13 per cent went straight to Labour and 11 per cent to the Liberal Democrats.[6] But how permanent are these converts? In its election campaign Labour promised little and seemed to have abandoned many of its past commitments, so there is a doubt about how solid its new support will prove. The new coalition of voters which Labour has assembled may be hard to hold together, and may melt away as soon as the inability of the new government to do much about the intractable problems which face all governments becomes apparent.

This may be true, but there is not much evidence that electoral volatility increased markedly in 1997 or that it had much to do with the Conservative defeat.[7] After the Conservative government took the pound out of the Exchange Rate Mechanism in 1992 opinion polls told a consistent story: Labour led the Conservatives by a large margin throughout the Parliament. Far from volatility the electorate displayed marked stability in its preferences. There was no pre-election recovery of Conservative support. Despite holding on to office to the very last moment, and despite a longer than normal election campaign, the Conservatives did not benefit.

A second feature of the 1997 election was the opportunity to vote for new parties. By far the most successful new party in 1997 was the Referendum Party, funded by James Goldsmith, which campaigned on the single issue of the need for a referendum on Britain's continued membership of the European Union and which polled almost a million votes across the country and an average 3 per cent of the vote in the constituencies it contested. The existence of the Referendum Party clearly hurt the Conservatives, but the assumption that most of these votes would have gone to the Conservatives in 1997 if the Referendum Party had not been standing is false. Post-election analysis shows that the Conservatives would have lost the votes anyway, and that the main loser from the presence of the Referendum Party was the Liberal Democrats.[8] The Referendum Party provided a vehicle for voters who had decided not to vote for the Conservatives. Otherwise there was no general surge towards new parties or third parties. The main surge was towards Labour, with alternatives on the left such as the Socialist Party and the Socialist Labour Party picking up a derisory number of votes. New Labour was able to retain the great bulk of old Labour support, while still broadening its base and winning over large numbers of former Conservative voters.

A third feature of 1997 which contributed to the Conservative defeat and the size of Labour's victory was the willingness of so many Labour and Liberal Democrat voters to vote tactically in a bid to oust incumbent Conservatives. In many constituencies this occurred on a large scale, and in twenty-four cases may have swung the result.[9] Such extensive tactical voting may not occur at the next election since there will no longer be an incumbent Conservative government, and therefore it may be harder to sustain the informal alliance between the voters of the two centre-left parties which undoubtedly existed in 1997. But this partly depends on how the relationship between the two parties develops during this parliament. If the parties co-operate on the constitutional reform programme and agree on the main lines of policy, they are likely to continue to treat the Conservative party as their main opponent rather than each other, and this could give their voters even greater incentive for tactical voting next time.

A fourth feature of 1997 was the low turnout (72 per cent). This was the lowest turnout in any post-war election and a 6 per cent drop from 1992. There is however no evidence that it was Conservative voters who disproportionately stayed away because of their dissatisfaction with the Government. The lowest turnouts were in inner city Labour seats, and in general turnout declined on average more in Labour than in Conservative seats.[10] The reasons for the low turnout are not entirely clear, but may be related to boredom with the campaign and to a feeling that there was little to choose between the parties. New Labour's inability to reverse the trend towards declining participation among the urban poor demonstrated that its appeal was not universal. The party did not succeed in convincing many of those in the inner cities that there was any good reason to turn out and vote. Low turnout in 1997 therefore penalised Labour more than the Conservatives and depressed its share of the vote, although it probably did not cost it any seats.

THE CONSERVATIVE ROUT

There is not much comfort for the Conservatives in any of this. Certainly commanding majorities can evaporate as quickly as they arise, and the 1997 result in itself does not establish any inevitability about the prospects of the parties in the next election. Nevertheless the strength of Labour's current position is formidable. 1997 was a historic defeat for the Conservative Party, its biggest since 1832. Labour secured its greatest ever lead in seats and votes over the Conservatives. The swing (at 11 per cent) was the biggest Labour has ever achieved at a general election apart from the special circumstances of 1945 when there had not been a general election for ten years. Again, apart from 1945 Labour had previously never managed to increase its share of the vote at a general election by more than 4 per cent. In 1997 it rose by 9 per cent.

Labour's achievement in 1997 was still more striking because of the strong showing of the Liberal Democrats and the nationalist parties. The Liberal Democrats did not increase their share of the vote but they did succeed in winning forty-six seats, partly aided by tactical voting, their highest parliamentary representation since the 1920s. When the Liberal Democrat and the Nationalist share of the vote is added to that of Labour, then the anti-Conservative majority among those voting is overwhelming (63 per cent). This is the weakest electoral result the Conservatives have had in the twentieth century, and it gives Labour and the centre-left in Britain a special opportunity. The position which Labour experienced after 1983 has been reversed. It is the Conservatives who must now achieve a swing of 11.6 per cent at the next general election to regain a majority in Parliament. They need an 8 per cent swing for a hung parliament, which the structural bias in the electoral system makes very hard to achieve. This structural bias is reflected in the fact that in 1997 it took on average 113,987 votes to elect a Liberal Democrat, 58,127 votes to elect a Conservative, but only 32,318 votes to elect a Labour MP.[11] The Conservatives managed to lose 4.5 million votes since 1992. Among the under 25s there was a 15 per cent swing to Labour, and Labour was ahead in every age group (except those over 65) and every income group (except the ABs). For the first time Labour won equal support from men and women; in every previous general elections it had always received a higher vote from men. The Conservatives are more than ever before a party of the South and East (three quarters of their seats are in the South of England). Their parliamentary representation was wiped out in Scotland and Wales as well as in most of urban England, and they ran second to the Liberal Democrats in Devon and Cornwall.

BREAKING THE PARTY MOULD

The scale of the Conservative defeat in 1997 cannot be explained simply as the result of special factors or the bias of the electoral system. Something more profound is going on. It is possible that the defeat heralds a change in the balance of the party system, and an end to the long Conservative hegemony in British politics. The Conservatives dominated British politics throughout the twentieth century. Labour only won three elections with clear parliamentary majorities – 1945, 1966, and 1997 – and never served two full consecutive parliamentary terms. Its first two spells in office, in 1924, and 1929-31, were cut short. The party was re-elected in 1950, but lost office in 1951. In 1964, elected with a majority of four, Labour governed for eighteen months before winning the 1966 election with a majority of ninety-eight. But the party was then defeated in 1970. It returned to government in 1974 as a minority government, and eight months later won a small overall majority. But by 1977 the party was a minority administration dependent upon the Lib-Lab pact to survive. This means that apart from the Liberal period of government from 1906 to 1916 and the wartime coalition in the 1940s, only the Conservatives have been in government for periods of more than ten years. They have achieved this feat not once but three times: 1931-1945; 1951-1964; and 1979-1997. They have been in government either on their own or in coalition for two thirds of the twentieth century (sixty-eight years). Compared to this the Liberals have been in government for only sixteen years and Labour for only twenty-seven.

1997 may prove to be another false dawn but it may also come to be seen in retrospect as the moment the centre-left majority in British politics, submerged for so long, at last broke through and created the basis for a different pattern of politics in the twenty-first century. One key condition for this will be whether or not the programme of constitutional reform on which the centre-left has embarked leads to a strengthening rather than the breakup of the United Kingdom. An event which greatly influenced the shape of the party system in Britain in the twentieth century was the withdrawal of Ireland from the Union. If Ireland had still elected eighty MPs for Westminster after 1922, the dynamics of the party system would have been very different. Concentration on the politics of the conflict between capital and labour, which came to dominate national party competition and party identity, would have been modified by much more prominent politics around the conflict between the metropolitan centre and the regional periphery. Regionally-oriented parties would have been much stronger in the UK polity. Party alliances (such as that which did exist between the Conservatives and the Ulster Unionists from 1922 to 1972) would have become more common, and many fewer elections would have resulted in a clear majority for one party, leading to more coalitions. The Conservatives would have been in a weaker structural position, both because anti-Conservative forces in the parliament would have been more numerous, and because at some stage an anti-Conservative coalition would very likely have initiated constitutional changes.

Constitutional reform is once again on the agenda and, if carried through, is likely to have far-reaching consequences for the shape of the party system and the balance of forces within it. Its success depends heavily upon whether or not the parties of the centre-left can co-operate, as they did in the 1997 referendum campaign for Scotland, and less certainly in the referendum campaign for Wales. If they fall out and fight one another again, the constitutional programme is likely to stall, and the main beneficiaries will be the Conservatives. Reforming the constitution does not guarantee political hegemony for the centre-left, but it is an essential condition for it. Ensuring that the centre-left majority in the electorate is reflected in the composition of government is the first step to building a wider hegemony over policy.

What became clear in the Thatcher years was that Labour's old strategy and politics for winning that hegemony was exhausted. In 1978 Eric Hobsbawm, reflecting on the conflicts and difficulties of the 1970s, suggested that the forward march of labour and the labour movement which Marx had predicted, appeared to have come to a halt: 'The development of the working class in the past generation has been such as to raise a number of very serious questions about its future and the future of its movement.'[12] The hurricane of Thatcherism was soon to answer those questions. Labour had not just halted but was in headlong retreat. The forward march had been primarily a march of the labour movement centred on trade unions, with a few allies among the professional groups. The steady advance of Labour reached its high point in 1945-51; Labour's highest ever share of the vote was actually achieved in 1951, the election in which it lost office. For twenty years Labour's electoral support settled on a plateau of between 41 and 47 per cent, before dropping sharply in the 1970s. The nadir was reached in 1983 when Labour's share of the vote returned to what it had been in the 1920s, below 30 per cent.

Hobsbawm argued that if Labour were to resume its forward march it had to re-learn how to put itself at the head of a broad progressive coalition. Parties elsewhere which had succeeded in breaking out of stagnation, decline, and political isolation had moved forward 'not only as class parties ... but as 'people's parties' with which the majority of their nation interested in progressive reform and change [could] identify.'[13] New Labour appears in one way the fulfilment of that hope, with the 1997 election returning Labour's level of support to where it was in the 1950s and 1960s. But this is hardly a resumption of the forward march, since the new coalition Labour now seeks to lead is so different from the old. The role of trade unions has changed, and they are no longer the centre of the party as they used to be. New Labour is neither a radical nor a conservative labour party; it is no longer recognisably much of a labour party at all. Instead it is a catch-all party of a familiar kind, a party of the centre which seeks to remain autonomous from all interest groups. If new Labour has a project it is not a project which would make sense in terms of the framework of the forward march of labour.

This is both a strength and a weakness for new Labour. It is a strength because the unions are no longer the force they once were and because the electoral and political strategy which gave priority to the concerns of the labour movement never succeeded in making the Labour Party politically dominant in British politics. The Conservatives were successful in organising an electoral coalition against it which always equalled and generally outvoted Labour's coalition. But it is also a weakness because the union link with Labour did in the past give the party an identity, an ethos and a purpose, for which new Labour has no real substitutes. The more new Labour defines the trade unions as part of old Labour and therefore as part of the problem, the less anchorage it has in the party's traditions and core attitudes.

CONSERVATIVE TRAVAILS

The opportunity for new Labour is all the greater because of the difficulties facing the Conservatives. The Conservatives have always prided themselves on the speed with which they have recovered after major election defeats. But the fact that they have succeeded in the past gives no guarantee they can succeed in the future. In several important respects they are weaker now than at any time in this century. The last time the party appeared to be in great difficulty was in the winter of 1974. They had lost four of the last five general elections, had lost office in 1974 in chaotic circumstances, and had seen their share of the vote go down to what at that time was its lowest level this century – 35 per cent.

The party did recover. It found a new leader and a new project, and between 1979 and 1997 enjoyed its longest continuous spell in government this century. But in a longer perspective the victories of the Thatcher years may come to seem illusory. Thatcherism expunged the pain of the memories of the bitter electoral and industrial defeats the Conservatives suffered in 1972-74. It gave them an unparalleled dominance in the 1980s. The opposition to them was split, and they commanded the political and intellectual agenda. For a time it seemed they might entrench themselves in government indefinitely.

But the achievements of Thatcherism, real though they were, can now be seen to have exacted a heavy price, part of which is today being paid by the Conservatives. The very success of the Conservatives in carrying through a programme of economic modernisation accelerated the erosion of the four pillars which had formed the basis of

Conservative political hegemony through the twentieth century and the era of mass democracy: the Union, the Constitution, Property and Empire.[14] The party had made itself pre-eminently the party of the nation-state and its institutions, but in its quest for economic modernisation the party found itself destroying the rationale for many of its past attachments.

By the 1990s the party still proclaimed itself the party of the Union, but it had failed to restore the historic links with the Unionists in Northern Ireland, and its support in Scotland and Wales had crumbled further. The party which had 50 per cent of the Scottish vote and half the Scottish seats in 1955 found itself in 1997 with no seats and less than 20 per cent of the Scottish vote. The decision by the party leadership to fight for a 'No No' vote in the Scottish referendum in September 1997 further isolated it from Scottish opinion, and underlined how much the party had become an English party, centred on the South and East of the country.

A second great cause, the British Empire, was also gone beyond recall. The Falklands episode could not revive it.[15] The handover of Hong Kong in 1997, negotiated by the Thatcher and Major governments, appeared to be the final chapter. This demise of empire helped underline the importance of the European Union and Britain's relationship to it. But encouraged by the open hostility of a key section of the Conservative leadership, including Thatcher herself, to the European project espoused by France and Germany, the party increasingly swung against further European integration. The party of Europe became the party of anti-Europe. The divisions in the party over the question of Europe have meant that the party has edged steadily closer to its first major split since before 1914.[16]

Towards the third pillar, the old constitutional state and its Establishment, the Conservatives still declare undying loyalty, but in practice during the Thatcher period they waged unrelenting war on many of the professions, institutions, and organisations which composed it. The state was hollowed, and many of the understandings and compromises on which it had rested were weakened or destroyed. The Conservatives themselves have been the gravediggers of the old constitution, and helped create the conditions in which radical reform of the constitution has become possible.

A similar story can be told in relation to the fourth pillar, property. Throughout the twentieth century the Conservatives were the party of property, the umbrella for the defence of all property interests against the threat posed by the spread of socialist ideas in the British Labour movement. They successfully portrayed Labour as the anti-business party, lacking economic competence. But the end of the cold war and the weakening of organised labour, partly through the actions of the Thatcher Government, have changed the terms of the domestic political debate. The business coalition behind the Conservatives has fractured, and the automatic identification of business with the Conservatives has ended. On certain issues such as the European single currency, significant sections of business are openly deserting the Conservatives.

The party therefore faces a very difficult task in rebuilding itself, facing a confident government with an overwhelming parliamentary majority. Apart from Europe, which continues to divide the Conservatives, there are few major policy differences between the two main parties. The membership of the Conservative Party is declining and ageing.[17] Its new leader, William Hague, may be an able parliamentarian, but has little popular appeal. He has instituted internal party reforms, but these will not by themselves be enough to broaden the party's support and rebuild its membership. What that requires is a fundamental rethinking of the party's programme and identity. Hague shows few signs of initiating it. He is a cautious centrist whose main strategy is to wait for the government to become unpopular and for the unity of the Cabinet to break up.

Many Conservatives think a much more positive strategy is required if the party is not to risk being permanently marginalised in British politics. There are two main alternatives. The first would be to make the Conservatives a pro-European business party again and accept the reshaping of the constitution as proposed by Labour and its allies. The Conservatives would move firmly back on to the middle ground and attempt to dislodge new Labour from it. This strategy is attractive to many senior Conservatives, but has little chance of being adopted. The drift in the party (which Hague's victory over Kenneth Clarke reflected) is entirely the other way, towards a programme based on national sovereignty, constitutional conservatism, and economic and social libertarianism. Policy on issues such as the single European currency would be based on clear principles, not on pragmatism. Such a stance would certainly precipitate the split John Major laboured so long to avoid, and might further damage the electability of the party, but the Conservatives could expect to attract a fervent and committed membership. This is a high risk strategy and would need a charismatic leader of the Michael Portillo kind. William Hague is certainly not the man.

TOWARDS 2002

Opportunities have to be grasped. Nothing guarantees new Labour success or condemns the Conservatives to failure. The Conservatives were rejected in 1997 primarily for their failures in government and the loss of their reputation for economic competence.[18] Sleaze and boredom were other key contributory factors. In time memories of the Conservative government will fade, and Conservative popularity will revive as that of Labour declines. New Labour and Tony Blair have yet to face real unpopularity. How they cope with it will be one of the factors in determining whether or not Labour succeeds in building on its May 1997 success and extending its period of government beyond 2002. Another factor is whether or not the Government finds ways of uniting rather than dividing the different elements of the centre-left. The constitutional programme is absolutely central here. It carries enormous risks and many of its elements have not been thought through. But it does offer the prospect of a fundamental and lasting change in the way Britain is governed.

The key components of new Labour's project are modernisation of the welfare state and modernisation of the constitution. Socialism is left far behind. New Labour is a coalition of the centre, with both radical and conservative elements, but it is still unclear whether the radical or the conservative elements will gain the upper hand. Both are represented in the Government and there is likely to be increasing conflict between them. The trade unions are still an element in this coalition but are much reduced in influence, and their role is likely to diminish still further. They have been marginalised because they remain reluctant converts to the need for modernisation. They cannot be removed altogether from the party, they still supply 50 per cent of the funding, but there is no way back to the position they once used to enjoy.

Other elements in the coalition are the remnants of Labour's socialist Left, the Liberal Democrats, and the social democratic wing of old Labour. The socialists in Labour's coalition have so far been marginalised. As the new Labour project unfolds many may simply walk away from the party, unable to support the policies which are being pursued. There is an attempt to build a left opposition within new Labour based around resistance to globalisation and seeking to embrace green and socialist groups outside the party.[19] It is hard, though, to see it making much headway unless there is a serious rift over policy as distinct from personality conflicts in the party leadership. The social-democratic wing may put up more of a struggle, particularly over the welfare to work programme, and concessions are likely to be made to them. But there is little doubt that the concessions will be few and far between, because the Government needs to make big savings on welfare in order to finance the promises for education and health upon which it intends to be judged at the next election.

The Liberal Democrats occupy an intriguing position within the coalition. On many policy issues they are now more radical than new Labour, but they have chosen to work closely with the Government and to keep their criticisms to the minimum. Their hope is that the constitutional reform programme, including electoral reform, will proceed, and that this will give them permanently higher parliamentary representation and make possible their early entry into government as a coalition partner. The Liberal Democrats depend on the success of new Labour. They are too close to the Government to benefit if it becomes seriously unpopular. They run the risk that their vote could collapse. This is not a new dilemma for the Liberal Democrats; their share of the vote fell sharply between 1964 and 1970 and again between 1974 and 1979. They have tended to do better under Conservative rather than under Labour governments. What may make it different this time is that they have established a regional presence, particularly in the South West, and they have a strong base in local government. They may be able to hang on to their support long enough to retain credibility as a coalition partner. They need, though, to reduce that proportion of their vote which is simply a protest vote, and enlarge the number of voters who positively identify with them. This will not be easy and if the Conservatives do revive, the Liberal Democrat vote may be the first to be squeezed.

Other threats to Labour's coalition come from the devolution proposals. The establishment of the Scottish Parliament and the Welsh Assembly will create a dynamic towards a less centralised state and the creation of regional assemblies in parts of England. The management of the relationship between Edinburgh and London will be difficult and if it is mismanaged the pressures for outright separation may grow. The detachment of Scotland from the United Kingdom would seriously weaken Labour's position in the Westminster Parliament, since fifty-six of its MPs come from Scotland. The over-represenation of Scotland will be corrected in future by the boundary commissioners, but any move to cut numbers further will be fiercely resisted by Labour.

New Labour is often accused of being too cautious, but the constitutional reform programme involves considerable risks. The prize is the transformation of Britain into a more decentralised and pluralist polity. If the Government does not self-destruct and goes on to win a second term it will have the opportunity of pushing through the main elements of its constitutional agenda: regional assemblies, elected mayors, a more proportional voting system, a reformed upper house, and freedom of information, all of which will entrench the centre-left coalition as the dominant force in British politics and be very difficult to reverse. The Conservatives will have to adapt to this new reality and find new allies within the reconstructed polity. The same is true of the single currency. If it goes ahead and is successful Britain will apply to join. The timing of the referendum will be crucial but it will be hard for the Conservative Party to win the referendum against an alliance of business, trade unions, Labour, the Liberal Democrats and senior members of its own party. If the referendum goes in favour of a single currency the Conservatives will be forced to accept it, just as they have had to accept the Scottish Parliament and the Welsh Assembly, or be permanently sidelined. The Conservatives are on the defensive over the constitution, and Labour's initiatives are likely to get bolder rather than more cautious. Just as the Thatcher Government pursued a programme of economic modernisation which Labour resisted but eventually had to accept, so new Labour has embarked on a political modernisation of Britain which the Conservatives are resisting but which eventually they too will be forced to accept.

New Labour plans to take fewer risks with the economy, but a major test is looming with its attempts to reform the welfare state and reduce its cost. These reforms are fraught with danger for the government as the size of the November 1997 parliamentary rebellion over cuts in benefits for lone mothers demonstrated. However, the new Labour project, to create a more inclusive society and remedy some of the underfunding of public services, depends on the success of its strategy for reforming welfare by ending the dependency culture and getting many of those on benefit back into jobs. This again is a high-risk strategy, with major implications for the structure of the state and of welfare.

New Labour already has a host of critics who accuse it of not being radical enough, or not being radical at all. In reality it is still a little early to judge. Governments sometimes acquire a momentum and a direction which were not present at the outset. If the reforms of the constitution and of welfare to which this government is committed are

carried through in the next five years, they will fundamentally transform the nature of British politics and create the opportunity and the
desire for further change. There are different and contrasting elements
in new Labour's coalition, and the more radical elements may yet come
to the fore if the Government is successful in maintaining its popularity and winning the next election. The real radicalism of Blair's project
lies in his determination to end the hegemony of the Conservative
Party in British politics. If that succeeds, other forms of radicalism will
be back on the political agenda in a way they have not been for a generation.

NOTES

1. The different points of view on this question are represented in contributions from Ben Pimlott, Samuel Beer, Colin Crouch, David Marquand,
Bernard Crick, Anthony Barnett, Colin Hay, and David Rubinstein to the
special issue of *Political Quarterly* devoted to the election, vol 68, number 4
(1997).
2. Stuart Hall, *The Hard Road to Renewal*, Verso, London 1988, p271.
3. The BBC exit poll in May 1997 showed that 87 per cent thought that
Labour would be good for all classes, while 71 per cent thought that the
Conservatives would be good for only one class. See Peter Kellner, 'Why The
Tories were Trounced', *Parliamentary Affairs*, 50:4, (1997), pp616-30.
4. Analyses of the general election can be found in the special issue of
Parliamentary Affairs, edited by Pippa Norris & Neil Gavin, 'Britain Votes',
50:4 (1997); David Butler & Dennis Kavanagh, *The British General Election of
1997*, Macmillan, London 1997; Patrick Dunleavy, Andrew Gamble, Ian
Holliday, & Gillian Peele (eds), *Developments in British Politics 5*, Macmillan,
London 1997.
5. See Patrick Dunleavy & Helen Margetts, 'The Electoral System',
Parliamentary Affairs, 50:4, (1997) pp733-49. They calculate that in 1997 the
Liberal Democrats' deviation from proportionality (how the allocation of seats
across parties deviates from the allocation of votes) in 1997 was 10 per cent,
smaller than in previous elections but still substantial. The mismatch between
seats and votes also varied enormously regionally, being higher than 40 per cent
in some areas.
6. Pippa Norris, 'Anatomy of a Labour Landslide', *Parliamentary Affairs*, 50:4
(1997), pp509-32.
7. *Ibid* p516.

8. Butler & Kavanagh, *op.cit.*, pp301-309. In their analysis of the results John Curtice and Michael Steed conclude that only a handful of Conservative losses in 1997 can be blamed on the intervention of the Referendum Party.

9. In Con-Lab seats the Labour vote increased on average by 13 per cent while the LibDem vote declined by 3 per cent. In Con-Lib seats the LibDem vote increased by 2-3 per cent while the Labour vote was lower than average. Variations in the swing cost the Conservatives up to 46 seats, 28 Labour and 18 Liberal Democrat. Norris estimates that up to 24 were lost as a result of tactical voting; Norris *op.cit.*, pp521-2.

10. David Denver and Gordon Hands conclude that the same pattern was visible as in previous elections: 'Poorer, urban, working-class seats with larger than average numbers of ethnic minority and young voters had much lower turnouts than more affluent suburban, small town and rural seats.' *Parliamentary Affairs*, 50:4 (1997) p728.

11. Norris, *op.cit.*, p530.

12. Eric Hobsbawm, 'The Forward March of Labour Halted?' in Martin Jacques & Francis Mulhern (eds), *The Forward March of Labour Halted?*, Verso, London 1981, p18.

13. Eric Hobsbawm, 'Observations on the Debate', in M.Jacques & F.Mulhern *op.cit.*, p179.

14. Andrew Gamble, 'The Crisis of Conservatism', *New Left Review*, 214 (1995), pp3-25.

15. The exceptional character of the Falklands War was clearly shown by the much more muted reaction of public opinion in 1991 to the Gulf War.

16. The depth of the Conservative split on Europe is analysed by Steve Ludlam, 'The Spectre Haunting Conservatism: Europe and Backbench Rebellion', in S.Ludlam & M.J.Smith (eds), *Contemporary British Conservatism*, Macmillan, London 1996.

17. Paul Whiteley, Patrick Seyd, and Jeremy Richardson, *True Blues: The Politics of Conservative Party Membership*, Clarendon, Oxford 1994.

18. Peter Kellner, *op.cit.*, pp616-630.

19. See the interview with Alan Simpson, *New Statesman*, 16/11/97.

SECTION TWO: MEMBERS, VOTERS
AND CRITICAL MASSES

THE PERMANENT
REVOLUTION OF NEW
LABOUR

Paul Richards

Re-reading the near-histories of the first term of the Thatcher government reveals how they accentuated long-forgotten rows and trivia, and
failed to predict the seismic shifts in social and economic policy which
came in the second and third Tory terms.[1] Thatcher's two and a half
terms in government are a useful benchmark for the future prospects of
the Blair government. The major changes Thatcher made – the privatisation and deregulation of the economy, and the centralisation of the
state – began years, more than a decade in the case of the water and rail
sell-offs, after her first general election win, and there was little sense
of them in the 1979 Manifesto or in the early phase of the first term.
The initial sell-offs of the state's holdings in ICL, Fairey Holdings,
Farranti, the British Sugar Corporation and Cable and Wireless yielded
modest receipts, and formed what Andrew Gamble has called 'a slow
and hesitant start' to the programme of privatisation which followed.[2]
It is not clear that there was any clearly defined plan for privatisation
of the major utilities, and that much of the precise detail of the mechan-
ics of privatisation was worked out after the event.

If this pattern repeats, then the lasting changes of the Blair government might not start to be implemented until the early years of the next
century, and their effects not properly felt until ten or fifteen years
later. Tony Blair certainly knows his chances of making an impact
depend on the party being re-elected, probably twice. He told the
Fabian Society in 1995, 'I am in this for the long haul ... it is not

enough to win an election.' In May 1998, in a letter to Labour members, Blair made the point again: 'We knew above all that we would need more than one general election victory to achieve our mission, that we would need an unprecedented second term in office.'[3] Committed modernisers need to settle in for a waiting game.

THE SHOCK OF THE NEW

Modernisation is rooted in the simple premise that whilst Labour's values – a belief in the essential worth of community, freedom of the individual, tolerance of others, fairness and opportunity for all, a moral objection to poverty, squalor or ignorance – are non-negotiable and timeless, the ways these values are expressed through policy and government action change. The values are what give us an anchor, and prevent the Labour Party drifting aimlessly, and stop us becoming rootless ameliorators or do-gooders. Most importantly, modernisers view the Labour Party as their legitimate home, and see the party as the only means for social and political reform. Whilst the party itself is not immune from the need for continual modernisation, it is viewed as the sole political institution capable of carrying out the modernisers' project. This may seem commonplace, but we should constantly remind ourselves of the mistakes made by well-intentioned socialists who believed the answers lay in the trade unions, in single issue pressure groups, in political sects, or even in a new social-democratic party.

Modernisation is a continuous process – a permanent revolution. That means that Labour's policies today must change again in the future. It should also mean that Labour's New Clause IV should be repealed and replaced on an on-going basis. Without this permanent revolution, Labour would still be debating issues that mattered to Keir Hardie (the Boer War, votes for women, temperance), or to Clem Attlee (demobilisation, colonial freedom, food rationing) or even to Harold Wilson (Rhodesia, the National Plan, the Cold War), instead of the issues that matter today (crime, jobs, Europe, the environment).

The methods and means change because the world changes, our understanding changes, the people's aspirations and conditions change, and a political party which does not change has no effective future. When Labour clung to outdated solutions such as state control of business or massive increases in personal taxation, the people we wanted to elect us moved on. Conversely, when Labour presents a platform which people trust and addresses their needs and aspirations, as in 1945, 1964 and 1997, Labour can win.

In this sense modernisation is not a new political method. The founders of the party were the original 'new Labour' because their understanding of changes in politics and economics led them to establish a brand new party and smash the Victorian consensus.

As Tony Blair told a Labour meeting in 1995: 'If you look back at why people came into the Labour Party in the early days of this century, they came in because the Labour Party represented to them the party of change, they didn't say the existing political structures and systems were fine for them. They said "Look the Liberal Party can't represent us. We need our own political party."'[4]

CAUSE FOR CONCERN

Tony Crosland wrote in his classic text of revisionism, *The Future of Socialism*, that 'state ownership of all industrial capital is not now a condition of creating a socialist society' but also that 'we no doubt want more nationalisation than we now have' as part of 'a society in which ownership is thoroughly mixed-up.'[5]

This view would place a modern Labour Party member on the hard left, and it stands in stark contrast to new Labour's Clause IV commitment to 'the enterprise of the market and the rigour of competition' and 'a thriving private sector'.

In the 1970s and early 1980s, revisionism came under an assault characterised by Tudor Jones as 'a severe ideological reaction ... against revisionist social democracy'.[6] The machinery of the party – the National Executive and the Conference – was captured by the hard left, coupled with a decline in membership of the party, making Constituency Labour Parties less representative of the mainstream. The process was described by Crosland as 'a revival of semi-Marxist thought in Britain.'[7]

The deaths of leading moderniser Tony Crosland in 1977, of John Mackintosh in 1978, the exile of Roy Jenkins to Europe in 1976, and the disappointments of the Callaghan government, allied to the departure of the social democrats in 1980, meant that revisionism was in retreat, and the Bennite insurgency could make significant gains, especially at the Conference and on the National Executive Committee.

Following the shock of the cataclysmic 1983 general election defeat, modernisation in its 1980s phase was centred on removing Labour's negatives. It was a product of the realisation amongst the left that the net effect of pursuing the policy agenda of the Labour Left, led by Tony Benn, would mean the Labour Party would never be elected again, and probably cease to exist.

The key figure was Neil Kinnock. Blair dates the start of 'new Labour' to the election of Neil Kinnock as Labour leader in 1983. In his acceptance speech as leader of the party in 1994 Blair said, 'It was a great achievement to make Labour electable once more, and we will never forget the contribution to us and to our country's history by Neil Kinnock.'[8] The defining document for modernisers in the 1980s was not a positive statement of belief: it was the 1983 Labour Manifesto, with its long, rambling, and inconsistent calls for state control of the economy, import controls, unilateral nuclear disarmament, and huge increases in taxation and public spending. The trajectory of modernisation was to take Labour as far away as possible from that document, and the political project was to remove all traces from Labour's future strategy and ideology. That was the point of the Policy Review, from 1987 to 1989, culminating in its final report *Meet the Challenge, Make the Change*, which ended the party's commitment to state control in its policies, if not in its constitution.

The debate over Labour's constitution, particularly the Clause IV commitment to nationalisation, had lain dormant since Hugh Gaitskell's failed attempt to revise it in 1959. After the 1992 defeat, two important statements were made to rekindle the question, and to pave the way for a new Clause IV. The first was Neil Kinnock's revising of Clause IV for a television programme on socialism in 1993, and the second was Jack Straw's pamphlet *Policy and Ideology* in 1993, which made a detailed case for a new Clause IV. Both initiatives were slapped down by the John Smith leadership.

The lessons of the defeats of 1987 and 1992 were two-fold. Firstly, Labour learned that relying on presentation and 'spin' alone, no matter how brilliant the 1987 campaign was, cannot compensate for policies which people don't support, and secondly, that the people knowing what you are not – not Margaret Thatcher, not Michael Foot – is never enough of an incentive to vote Labour as understanding what you are for.

In 1997, the lesson had been learned. The negatives had been largely removed. The Tories' lines of attack – Labour will put taxes up, let the unions run riot, sell out to Europe – didn't work as they had in previous elections. But, crucially, there was a much clearer idea of what Labour was for.

Tony Blair was a leader who inspired trust and enthusiasm. In 1995, the adoption of a New Clause IV – the ultimate act of revisionism – proved beyond doubt that Labour had changed. The significance of this move, not merely in electoral terms, but in ideological terms, is explained by Tony Wright:

> The Blairite revolution, converting socialism into 'social-ism' and constructing a liberal communitarianism anchored in a broad intellectual inheritance of the centre-left, succeeded where the putative revisionism of a generation earlier had failed. The means and ends of socialism had finally been disentangled, not through evasion or obfuscation but through a direct and explicit process of theoretical reconstruction. On any test it was a decisive and defining moment for the British Left, both politically and intellectually, with a significance for socialism that went wider still.[9]

Moves like the Road to the Manifesto ballot and the introduction of members' policy forums made the party more democratic and inclusive. The importance of these mechanisms for consultation is that they move Labour away from the delegatory democracy of general committees, regional executives and activist-based conferences, towards a direct membership democracy. Labour's old structure depended on an elitist, two-tier structure, where those with the stamina to attend countless meetings were given more power than 'ordinary' members. The old model, based on the Soviet system, meant that a member of a general committee could pass resolutions in the name of the constituency party, hold the local MP to account, elect and mandate the conference delegate, decide on the local party's affiliations to outside groups like Campaign for Nuclear Disarmament, and stand for local party office, while the rank-and-file branch member could not. That structure automatically favours the ideologically-driven or slightly eccentric members, and explains the success of Trotskyist infiltration in the 1970s and 1980s while excluding mainstream activists with work, family or social commitments outside the Labour Party. The reform of the old party system has begun, but is in no way over, and will not be successful until the General Committee system is abolished in favour of all-member democracy. This becomes more, not less, important when Labour is in power.

One Party, Many Modernisations

New Labour's modernisation is not a homogeneous project. There is no secret single blueprint. There are deep fault-lines in the moderniser camp, just as previous generations like the Gaitskellites were divided over fundamental questions such as European integration. This is not necessarily a problem, of course. There are broad churches even within broad churches, and because modernisers in the Labour Party are not democratic centralists or entryists, the lack of a uniform platform is a strength not a weakness.

There is even a debate about what the purpose of inventing 'new Labour' was. Some modernisers would argue that the creation of 'new Labour' was a scorched-earth, year-zero rejection of all the failures of the past, and that all that was old was bad. In that sense 'new Labour' is literally a new party, and old Labour is, if not quite dead, certainly not feeling too well. The alternative position is that 'new Labour' stands in a lineage of ethical socialism which has been part of the party since its inception, but is now being rediscovered and given new life. Tony Blair himself has referred to influences as varied as Keir Hardie, William Temple, John MacMurray, R. H. Tawney and Lloyd George.

Modernisers can belong to different groups within the party with differing agendas, while staying on the same side. Although today's internal pressure groups have nowhere near the influence or saliency of groups which were active during the height of Labour's factional warfare, such as the Campaign for Labour Party Democracy (CLPD), the Rank and File Mobilising Committee or the early Labour Co-ordinating Committee (LCC), there are some which are important. The LCC's role has diminished from the days when it acted as an outrider for Kinnock's reforms, as an organisational platform in local government, and as the backbone of the National Organisation of Labour Students, and when its policy papers would be reported in *The Guardian*. The LCC is in some ways the victim of its own success. With one of its own members installed as prime minister and a PM's wife who once served on the LCC national committee, the need for a party faction acting as a 'pressure-group' on the leadership is less necessary. When Blair was leader in opposition, he was changing policy and organisation so fast, groups like the LCC struggled to keep up. (The LCC has voted to wind up its operations.)

The LCC 'journal of Labour politics' *Renewal*, edited by Paul Thompson, has been more significant. Launched in January 1993 in response to Labour's 1992 general election defeat, with Tony Blair, David Miliband, Tony Wright and Patricia Hewitt on the editorial board, the journal has provided space for commentary and analysis of the Blairite progress with articles on modernisation, globalisation, stakeholding, and communitarianism.

It was founded on the premise that the 'one more heave' school of thought – that Labour needed merely to hang on in there for a further five years before victory would fall into their laps – was fundamentally flawed. Despite the huge affection with which the late John Smith was regarded, some modernisers had begun to criticise the slowing in pace of modernisation under his leadership.

Instead, further reform, re-thinking and reappraisal was necessary. Tony Blair made the point in an essay for *Renewal* in October 1993, based on the premise that Labour lost in 1992 because the electorate felt that changes to Labour 'were superficial' and that 'society had changed and we did not change sufficiently with it. Policy prescriptions for one generation became confused with basic principles that are timeless'. Blair concludes 'the process that is called modernisation is in reality the application of enduring, lasting principles for a new generation, not just by creating a modern party organisation, but by inspiring a programme for a modern society, economy, and constitution.'[10]

Renewal has allowed a theoretical underpinning of some of the concepts which might otherwise have remained unclear buzz-words. Editor Paul Thompson's aim, to make *Renewal* be a focal-point for in-depth, strategic debate for Labour and centre-left' has largely been realised.[11] Another important spin-off from the LCC is Nexus, the meeting point for new Labour-inclined academics to join in the debate at a more practical level, and sanctioned by Tony Blair's belief that 'I want Labour to be able to draw on a coalition of thinkers, including people outside the party'.[12]

Progress is both a pro-Blair glossy magazine and a training and political organisation. It works through briefing seminars and weekend schools to reach the activists in ward meetings and council chambers, and arm them with pro-government ammunition. Despite support at the very highest levels and high-quality training events at trade union colleges for Labour members, *Progress* does not yet reach the numbers of Labour members needed to have a major effect on the psyche of the party. However, as the confusion over welfare reform shows, the party leadership's need to communicate directly with party members, rather than through the distorting prism of the media or local party leaders, will become ever more important, and *Progress* could be the means of doing it.

The Fabian Society, which predates the party itself, was used as a platform for party modernisers in the 1990s. By performing a traditional think-tank role, the society kept the policy debate moving forward, and attracted modernisers onto its staff and executive. Stephen Twigg was for a short while its General Secretary. Ian Corfield was Director of Research. In the period between 1992-97, the Fabian Society acted as a focal point for Blair's modernisation project. He used a Fabian conference in 1994 to stake out his ideological position during the Labour leadership contest, and as leader used the Fabian Society's celebration of the fiftieth anniversary of the 1945 government to further set out his philosophy. In the immediate pre-election period, the Fabian Society enjoyed a key position in new Labour's firmament, providing behind-the-scenes expertise as the plans for government were drawn up, and hosting seminars and discussions with business leaders and politicians. A key task was a series of firmly off-the-record sessions at Birkbeck College, hosted by Ben Pimlott, with the Shadow Cabinet and their advisers, and former senior civil servants. The seminars formed part of the training in governance which Blair's team underwent before the election.

Ian Corfield, Research Director at the Fabians during this period, recalls 'the Society's main role was behind the scenes. In the lead-up to the election, we were not going to rock the boat, but could play a role in helping Shadow Ministers get ready for the real thing. Although the Fabian Society remained a forum for debate, it was used to advance the ideas of a core group of modernisers.'[13] All of the Fabian Society's staff were seconded to the general election campaign, with Corfield working on Blair's speeches at Millbank Tower.

Even more important is the role of the Young Fabians, the semi-autonomous 'young members section' of the society. The Young Fabians is home to the cutting edge of the modernisation project. Since the election, the Young Fabians have hosted debates and conferences on issues from trade union reform, the welfare state, and defence and been unafraid to tackle difficult issues. Their membership is metropolitan, mid-twenties, and fiercely loyal to Tony Blair. Young Fabian activists form the leadership of an important network of activists with every intention of remaining active in the party.

Peter Metcalfe, former Young Fabian Chairman says: 'Young Fabians are young enough to have never been in the party when the left was in ascendancy. Many joined because of modernisation, and do not see the process as a shock to the system but as common sense. We will continue to be in the vanguard of change.'[14]

Criss-crossing this network of groups are the other think-tanks: Demos, the Institute for Public Policy Research, and the Social Market Foundation. The think-tanks of the centre and left have not had the impact on Labour policy that the Adam Smith Institute or Institute of Economic Affairs had on Thatcherism. However, as Labour's existing policy programme is either superseded by events or implemented by government, the role of the think-tanks in recrafting the policy agenda becomes even more important. Already they have provided personnel for the government's machine: Geoff Mulgan went from Demos to the Number Ten Policy Unit, Dan Corry went from the IPPR to the Department of Trade and Industry. Youth is a highly visible trait of modernisers grouped around *Progress*, the Young Fabians, the network of former Labour Students in and around Westminster, and others drawn to the new Labour banner. The National Organisation of Labour Students formed an important training ground throughout the 1980s in colleges, and as the leadership of the NUS, and four recent Labour presidents of NUS are now Members of Parliament: Jim Murphy, Stephen Twigg, Lorna Fitzsimons, and Phil Woolas.

The average age is twenty-something in these groups. This is the generation which cannot remember the last Labour government, and has some difficulty remembering Neil Kinnock. Many came into activity after Tony Blair was elected leader, or even because he was elected leader, and have known nothing but the Blair Labour Party. Unlike the membership of the party as a whole, this cadre of activists is instinctively loyal to the party and its leaders. This group forms a network of alliances and friendships, usually going back to student days, which reaches into the trade unions, particularly MSF and the AEEU, constituency parties, local government, the think-tanks, Labour staff at Millbank and the regional offices, the political staff at Number Ten and Special Advisers. As the fledgling careers of members of these networks develop, in local parties, local government, the unions, the voluntary sector, and the political system, the influence of modernisers will grow.

THE IMPORTANCE OF PETER MANDELSON

Peter Mandelson's role is hugely important, and of far greater significance and lasting effect that the insubstantial newspaper coverage of his activities would suggest. His role as Director of Communications is well documented, and he played an important part in the modernisation of the party's image and presentation. For example Andy McSmith describes his contribution thus: 'Within an organisation long accustomed to the idea that second-best will do, he displayed an exacting professional standard and demanded it from others.'[15]

But presentation is only part of Mandelson's contribution. Whilst new Labour's young cadres owe their political loyalty to Blair, they look for inspiration to Mandelson as their political godfather. The Young Fabian reception at Labour's annual conference is one of the few which can rely on Peter Mandelson's appearance and he provides a tangible link between the party leadership and the young people on the ground who want to support Labour's leadership. He has also forged a youthful base of support that can only become more influential and weighty within the party over the next ten years.

MIND THE GAP

There remain political issues, which divide the modernisers.

Some see the speed and extent of party reform as a luxury which the Government cannot afford, given the levels of opposition it would undoubtedly produce from Labour's vested interests. The alternative view is that in order to avoid the splits and rancour that the Callaghan government produced, the party structures, which exclude the voice of the ordinary member in favour of the constituency activist, need to be opened up.

Flowing from this is the debate around the role of the trade unions. Those wanting a total divorce have had their main argument, that the institutional link deters people from voting Labour, destroyed by the landslide in May 1997. Yet the argument for divorce can still be framed as beneficial to the unions themselves, alongside the introduction of state funding for parties. For example, Donald Sassoon, writing in *Renewal* in January 1993, said that under such an arrangement unions would 'become a more effective lobbying organisation ... and they would still have considerable influence with the Labour Party.'[16] A new, ultra modernisers' group launched at the 1998 Party Conference, 'Second Term', is committed to ending the party-union link.

The importance of the unions within the party is not lost on modernisers. Many former Labour Students activists have put their organisational and political skills to work within the trade union move-ment. Lee Whitehead, campaigns officer at MSF and new Labourite, says: 'Many young modernisers recognise that trade unions have a legitimate role to play. The cementing of the relationship came when unions agreed the cutting of the block vote at conference, giving power back to individual members. This proved that the relationship could be constructive and based on individual membership, a principle very important to new Labour.'[17]

Reform of the constitution is another major fault-line in modernisa-tion. This revolves around the extent to which the Labour Party should accommodate the Liberal Democrats to forge a new political consen-sus, which could keep the Tories out of power for fifty years or more. The main proponents of such arrangements, the Labour Initiative on Co-operation (LINC), decided to fold in the wake of Labour's land-slide, but it seems Blair would be willing to attempt such a mould-breaking exercise. He has remarked that the philosophical parents of the 1945 Labour government were Beveridge and Keynes, both Liberals. In this he would meet bitter opposition from Labour chau-vinists. The debate over electoral reform pits moderniser against moderniser. The Labour Campaign for Electoral Reform is bitterly opposed by supporters of first-past-the-post, whilst amongst those who support electoral reform there remains the dispute over which kind of system should be adopted.

In other political areas, from changes in the system of local govern-ment, the progress and extent of European Monetary Union, the struc-ture of the taxation system and the introduction of hypothecation, the scope of welfare reform and the ending of universality as the guiding principle, and the future of the health service and education system, there are many arguments still to be had. However, this lack of a coher-ent shopping list of policy is no bad thing: it enables tactical flexibility and lets Government govern as circumstances change. The Tories in 1979 had a vague sense of wanting to extend the free market, but the precise mechanism – privatisation – hadn't even been invented yet. Labour will make progress in the same way: guided by values, but capable of innovation.

The lack of a firm code of belief amongst Labour's modernisers is a result of the lack of serious opposition. Those who reject the trajectory of modernisation, who voted against Tony Blair, the New Clause IV, and the manifesto, form a tiny minority within the party. Even votes for leftwing candidates for the pre-reformation NEC can be explained by the beauty-contest character of the voting, rather than as an expression of ideology. Those seriously arguing for nationalisation, such as Arthur Scargill or Hugh Kerr, are either on the margins or no longer in the party. Even grass-roots groups like Labour Reform, a new organisation opposed to the changes to the party constitution under Blair, are confused over what they stand for or want. New Labour is still the only serious game in town.

Towards the third term

The electorate which faces the general election in 2007 will probably have lived under a Labour government for a decade. Many first-time voters will have no recollection of the Conservatives in power. People will have trouble remembering who John Major was. It is entirely possible that Labour will be viewed as the natural party of government.

Tony Blair will face the electorate as one of the country's longest serving Prime Ministers. The personalities of the first Labour Cabinet will have long since been replaced by men and women whose names we do not yet know, some of whom are not even yet in the House of Commons. His governments will have been rocked by political falling-out and sporadic scandals, as all governments are. But as election week approaches, the polls will show a healthy support for the Labour Party, the 'new' will have long-since been dropped as unnecessary.

In ten years, much will have changed. Britain will have joined the single currency. The changeover will cause little fuss once the decision is made, just as in the 1970s when the Tories brought in decimalisation. The Old Money will look as curious and dated as threepenny bits and half crowns. Businesses, the financial services and tourists will all take the Euro for granted.

As people travel around the United Kingdom they will see greater fairness in the distribution of jobs and investment between North and South. The Regional Development Agencies will have worked with local employers and inward investors to ensure all parts enjoy prosperity. London will have a mayor with executive powers, heading up an elected London assembly.

The Scottish Parliament and Welsh Assembly will have staved off the demands for independence, but demands for greater political and fiscal freedom will characterise the relationship between the Welsh, Scottish and Westminster Parliaments. Northern Ireland will have its own Parliament too, and the province will have enjoyed a longer period of peace than at any time since 1969.

The chances are our travellers will have left their gas-powered car at home and taken a 'Prescott' train, one of the state-subsidised services designed to get people onto public transport. Looking from the window of the train, they will no longer see the great sink estates and inner-city deprivation which the Tories caused, and then ignored. The first great intervention to tackle unemployment – Gordon Brown's windfall tax and New Deal – will look like small beer compared to the great radical initiatives later taken to end unemployment.

The Millennium will have come and gone. People will remember the day they spent in Greenwich at the Millennium Experience for the rest of their lives. It will be a success. The Dome will still be standing, like the South Bank or the Crystal Palace before it, a testament to political courage. England's performance in the World Cup 2006, with the thrilling final at Old Trafford, will be entering popular folklore.

The welfare state will have been transformed. The availability of work, the access to training and skills via the University for Industry, and the laser-like accuracy of the targeting of benefit thanks to new IT-based solutions, will mean that the welfare bill will have halved in ten years. The Government will have diverted resources away from the bills for failure and into the investment in schools and the health service that people voted for in 1997 and 2002. Just as in the 1940s when international visitors marvelled at the new NHS, once again the Health Service will be a symbol of Britain's success.

Britain will not have changed beyond recognition. Changes will have come incrementally and slowly. But Britain will have changed. New laws banning fox hunting will have been introduced. Childcare will be available to all. Trade unions will have a place at the top table, alongside employers. There will be a national minimum wage covering all workers. Smoking will be on the decrease amongst the 11-16 year olds for the first time, following bans on cigarette advertising and smoking in public. Crime will have been cut through better use of crime prevention methods. People will be living in city-centres once more, breathing new life into run-down areas. The House of Lords will have gone, the Monarchy will have been reformed. Queen Elizabeth II, still on the throne, will spend the final years of her reign in a process of modernisation of the monarchy's constitutional and financial affairs which will allow the institution to survive alongside the extension of democracy and new structures of government which will be Labour's lasting monument.

The system of taxation will have been transformed. Labour will have realised that only through hypothecation of taxation can the taxpayer be reconnected to the tax system. By directly linking taxes and the benefits they pay for, new Labour will manage to raise extra revenues without creating a tax revolt amongst its middle class supporters.

The memory of homeless teenagers on the streets will seem as alien and offensive to our twenty-first century voter as the sight of First World War veterans selling matches did in the 1930s. The ending of the worst excesses of squalor and poverty will be demonstrable by statistics and people's everyday experience.

There will be greater tolerance of racial minorities and gays, with an equal age of consent, the lifting of the ban on gays in the armed forces, and new laws outlawing racially motivated violence. A new sense of security at work will replace the fear and uncertainty of the Tory years.

The voter making his or her mind up in the general election of 2007 will be faced by the choice of the Labour Party led by Tony Blair, the Conservative Party led by Chris Patten, the New Conservatives – the Euro-sceptic, nationalist breakaway led by John Bercow – the Liberal Democrats under Lembit Opik, and the newly emergent Green Party.

The election will be fought under proportional representation for the first time, the Additional Member System, although similar PR systems will have been working well in the Scottish Parliament, Welsh Assembly, the Parliament of the North, local government, and the European elections for years. Voting will take place over a weekend in shopping centres across Britain, with the option of cyber-voting from home.

As Tony Blair faces his third general election campaign at the head of the Labour Party, he will be filled with confidence that people support his policies and vision, even more so after a decade in the job as Britain's most radical prime minister since Lloyd George. His first and second governments will have proved that government can make a difference to our lives, that politics still matters in the face of the globalisation juggernaut.

In 2007, in a hundred small ways, and a number of big ways, Britain will be a cleaner, safer, brighter, happier, more confident place. Many of the changes will be imperceptible, and soon taken for granted, such as new road safety laws, the ending of passport controls, the liberalisation of the licensing laws to allow 24-hour pub opening, and the introduction of national identity cards containing all our bank and personal details. Some of the changes will be major, and their implementation will cause division and debate.

Modernisation is a process without an end point. The modernisation of party and country is a revolution that never stops. It is a permanent revolution, or it is nothing.

NOTES

1. D. Bell (ed), *The Conservative Government 1979-84*, Croom Helm, London 1985; J. Bruce-Gardyne, *Mrs Thatcher's First Administration*, Macmillan, London 1984.
2. Andrew Gamble, *The Free Economy and the Strong State – the Politics of Thatcherism*, Macmillan, London 1998.
3. Tony Blair, *New Britain*, Fourth Estate, London 1996.
4. Tony Blair, *op. cit.*
5. Anthony Crosland, *The Future of Socialism*, Jonathon Cape, London 1956.
6. Tudor Jones, *Remaking the Labour Party – from Gaitskell to Blair*, Routledge, London 1996.
7. Anthony Crosland, *Socialism Now*, Jonathan Cape, London 1974.
8. Tony Blair, *op.cit.*
9. Tony Wright, *Socialisms*, Routledge, London 1996.
10. Tony Blair, 'Why Modernisation Matters', in *Renewal*, October 1993.
11. Paul Thompson, *Renewal*, January 1993.
12. Giles Radice (ed.,) *What Needs to Change*, HarperCollins, London 1996.
13. Interview with author April 1998.
14. Interview with author April 1998.
15. Andy McSmith, *Faces of Labour*, Verso, London 1996.
16. Donald Sassoon, *Renewal*, January 1993.
17. Interview with author April 1998.

SHIFTING TO THE BRIGHT: IN SEARCH OF THE INTELLECTUAL LEFT

Geoff Andrews

To make any assessment of the Blair project, it is necessary to engage critically with new Labour's attempt to articulate a new concept of governance, and a new ideological framework for the centre left. Hence recurring themes in such assessment are uncertainty over the ideological provenance of new Labour, discussion of its progress in attempting to articulate a third way between traditional left and right, and the debate about the extent to which it departs from social democracy or accepts the logic of neo-liberalism. Success in these areas will depend crucially upon new Labour's relationship with intellectuals. Tony Blair has shown an openness to intellectuals that marks a departure from the conservative, cautious, at times hostile, approach of traditional labourism. He has welcomed the new intellectual networks that have been set up such as Nexus and he has encouraged the greater intellectual pluralism that is a feature of contemporary politics. He has gathered an impressive range of thinkers around him, such as Anthony Giddens and John Gray of the London School of Economics, while one of the most iconoclastic and free thinking of contemporary intellectuals – Geoff Mulgan director of Demos has found his way into the Downing Street Policy Unit.

Yet few can speculate with any confidence about the outcome of this new *rapprochement* with intellectuals. Much will depend upon the boldness of new Labour as it faces the reality of governing. We must also ask if intellectuals any longer have the capacity to make a difference. Have the technological, demographic, global and cultural trends of late modern societies rendered intellectuals redundant as political agents?

We are now approaching a critical moment in the history of intellectual influence upon public debate. For Michael Ignatieff there has been a 'crisis of authority' in the public role of intellectuals. He laments the decline of those public intellectuals, in the tradition of Voltaire and Sartre, who helped to shape the development of democratic and progressive thought and whose audience was not the 'monastic few', but the 'educated many'. 'Where' Ignatieff asks, 'are the independent, public intellectuals now? ... Worthy professors, cultural bureaucrats, carnival barkers and entertainers. The death of the intellectual has left a void in public life; in place of thought we have opinion; in place of argument we have journalism; in place of polemic we have personality profiles'.[1]

This public and independent status that Ignatieff identifies is crucial to an understanding of the role of the intellectual. The defining feature of intellectuals is the rejection of wholesale loyalty to party lines or convenient public opinion: they assume responsibility for critical and independent thought. Intellectuals should also take on the responsibility of intervening in the public domain, and of being actively involved in re-shaping or challenging prevailing world views. Thus intellectuals inevitably have a political role. For some this has been the problem, while for others it has been the way in which tyrannies have been challenged and the universal concepts of justice, freedom and enlightenment upheld.

THE PERILS OF PROFESSIONALISATION

It is these two dimensions – maintaining independence in the pursuit of truth and taking responsibility for articulating ideals to a wider public – which many have seen as being under threat. Edward Said, in his 1993 Reith Lectures, identified the pressures released by the drift towards 'professionalisation' as the basis of this problem. The professionalisation of intellectual life had seen off the ' true' intellectual who had been reduced to the role of 'manufacturing consent' for various forms of authority. Professionalisation had brought into being tendencies of specialisation and the obscure – and an obsession with expertise to the extent that intellectuals must often face forms of 'certification' before their status is accepted and they can be assimilated into the power structures of state institutions. Said asks the crucial question: can there be 'anything like an independent, autonomously functioning intellectual, one who is not beholden to and therefore constrained by his or her affiliations with universities that pay salaries, political parties that

demand loyalty to a party line, think tanks that while they offer freedom to do research perhaps more subtly compromise judgement and
restrain the critical voice?'[2]

Said also dismisses the concept of a 'private intellectual', since 'the
moment you set down words and then publish them you have entered
the public world'. The domain of the intellectual is therefore both independent and public, the values universal, the temperament unorthodox
'embarrassing, contrary even unpleasant rather than making people feel
good'.[3]

THE ACCOMMODATING ACADEMY

The extent to which the public and independent roles of intellectuals
have been compromised is illustrated by the state of contemporary
academia. Although the academy is often misleadingly seen as the epitome of academic life (it was never that), it is now one of the last places
one might expect to find the kind of intellectual that Said describes.
Academics have become increasingly marginal to mainstream public
debate. On the back of the dominant ethos of the new managerialism,
which has transformed the balance of power between academic and
managerial staff in universities, there has been a retreat into obscurity,
as well as a surrendering of independence.

This is nothing new in itself, nor is it due solely to lack of courage
and imagination by academics who have to meet strict research, funding and administrative criteria. These most recent trends, though, do
mark a fundamental shift in the status of academics, who now face a
choice between two roles. One alternative is to become 'research
hermits', engrossing themselves in the need to increase their research
assessment rating by writing for obscure 'refereed' journals, or by
keeping up appearances on the academic conference circuit, a process
that is becoming increasingly tedious, with often mediocre outcomes.
On the other hand they can become 'career bureaucrats', immersing
themselves in the demands and details of administration and foregoing
any kind of intellectual activity.

The cumulative effect of these two roles is that many academics have
forgotten how to be intellectuals. Their contributions to generalist
public debates in civil society are at best peripheral, at worst irrelevant.
Moreover there is little impetus from within universities themselves for
the situation to change. After all, the rewards and promotions which

await academics are based either on research assessment rating or more usually, on an increase in administrative tasks. Teaching and wider public intellectual energies count for little. No wonder that heresy and iconoclasm are becoming rare in academia or that cynicism has replaced scepticism, that essential component of an intellectual. In the wider picture of the organisation, policing and management of university life, there is little space for dissent. Indeed academic freedom itself may now be a luxury.

THE MUDDY WATERS OF THE POST-ENLIGHTENMENT

These shifts in academic life represent a much broader dilemma: whether or not intellectuals can keep faith with their original calling. Those intellectuals who emerged from the Enlightenment as confident unmaskers of truth, and articulators of the universal principles of freedom and justice, had a clear perception of their role. In their condemnation of the prejudices and superstitions of prevailing beliefs, they sought critical independence, many coming into conflict with authorities or other defenders of received opinion. Through the *Encyclopédie,* salons and popular pamphlets the wider public audience became involved. In this Age of Enlightenment, when classical ideologies were in embryo and new forms of media had yet to develop, a consensus in the idea of 'progress' emerged. The role of intellectuals was clear: they were purveyors of truth as well as justice. They would not give in to popular opinion or prejudice. They were outsiders yet simultaneously in conflict with orthodoxies.

The concept of the intellectual which came out of the Enlightenment was based therefore on the necessity of a public role and, following the liberal tradition of reason and progress, prioritised the seeking of truth and certainty. However questions remained over the extent to which intellectuals should take on an overtly political role. Modernity itself brought major dilemmas. The rise of classical ideologies, or the 'grand narratives', provided a framework for intellectual activity, yet threatened the priority of seeking 'objectivity' and 'truth' .

Further dilemmas arose with the development of the state and other forms of social organisation, the outcome of what Foucault has termed the 'disciplinary society'.[4] This reveals the contradictory impact of modernity on intellectuals. In Mannheim's view[5], it allowed a 'relative autonomy' to intellectuals as a new social strata. Yet it also provided forms of assimilation and control, which compromised intellectual work. The nineteenth-century demand for experts, as the new rulers of modern societies, has been followed in the twentieth century by professionalisation. Intellectuals face the choice of being 'insiders' or 'outsiders', and greater integration threatens their role as independent critics.

INSIDERS AND OUTSIDERS

There have been two major responses to these dilemmas. The first position is that identified with the Italian Communist leader and Marxist theoretician Antonio Gramsci. Gramsci's classic distinction was between traditional intellectuals, those 'true intellectuals', the men of letters who carried out what he saw as aloof and non-directive roles, and 'organic' intellectuals, who had a more concrete historical and ideological role in shaping the world view of particular social groups. He describes the emergence of the new concept of organic intellectuals in this way:

> The mode of being of the new intellectual can no longer consist in eloquence, which is an exterior and momentary mover of feelings and passions, but in active participation in practical life, as constructor, organiser, 'permanent persuader' and not just a simple orator ... from technique-as-work one proceeds to technique-as-science and to the humanistic conception of history, without which one remains 'specialised' and does not become directive.[6]

'Directive' in the Gramscian lexicon would eventually come to mean 'hegemonic'.

When Gramsci described intellectuals as 'permanent persuaders' he assigned them the major task of taking social groups beyond common sense, to help fashion a 'national-popular' will and to help create political blocs. It is vital to note the period in which Gramsci was writing, a time of mass politics, mass parties, clearly demarcated political ideologies and relatively homogeneous social groups combined to make political change. Parties were crucial in organising these directive impulses of Gramsci's hegemony, because they were a main vehicle for ideas and influence. His famous statement – 'all can be intellectuals but not all have the function of intellectuals' – provides a much broader concept of the intellectual. Intellectuals operate according to this concept in a variety of spheres, as 'permanent persuaders' in a range of specialised functions. The decline of mass society and the technological transformation of work and the economy have therefore released intellectuals into an increasing number of such functions.

This suggests that intellectuals continue to be defined by their political role. The significance of Gramsci's view, which has been described by Bellamy as the 'intellectual as social critic' position, is that intellectuals in the modern sense cannot be neutral.[7] The truth seeking intellectual has been rendered obsolete by the transformative processes of modernity. Gramsci didn't argue, as others have, that intellectuals are by definition radical; the bourgeoisie had its own array of intellectuals essential to maintaining its own hegemony. What was crucial was the social and political domain that intellectuals had allegiance to in the modern world. It was the function of intellectuals as part of the superstructural apparatus that was fundamental for Gramsci, not the pursuit of truth.

This conflicts with the second position, which has a number of different dimensions, combining ideas first associated with Karl Mannheim with more recent work which gives attention to the outsider status of intellectuals – a view articulated by Edward Said in his Reith Lectures. According to Mannheim, intellectuals in the modern era were a 'relatively classless stratum', who were neither a class themselves nor part of a class. This distinguished his position from Gramsci's. What really distinguished intellectuals was their ability to work free from social constraints. For Mannheim the development of the strata of intellectuals marked the last stage in the growth of social consciousness. Mannheim argued that intellectuals 'were the last group to acquire the sociological point of view, for its position in the social division of labour does not provide direct access to any vital and functionary segment of society'.[8]

While Mannheim's theory helps move the argument on from deterministic or reductionist theories associated with the debilitating restrictions of some aspects of traditional Marxism and functionalism, it suggests that the heterogeneous nature of intellectual life allows these thinkers a special place to develop their ideas. Said in his Reith Lectures takes this view further, combining elements of Mannheim's position with those of Gramsci. For Said the true intellectual is an 'outsider' who leads a 'lonely existence', one who lives 'on the margins' in 'self-imposed exile'. It was the:

spirit in opposition, rather than in accommodation that grips one
because the romance, the interest, the challenge of intellectual life is to be
found in dissent against the *status quo* at a time when the struggle on
behalf of under-represented and disadvantaged groups seems so unfairly
eighted against them.[9]

For Said, now moving away from Mannheim, intellectuals must take
on a political role; they need to make choices.

DANGER! INTELLECTUALS AT WORK

Of course many have found the political interventions of intellectuals
objectionable. Britain has a particular disdain for intellectuals, reflected
in the empirical traditions of British history and social science.
Intellectuals here have always had a lower profile than in most other
European countries. A distrust of intellectuals, reflected in Edmund
Burke's response to the attempts by French revolutionaries to 'remake
society from its roots', has been sustained by a deferential and antiquated political culture. Thatcherism, with its contempt for traditional
intellectual institutions, notably Oxbridge, and its drive to marketise
arts and literature reasserted this distrust. For many on the right the
problem of socialism became inextricably linked to the problem of
intellectuals, who 'preached' to ordinary people about how to lead
their lives, offered utopian schemes, often hypocritical in the way they
conducted their own lives. The disjuncture between an intellectual's
personal life and his or her high-minded ideals has been a feature of
much critical commentary from right-wing thinkers. Left-wing intel-
lectual-turned-right-wing-populist Paul Johnson notes 'a growing
tendency among ordinary people to dispute the right of academics,
writers and philosophers, eminent though they may be, to tell us how
to behave and conduct our affairs'.[10] John Carey in *Intellectuals and
the Masses* has also attacked the elitism, as he sees it, of left-wing intellectuals from the Bloomsbury Group to the Fabians.[11]

It is grossly misleading however to imply that the left by nature
exhibits intellectual energy, and the right merely an anti-intellectual
paranoia. The success of the New Right in Britain in putting together
an intellectual project which has altered politics for a generation – for
good some would argue – has been in no small part due to the ability
of some organic intellectuals in think tanks such as the Institute for

Economic Affairs and the Centre for Policy Studies. Both have influenced the New Right's policy agenda in the direction of an alternative world view.

Moreover the British left itself has strong anti-intellectual traditions. Within the Labour Party those such as the Fabians and the Bevanite/Tribune left have always sought to plough their own furrow between the labourist ethos of electoralism and trade union conservatism. Even outside the Labour Party mainstream, where there was more space for critical intellectuals, uncomfortable questions kept re-emerging. The Communist Party [CPGB] produced a range of impressive intellectuals, notably the Marxist historians group and a later generation associated with the Communist University of London and the magazine *Marxism Today*, yet it also showed much impatience with the intellectuals' lack of discipline, claims to autonomy and concern with higher ideals rather than local campaigns. The height of this tension was of course 1956 when many intellectuals left the party and helped to form the more intellectually prosperous New Left.

Further reverberations were heard in the 1980s when groups such as the Militant Tendency declared that the prominence given to middle-class intellectuals contributed to the dilution of working-class values. In agreement with Johnson and other critics from the right, the overtly 'workerist' Militant saw the *social position* of intellectuals as responsible for distorting the real life experiences of ordinary people and leading them down avenues of defeat. Not only did right-wing and left-wing populist views converge in their dislike of intellectuals, they both missed the point: the role of the intellectual had been transformed.

TOWARDS THE POSTMODERN INTELLECTUAL

This left anti-intellectualism of the 1980s marked a departure from the optimism of the 1960s and 1970s, during which time a new generation of student-intellectuals had challenged the political establishment and the inadequacies of existing political structures. A renaissance of Marxism, resurgence of feminist ideas, and Eurocommunism, had each suggested healthy prospects for a revival of the left. Intellectuals again became important. Yet in retrospect the real legacy of this period was the transformation of intellectual modes of work, and the decentring of the intellectual, as we have known him/her. This transformation and decentring was driven by the inability of classical ideologies to organise belief systems. Events in 1989 confirmed this.

Whether or not intellectuals can still aspire to a critical and engaged public role will be decided in the context of the crisis of modernity. The moment of 1968 remains crucial in this respect. The 1960s left emphasis on the micro as well as the global, the 'personal is political', and the view, conceptualised in the works of Foucault, that power resides in a multiplicity of spheres, gave new impetus to the belief that critically engaged intellectuals could effect change. Yet it also raised doubts about the extent to which intellectuals could operate within formal political structures, notably that of the political party. Since 1968 the space for critical intellectuals has increasingly become one of 'outsiders kicking in'. For Boggs this has meant that future organic intellectuals will have to organise 'around multiple centres of resistance and sites of popular struggle [in which] it becomes commonplace for critical intellectuals to perform more distinctly loyal and organic functions tied in some way to social movements. It is here that theory, culture and politics finally merge'.[12]

As Boggs argues, there will be more space for intellectuals: 'The future erosion of a rational ordered world presided over by corporate elites and institutional managers could allow for a new sense of time and space leading, potentially, to a revitalised public sphere in which critical public intellectuals can fully participate as political actors'.[13]

Today there is a more complex relationship between ideas and intellectuals than ever before. Neither liberalism nor social democracy can any longer wholly account for the phenomena of globalisation, the fluidity of class structures, the transformation of gender roles, the pluralisation of identity and the structural decline of the political party. It is more difficult to be a committed intellectual on the left, but also easier to take on the function of an intellectual – as Gramsci predicted – as the old barriers between the intellectual and the non-intellectual break down.

The decentring of the intellectual, in terms of both ideology and function, raises the prospect of the emergence of a postmodern intellectual. The resurgence of civil society in more diverse and fluid forms offers a favourable setting for the iconoclast, who is freed from the twin trappings of orthodox political cultures and traditional spheres of influence. As these more sophisticated and complex societies emerge, it becomes more, not less, necessary for intellectuals to use their influence in public debate.

FUTURE TENSE: NEW LABOUR AND THE INTELLECTUAL DIASPORA

These dilemmas posed by intellectuals have only partly been addressed by new Labour. It has learned from the long hard winter of Thatcherism the necessity to construct a 'project' – a favourite Blairite phrase – to sustain the next generation, one that would have to involve those outside the Labour Party ranks. The need to distinguish between the long-term, and the short-term, the need to deal with structural causes, and the need for conviction have been there from the outset. Blair himself wants to feel at home in the intellectual diaspora, welcoming ideas from both traditional left and right, and indeed describing his approach as a 'third way' between these traditions. The thinkers most associated with him reflect this new pluralism, where 'no fixed ideological abode' is a distinguishing feature of new forms of intellectual engagement.

The influence of *Marxism Today* was important in the commitment to a 'project'. Indeed, to Stuart Hall and Martin Jacques, Blair was the '*Marxism Today* candidate' for leadership of the party, precisely because of his determination to learn from Thatcherism and to break free from labourism, and because of his ambition to root an alternative approach in the context of social, cultural and economic change.[14] Both Hall and Jacques, though, remain unconvinced about the scope of Blair's project, seeing only a limited attempt at modernisation and an approach which remains culturally conservative. Indeed for all Blair's modernisation of the party, crucial as it was in departing from labourism, there was no clear vision of modernisation for the country. Nor did it have a clear sense of its enemies and allies – crucial for the success of any *hegemonic* project.[15]

For Blair, then, while intellectuals matter, dilemmas remain. His enthusiasm in encouraging the Nexus network, in order to maintain the intellectual resources of the project, such as it exists in its 'impermanent'[16] and 'uneven and incomplete'[17] forms, confirms his more open and free-thinking approach. A dual message was sent to intellectuals – that they matter, more perhaps than Labour had been prepared to admit in the past, but they must not be 'aloof'.

The intellectuals who become 'insiders', however, do so in a very narrow sense. The focus of Nexus is very much policy-orientation: connecting intellectuals in its different topic groups to policy agendas and holding seminars which bring together policy-makers, academics and the business community. It is uncertain how much direct influence this kind of work produces, which raises the question of how seriously new Labour treats its intellectual allies and where the balance of power lies between intellectuals and politicians. Labour remains suspicious, waiting to extract a loyalty from intellectuals as it increasingly does from any other part of its constituency. However intellectuals cannot offer this same degree of loyalty. And they have no business doing so. It is not the vocation of intellectuals to be 'trusted'. The critical functions they adopt in their work must be allowed to flourish.

New Labour often exhibits a one-sided heresy in questioning the basis of social democracy for specific ends, notably the reform of the welfare state, the challenge to redistributive taxation and flexible labour markets. In other areas, such as the family, the impact of risk and insecurity and other general trends of a post-traditional society, it has shown little sign of heretical engagement. New Labour has plenty to say about the end of social democracy, but little about the more pluralistic cultures, and loose networks of ideas, that were providing new forms of allegiance and identity long before.

We need to 'out' intellectuals by demanding that they take up a more public and critical role during this decisive period in politics.[18] Being an 'insider' intellectual should not necessarily mean being a party loyalist. It should carry a responsibility for helping to shape public debate, with an influence on political decision-making being only a part of this role. Intellectuals need also to be outsiders: sufficiently detached to develop critiques and to look for the wider picture, and the long-term perspective – going against the grain where necessary. The outsider intellectual also needs to be able to recognise the limits of party form, rejecting the assimilative pull of managerialist bureaucracies and reconnecting with the diversity of the public realm.

NOTES

1. M. Ignatieff; 'Where are they now?', *Prospect Observer* Taster 197.
2. E. Said, *Representations of the Intellectual*, 1993 Reith Lecture, Vintage, London 1994 p51.
3. *Ibid.*, p9
4. M. Foucault, *Discipline and Punish*, Allen Lane, 1979.
5. K. Mannheim, *Essays on the Sociology of Culture*, Routledge and Kegan Paul, London 1956 p101.

6. A. Gramsci, *Selections From Prison Notebooks*, Lawrence and Wishart, London 1971 p10. See also A. Showstack Sassoon, *Gramsci's Politics* , Hutchinson, 1987. [Postscript]

7. R. Bellamy, 'The Intellectual as Social Critic' in J. Jennings and A. Kemp-Welch, *Intellectuals in Politics; From the Dreyfus Affair to Salman Rushdie*, Routledge, London 1997 pp25-44.

8. Mannheim, *op. cit.*

9. Said, *op.cit.*, pxv.

10. P. Johnson, *Intellectuals*, Weidenfeld and Nicholson, London 1988 p342.

11. J. Carey, *Intellectuals and the Masses*, Faber and Faber, London 1992.

12. C. Boggs, *Intellectuals and the Crisis of Modernity*, State University New York Press, p10.

13. Boggs, *op. cit.*, pxiii.

14. See the three conversations between Martin Jacques and Stuart Hall in the *New Statesman*, 22 November 1997, 29 November 1997, and 5 December 1997.

15. M. Jacques, 'He has a project for the party but what about his project for the country', The *Guardian*, 26 September 1996.

16. See K. Davey, 'The Impermanence of New Labour', in M.Perryman (ed), *The Blair Agenda*, Lawrence and Wishart, London 1996.

17. M. Kenny and M.J. Smith, '[Mis]Understanding Blair', *Political Quarterly*.

18. G. Andrews, 'Breaking Free; Intellectuals and New Labour', *Renewal* Vol 5 No 1, February 1997.

CURRYING FAVOUR?
RACE AND DIASPORA IN NEW BRITAIN

Rupa Huq

It's the summer of 1997 and celebrations are about to mark fifty years of Indian independence; itself the fruit of an earlier Labour landslide ushering in a new dawn. It's as if things have come full circle. The British South Asian diaspora – the natural consequence of Indian independence – have returned the favour by placing their faith in the People's Party, helping to deliver them power on a scale unimaginable in any of the intervening years. Fast forward to Spring 1998, nearly a year on, and post-election euphoria is subsiding. The death of Enoch Powell jolts the national consciousness, raising the spectre of a figure from a pre-new Labour age and issues long thought to be dead in British politics: race, patriotism and immigration.

Powell's original 'rivers of blood' anti-immigration speech of 1968 contained the warning: 'In 15 or 20 years' time the black man will have the whip hand.'[1] Even in death, it seemed Powell split the country; this time over the question of whether his body should be allowed to lie in state. The Bishop of Croydon, the Rt Rev Wilfred Wood (vehemently opposed) remarked: 'Enoch Powell gave a certificate of respectability to white racist views which otherwise decent people were ashamed to acknowledge'.[2] Tony Blair was more charitable stating: 'However much we disagreed with many of his views, there was no doubting the strength of his sincerity, or his tenacity in pursuing them, regardless of his own political self-interest'.[3]

Although Powell's central prediction remains far from realised three decades later, its legacy has been to instill the common perception of Labour as 'soft' on immigration and the Conservatives as taking a contrastingly hardline approach. However practice and implementation have proved otherwise. The race/immigration issue has largely been a consensus one; both parties adhering to the dictum 'keep them put, keep those who are in happy', encapsulated in the Tory manifesto statement: 'Fair but fair immigration controls underpin good race relations'. Both the Conservatives and Labour have introduced immigration limiting measures in government, the main distinguishing factor being that Labour has also introduced race relations legislation – notably the 1976 Race Relations Act. As a result, race and immigration have remained largely dormant day to day in British politics, emerging only during general election campaigns as Tory anti-Labour scaremongering tools to highlight non-existent differences – particularly when the result promises to be close. Examples include Thatcher's 1978 warning of Labour 'swamping' the country with immigrants and Winston Churchill's similar admonition on the eve of the 1992 poll.

Despite fears of a 1997 re-run – the Labour candidate handbook warned of a leaked internal Conservative document advising that immigration had 'potential to hurt' Labour as an election issue – race seemed to have practically dropped off the agenda at the last election. (The main exception to this rule came in the shape of Tory MP Nicholas Budgen, occupant of the Wolverhampton seat once, ironically, represented by Enoch Powell, who claimed: 'Immigration is an electoral issue because it has changed the culture and population of large areas of our inner cities' bringing with it 'considerable social tensions'.[4] He was ticked off by Major for his pains and in the event lost his seat to Labour). Instead, politicians from the main parties did their utmost to ingratiate themselves with Asians; photos of Major garlanded with flowers in the subcontinent vied for press space with pictures of prospective parliamentary candidates with respectful headgear donned in canvassing visits to local temples and mosques.

Race as an electoral theme coming to an end appeared to mark the fact that Labour had become pragmatically indistinguishable from the Tories on the subject. In the words of Hans Kundnani of the Commission for Racial Equality's (CRE) policy group: 'Both parties were really saying the same thing. With Labour saying that they weren't going to repeal the Immigration and Asylum Act, immigration *couldn't* really feature as an issue'.[5] More positive is the implication that Powellite sentiment really has dampened down over the decades and that race negativism is no longer a vote winner among the white electorate. At the same time the evidence suggests that immigration is no longer a concern to settled ethnic communities either. The five pledges on education, crime, health, youth unemployment and tax, which formed the backbone of New Labour's electoral strategy, were equally central to the party pitch made to Asians. A video cassette of fairly anonymous packaging, entitled simply 'A Personal Message from the Rt Hon Tony Blair MP' was sent to Asian households in marginal seats identified from the electoral register. Blair was pictured amongst Asians. His speech to camera included the soundbite 'ambition and compassion' but no mention of immigration. Indeed a MORI/Zee tv poll of February 1997 showed that 18 per cent of Asians believed that UK immigration laws were 'not strict enough'. An Asian businessman in the *Daily Telegraph* puts the position in terms that no political party serious for power would risk using: 'Many Asians now have a stake in British society. They don't want to see the economy bled dry by opportunistic outsiders'.[6]

BULLDOG TACTICS

In place of the Conservative 'Land of Hope and Glory' jingoism that one had come to expect since the Thatcher years, in 1997 it was Labour who used both the Union Jack and the British bulldog in their campaign – the latter in the form of a real live mutt called Fritz who featured in an election broadcast. Labour back-bencher Bernie Grant labeled the stunt 'offensive and a damn disgrace', commenting: 'For people who grew up with the Empire, the British bulldog was used as a symbol too keep people in their place'.[7] Faz Hakim of Downing Street's Political Unit explained the rationale. 'Everyone can instantly understand what it means. It's supposed to make you laugh. You look at it and go "aah cute".'[8] A simultaneous reappropriation of the Union Jack took place. Certainly Britishness itself is not a static concept. Blair has expressed a desire to redefine it but using such arch-traditional symbolism with its far-right associations opens up accusations of retardation rather than modernisation.

Archbishop George Carey has urged: 'We may be patriots but we cannot be exclusive nationalists'.[9] In practice the territories of the two concepts have contested borders. 'I'd still find it difficult to wave a union flag, it doesn't come naturally,' Hakim admitted, 'but the idea is that the flag is for everyone. The whole thing of new Labour is the centre ground for the majority. We're here for everybody, that includes ethnic minority voters.' Statistics have frequently shown solid Asian Labour support, across the class spectrum.[10] MORI's figures for 1997 show this at 66 per cent.[11] So why has this constituency been so consistently loyal to Labour unlike some of the party's more voguish white target groups: Worcester Woman, Essex Man, the Sierra-driving family?

ASIANS AND LABOUR
LOVE AFFAIR OR ARRANGED MARRIAGE?

Most electoral analysts take an 'othering' line *vis-a-vis* new Commonwealth immigrants. Dennis Kavannagh writes 'While Irish, French, Huguenot, and Jewish immigrants had been assimilated in earlier waves, the skin colour and traditional beliefs of many of the new arrivals made this a difficult process.'[12] Bill Coxall and Lynton Robins concur, using the phrase 'visible as strangers', adding that this 'made it more difficult still for the new black immigrants to adapt to Britain's traditional culture.'[13] Meanwhile Oakley in his description of British society aimed at foreign readers writes: 'These newcomers have now increased and are now in a broad range of occupations. Some, particularly the Asians, have been contributing much to British life.'[14]

When discussing 'Asians' one must be cautious in using catch-all terminology to homogenise peoples of diverse religious, cultural and linguistic practice. The particular British use of this term is unnaturally narrow, reducing an entire continent to effectively a small handful of its ex-colonies in the Indian subcontinent. Keith Vaz MP has spoken of tensions *between* different ethnic communities in his constituency. 'People say "why can't we [Asians] be more like the Jews?" but religion divides us and the subcontinent divides us. When I held a celebration for the fiftieth anniversary of India in my constituency I got a letter from a Bangladeshi man who said "but you didn't do one for Bangladesh"'.[15] The Asian community is not homogeneous, but then no community is. Labour MP for Southall Piara Khabra told me 'Labour is seen as the friend of the Asians'. He cites the granting of Indian independence by Attlee as a central factor.[16] Memories of the rivers of blood also run deep. Both the septuagenarian Khabra and the twenty-something Faz Hakim mention Powell's Birmingham speech as a reason for the Asian vote's identification with Labour. Virendra Sharma, a former Labour Party ethnic minorities officer and now a Labour councillor in Southall, comments: 'The three outstanding factors are welfare, equality and justice ... The Party stands for liberty, equality and fraternity ... The basic philosophy is at one with the basic philosophy and explains why Asians across all classes vote Labour'.[17]

Tariq Modood, Professor of Sociology at Bristol University, identifies among traditional Asian values the extended family, community languages, arranged marriage and above all, religion. He claims that for first generation immigrants, religion is key to cultural identity providing 'moral structure, with its emphasis on familial obligations and opposition to a materialist, hedonist and selfish view of life'.[18] Blair is strongly associated with Christian socialism which shares these same values. Despite his personal convictions he has distanced himself from overt Christian triumphalism.

With research showing that British Asians contribute five billion pounds annually to the British economy, both the Conservatives and Labour actively chased the Asian business vote in 1997.[19] Raj Bagri, chairman of the London Metal Exchange and the millionnaire industrialist Suraj Paul were ennobled by the Conservatives and Labour respectively and paraded as party supporters to the Asian business community during the election campaign. John Major addressed Asian businessmen at the Commonwealth Institute in January. Lord Paul and successful restaurateur Amin Ali starred in Labour's Asian video; warning voters against tax rises. This frequenting of the upper echelons of Asian business has continued in government with TV chief Waheed Ali of Planet 24 Productions appointed to Blair's creative task force and subsequently knighted. Tony Blair, accompanied by a be-saried Cherie, dined with Britain's 200 wealthiest Asians at a London reception in March 1998 and declared that this group was 'a credit to the country as a whole, not just the Asian community'.[20]

Yet the average Asian small business, representing 65 per cent of all independent retailers nationally and 85 per cent in London according to the London Chamber of Commerce (1996), is however of a different nature. 'The majority of Asian businesses are very poor,' Atma Singh, secretary of the National Black Alliance claims. 'They're two to three people – what could be described as *micro*-businesses'.[21] Out of town supermarket sitings, the monopolisation of the newspaper trade and rising business rates had turned the Thatcherite grocer shop dream sour for Asian business. As Kamaljeet Jandu, ethnic policy officer at the TUC, said of the Blair/Asian millionnaires dinner: 'This list does not give a complete picture and there is a danger of replacing old stereotypes with new ones. Not all Asians are wealthy and many have limited opportunities'.[22]

The stereotypical picture of Asians is that they are socially conformist yet still determined to retain features of their culture of origin and links with their homeland, rejecting total assimilation. Tariq Modood describes the Asian community's self-perception as 'law abiding, hard working citizens at peace with British society but culturally distinct from it'.[23] Asian Tory Peer Baroness Flather has claimed that Asians are natural conservatives: 'They believe in continuity of structures, self-help ... They are certainly capitalists'.[24] Business and property owning are also favoured. 'I don't know if there is a natural party for any voter,' Faz Hakim commented. 'If you take away all the things that make people up, the low tax thing affected all voters.' Piara Khabra used Major's reverse Midas touch – everything that he touched seemed to turn to sleaze – to scorn suggestions of Asian Tory bias: 'The Conservatives have been involved in corruption morally, socially, economically, politically, you name it. That's not family values. If you say Asians and Conservative have the same values you're talking nonsense'.

So what difference did new Labour make to this traditional heartland of the party's support? Labour councillor Mustafa Kamal, deputy leader of Leicester Council, commented: 'Tony Blair's values fit in nicely with Asian values of the family, law and order, philanthropic business, ethics and consensus'.[25] Claude Moraes, director of the Joint Council for the Welfare of Immigrants, puts it this way: 'Blair had added appeal. Combined with that basic [Asian-Labour] tradition was an additional psychological factor. He and his wife are both lawyers and hugely attractive. His whole image of modernity appealed to middle class Asians as it did to the white middle class. Asians in Harrow, Slough and Leicester were the kind of votes Labour wanted'.[26] Asian professionals were used heavily in the new Labour Asian voter video. A doctor and a barrister were among its talking heads decrying the Tory record and urging a Labour vote. Indeed this document is almost entirely aimed at Asian achievers and aspirationalists. There is no mention of how new Labour, with its introduction of a minimum wage, can help the sweatshop worker in Bradford paid a pound an hour. 'Clearly new Labour has got a particular relationship with the Asian middle class that's profited from Thatcherist economic policy,' Hans Kundnani told me. 'That's obviously part of the wider move towards being closer to business generally. You've got to look at new Labour's relationship with some of the more disadvantaged strata of the Asian community and there it's probably a more problematic relationship.'

MAKING A DIFFERENCE

As Professor Mohammed Anwar of Warwick University's Centre for Ethnic Relations has pointed out, figures of Asian voting from 1997 mask huge differences in individual constituencies.[27] Contested selections involving both Asian candidates and party members in the run-up to the election go some way to explain this. The first test of the much trumpeted Labour Party one member, one vote reform did not proceed as smoothly as some would have wished. Membership buying was widely alleged. Faz Hakim, then Labour Party ethnic minorities officer, led the internal investigations into membership abuse. 'Nobody knew how to deal with it because we'd never had one member one vote before where getting selected depended on how many people you had signed up.' The old electoral colleges had been deemed undemocratic but the potential for manipulating the new system meant that it was in some ways no better. 'Before, you had to work in groupings that already existed, trade union blocs and so on. Disproportionate influence was what we were meant to get rid of but it gave us a new problem,' she recalled. At party level no records of Asian membership are kept, although a voluntary monitoring system has been introduced recently.

Atma Singh of the National Black Alliance claims that in the run-up to the general election four thousand Asians were expelled. A number of constituency parties were suspended from the Labour Party by its ruling NEC for membership irregularities. Bradford, Tower Hamlets, Manchester Gorton, Glasgow and Birmingham hit the national headlines, causing acute embarrassment to the leadership's anti-sleaze stance. In the months preceding the May 1998 council elections, accusations of Labour racism resurfaced when it emerged that some 50 non-white Labour councillors had been deselected in London alone. According to the National Association of Black, Asian and Ethnic Minority Councillors' secretary Lester Holloway – himself dropped as a councillor in Hammersmith – this is due to the tendency of such individuals to address the 'race' agenda and its incompatibility with new Labour priorities. Faz Hakim however asserts that expulsions were due to malpractice and no other reason: 'It's not just an Asian thing. It happened all over the country ... in some parts of Scotland where there's no Asian community anyway.' Meher Khan, former Mayor of Waltham Forest and the UK's first Muslim mayor, rejects this however: 'New Labour is hypocritical sexist and racist'.[28]

In Manchester Gorton and Birmingham Sparkbrook white candidates were eventually selected, despite strong Asian showings in the selection process. In Sparkbrook, the outgoing Roy Hattersley expressed the rank and file members' wish to be represented by a candidate from one of the minorities, and warned that 'the outcome for the constituency would be catastrophic' if this did not happen.[29] Elsewhere ethnic candidates were selected but not of the pre-dominant minority of the locality. Oona King, a Jewish Afro-Caribbean, stood in Bethnal Green, an area with a high Bangladeshi Muslim population. In largely Muslim Bradford, Marsha Singh – a Sikh – was selected. The Conservatives, who had stood Bengali and Pakistani candidates respectively, saw swings to them from Labour, against the national trend. Ruhul of Tower Hamlets youth pressure group Bangla 2000 told me of the Bethnal Green case: 'Bangladeshi people wanted a Bangladeshi candidate, a role model. Bangladeshis who on the whole vote Labour voted for Khabir Uddin Chaudhury [Conservative candidate] because he's seen as part of the community'.[30] He believes that it now looks unlikely that Britain will get a Bangladeshi MP in the foreseeable future. 'A Bangladeshi could have got in and done a crap job,' he admits, 'but it was a disappointment to the Bangla community.' Certainly King has an assured lengthy parliamentary career ahead, having been elected at the age of 29. As the steadily increasing majorities of Keith Vaz and Piara Khabra testify, sitting MPs benefit from the incumbency factor. The reduced Labour vote of 1997 in both Bethnal Green and Bradford can be thus attributed to psephological blips.

SEEN BUT NOT HEARD

Labour's election year 1997 also marked ten years since the first four black members in recent times were elected to Parliament, including Keith Vaz, the first Asian since 1924. Direct representation has seen an erosion of what Wainwright calls 'the "Hatterjee" or "Bidwell Singh" syndrome', by which white MPs would exercise a patronising patronage over Asian interests in return for votes. Hilary Wainwright writes, 'This produces a colonial mentality'.[31] Since 1987 black representation in parliament has crept up disappointingly slowly. There was a net gain of just three black MPs in 1997; eight compared to five in 1992, as the Asian Conservative Nirj Deva was defeated in Brentford and Isleworth. The 1997 total included four Asians out of a total of 657 members. If this is the position in Labour's best ever year, with an all-time high total of 419 MPs, the omens are not encouraging for reaching the figure of twenty Asian MPs that would accurately reflect the national ethnic composition, on Mohammad Anwar's calculations. Of the original 1987 intake, in the first distribution of government jobs Keith Vaz and Paul Boateng were demoted from their shadow positions. At European level Mark Hendrick is the one black British MEP. At local government level Anwar estimates that there are 400 black and Asian councillors, out of a total of 23,000 altogether, and 11,000 Labour councillors.

Sir Herman Ousley of the CRE expressed his displeasure at the racial distribution of power: 'Just look at the inner circle [of the Cabinet]. Who do you see there? It's just not happening. There is no visibility. In the outeer circle there are only one or two people. The frustration is building up'.[32] In March 1998 the CRE suffered a funding cut of £1m, predictably enough blamed on the previous administration by Home Office minister Mike O'Brien: 'The cut has been implemented as previously planned because of the severe pressure on public expenditure overall'.[33] Of the 'kitchen cabinet' inner circle, Faz Hakim, assistant political secretary to the Prime Minister, is of Indian Muslim descent. She declares herself in total agreement with Ousley's comments about under-representation of Asians in the civil service. 'This whole governmental machinery has thrived on bringing the same people together. It's nice having us around'. Keith Vaz's report *The Glass Ceiling*, on ethnic minorities in the civil services confirmed this. 'I'll publish it anyway, even if the numbers are all zero zero zero,' he vowed a month before its release. Blair himself acknowledged the problem in his 1997 Labour Party conference speech when he declared, 'We cannot be a beacon to the world unless the talents of all the people shine through. Not one black High Court judge, not one black officer above the rank of colonel. Not one Asian either. Not a record of pride for the British establishment ... I am against positive discrimination, but there's no harm in reminding ourselves just how much negative discrimination there is'.[34] Changing the whole civil service culture will take time, but such pronouncements are encouraging.

Mohammad Anwar has outlined ten priorities for new Labour in government.[35] Among these are the pursuit of equal opportunities within the party and outside; extending Northern Ireland laws on race discrimination to Britain; the instigation of the 1992 CRE proposals to strengthen the Race Relations Act; increased punishment for racial attackers/harassers; monitoring government contracts; and a positive commitment to ethnic diversity. Most contentious of all is likely to be the proposition to introduce targeted programmes to tackle unemployment amongst Pakistani and Bangladeshi youth, a measure *a priori* incompatible with the new Labour 'inclusive' general approach which rejects the treatment of ethnic minorities as 'special cases' assumed to be 'oppressed'. At the same time the ethnic politician is frequently ghettoised to the policy brief of minority interests, unlike their white counterparts who can develop wider interests. Piara Khabra's parliamentary interventions to date have had a strong 'Asian community' bias, in addressing the compulsory wearing of protective headgear by Sikhs and immigration appeals. Similarly Keith Vaz made his name by championing the rights of Asian investors in the collapsed BCCI investment bank and calling for the withdrawal of Salman Rushdie's *Satanic Verses*.

TESTING TEBBIT

Under Conservative rule the ethic of cultural pluralism took a battering: the 1988 Education Act stipulated that schools must provide an act of Christian worship, and throughout the Major years government chief education adviser Nicholas Tate repeatedly stated that children should be taught 'the value of Britishness'.[36] His particular conception of this was naturally a white 1950s Ealing comedy version rather than a 1990s multi-ethnic Ealing Southall one. Multiculturalism also had a bad press from exaggerated Tory tabloid tales of Labour local authority excesses in the 1980s, dubbed 'Loony leftism'. Tony Blair signalled a break with this, however, when he claimed in March 1998, 'The single most important thing we can do is to make an absolutely clear statement on behalf of the Government ... that we believe in, and actually welcome, a multi-racial and multi-cultural society; that it's a good thing, that it's not something to be frightened of'.[37]

Norman Tebbit's contrasting assertion that multiculturalism was 'divisive', at the 1997 Conservative Party Conference, earned him the rebuke of 'dinosaur' from the party leadership, but simultaneous applause from some sections of its membership. Tebbit evoked memories of Powell when he declared: 'You cannot have a whole load of cultures in one society. You have one culture for one society and if you get different societies mixed up and living close, cheek by jowl, you will splinter our society in the way devolution is splintering the United Kingdom'.[38] Media reactions were a near-universal pouring of scorn on the remarks, in opinion pieces from all quarters ranging from the liberal press (eg, the *Independent*'s claim 'Even Canute would not try to turn back the tide of multiculturalism'[39]) to the more traditionally reactionary titles ('Britain is strong enough to absorb new cultures', claimed the *Telegraph*[40]). Interestingly, William Hague's attendance at the Notting Hill Carnival and the choice of the well-received Asian young Tory, Munish Chopra, to open the 1997 party conference showed a willingness to engage in a more positive attitude to race than that for which the Conservatives are usually known. 15-year-old Chopra, of Solihull, evoked irresistible comparisons with the young Hague by telling delegates that he had been fortunate to have lived most of his life under Conservatism, and declaring: 'My Indian upbringing has seen that respect for authority, a high moral standard and an environment of hard work have been instilled in me'.[41]

THE SECOND GENERATION
BLUES AND REDS

Over fifty per cent of UK Asians today were born in the UK, with English as their first and often only language. Late twentieth century immigration is unprecedented: enabling people to uproot and relocate on the other side of the globe while retaining constant contact with the country of origin via telecommunications, global media and air travel. Perhaps conscious of this, Enoch Powell in 1968 claimed: 'The West-Indian or Asian, does not, by being born in England become an Englishman. In law he becomes a United Kingdom citizen by birth; in fact he is a West Indian or Asian still'.[42] Academic writing on young Asians has traditionally tended towards negative aspects such as 'paki-bashing'. Dick Hebdige, for example, wrote: 'Less easily assimilated than the West Indians into the host community ... sharply differentiated not only by racial characteristics but by religious rituals, food taboos and a value system which encouraged deference, frugality and the profit motive, the Pakistanis were singled out for the brutal attentions of skinheads, black and white alike'.[43] More recently, however, Asian youth are proving to be more visible than their parents across a number of domains, including new Asian musical styles, film, writing and comedy. In their singer, the second generation Punjabi Sikh

Tjinder Singh, the band Cornershop reaching number one in the charts in Spring 1998 marked the first 'out' Asian to achieve the feat. Simultaneously, the all-Asian comedy show *Goodness Gracious Me* scored high ratings for BBC2. One can only hope that the new found media attention aroused by such initiatives is more than empty hype; and that it does not represent the media exoticisation of people who are picked up one day and dropped the next.

A duality, nay multiplicity, of identities shapes second, third and fourth generation cultural bearings, rather than the idealised past of 'home' of the first which was reflected in practices of sending back money etc. Inder, rapper with Bradford band Detrimental, retains strong attachments to his spiritual (rather than real) 'homeland' wearing a turban onstage. 'I've actually got a stronger Asian culture than some people in India,' he claimed.[44] Respect for elders is central to 'Asian values', which continues. Ruhul, of Bangla 2000, told me, 'Our parents came from a very different background to us. They came from a background of survival, whether it was ploughing fields or fishing or whatever. Everyday was a hustle.' Dipen, also of Bangla 2000, added, 'Our generation would probably do worse if we were kicked out of this country because we haven't got that survival instinct'.[45] Inder's remarks, however, reflected an assertiveness of expression that was absent among the first generation: 'Our parents have done a lot of hard work for us, getting us through to where we are today. They did what they had to do, bowed down. Now it's ... "you called me Paki, I'm gonna fucking sort it out."' An Asian during the Blackburn and Burnley riots claimed: 'We proved that Indians are not chicken'.[46] Further outbreaks of youth violence in Bradford and Luton in 1995 continued to puncture the hardworking, passive Asian image.

As the first generation, with their memories of 1947 and Powell fade, a de-alignment of the Asian vote may follow. Class orientation is difficult to ascribe to the first generation. On arrival to the UK, Asians across the class and caste system found themselves equal in the eyes of the host community. For this reason Councillor Mustafa Kamal sees the monolithic bloc term 'Asian community' as one of historical validity with decreasing relevance in the light of a growing recognition of Asian differences in white eyes (Sikhs wear turbans, Muslims worship in mosques, etc), and multiple paradigm shifts in the second generation. 'Many young Asians are rediscovering Muslim, Sikh and Hindu identities that parents downplayed,' he explains. At the same time he sees fragmentation resulting from 'less knowledge of Asian languages, a weakening of the extended family and young people being educated away from home and becoming successful professionals thus sharing the lifestyle of their peers.' Any political repositioning of young Asians is dependent on class mobility rather than simply just a rebellion against their parents' traditional indebtedness to Labour as the 'equality' party. Some see this rupture with parental attitudes already underway. *Time Out*'s TV critic Alkarim Jivani contrasts 'first generation British Asians who feel like guests in this country who ought to be on their best behaviour', with the second generation who 'behave as we please, which pisses off the older generation who think we shouldn't be doing it in front of the whites'.[47] Faz Hakim states: 'People will make up their mind on the issues, which I think is better.' The Oxford geographer Ceri Peach meanwhile has predicted a post-diasporic diaspora, with a Jewish future for Indians and some Pakistanis (wealth bringing a flight to the suburbs), and an Irish future for Bangladeshis (condemned to languish in the ghetto).[48]

A COMMUNITY OF DIFFERENCE

UK Asians span different countries, religions, castes, at least seven major languages, multifarious dialects and now generations. Tariq Modood claims that differences between ethnic groups are now more significant than any black-white divide, with East African Asians and Indians succeeding professionally and in education, while Pakistanis and Bangladeshis are under-achieving.[49] Perhaps it makes more sense then to talk of the UK's Asian communities rather than a singular community. The Blair landslide was a feat of staggering proportions, achieved with the support of Asian electors. However, as Anwar warns, 'Political parties cannot rely on Asian support without something in return'.[50] Ways must be investigated to encourage increased ethnic participation and representation at all levels of the political process. To date new Labour has been met with cautious optimism. Piara Khabra said: 'Nothing is 100 per cent right but in my opinion it's better than it has been in the last 18 years'. When I asked the National Black Alliance's Atma Singh how impressed he was so far, he retorted, 'It's not about getting impressed. Black people are too cynical for that. They've been let down by too many Governments in the past to think that this Government will automatically deliver.'

Asians have been included in new Labour's election strategy, but in government the indications show that, specific race relations legislation aside, ethnic minorities are to be largely treated as part of the British population *per se*. The colour blind approach does raise tensions. 'This time round there was an absence of anti-immigrant feeling but at the same time there was an absence of the Labour Party standing up for black people', commented Rajinder Sohpal, director of Reading Race Equality Council. Encouragingly, open racism is, it seems, less acceptable than before in British society. 'I haven't been called a wog or nigger to my face for years,' Keith Vaz stated in 1997. One can only hope that the apparent fading from importance of immigration as a negative electoral factor continues and a positive race relations debate is opened in its place. As Ruhul put it: 'The Labour Party banked on the Asian vote and on the whole they got it. Just because they got in we don't say it's all cool. We welcome those things that Jack Straw's done but there's still a long, long way to go. It's not a question of doing a few quick things to pacify people. We would like to see a lot more in place before the next general election when the Labour Party really will be judged by Asian people.'

NOTES

1. Speech to the Annual General Meeting of the West Midlands Area Conservatives at the Midland Hotel, Birmingham, 20 April 1968.
2. 'Powell to lie in state but not in abbey, critics told', *Guardian*, 16.2.98.
3. 'Powell's Heart of Darkness', *Observer*, 15.2.98.
4. 'We Ignore Immigration at Our Peril', *The Times*, 18.3.97.
5. Personal Interview, CRE, London 14.7.97.
6. 'Race is No Longer a Black and White Issue say Voters' *Daily Telegraph*, 21.3.97.
7. 'Bernie Snaps at Labour's Bulldog', *Evening Standard*, 28.4.97.
8. Personal interview, 10 Downing Street 11.9.97.
9. TUC conference 9.9.97.
10. Mohammad Anwar, *Race and Politics*, Tavistock, London 1986; and Ivor Crewe, *Decade of Dealignment: the Conservative Victory of 1979 and Electoral Trends*, CUP, Cambridge. There were over 40 seats in 1997 where the Asian population outweighed the 1992 margin of victory, giving this section electoral influence disproportionate to its accounting for 1.5 per cent of the population.
11. MORI British Public Opinion Survey, May 1997.

12. Dennis Kavanagh, *British Politics: Continuity and Change*, OUP, Oxford, 1990 pp15-16.

13. Bill Coxall and Lynton Robbins, *Contemporary British Politics*, Macmillan, Basingstoke 1994, p408.

14. John Oakley, *British Civilisation: an Introduction*, Routledge, London 1991, p40.

15. Speaking at public meeting 'South Asians and the New Labour Government, expectations and reality', 10.9.97 ULU, London.

16. Interview with Piara Khabra, Ealing Sherman Labour Hall, London 8.9.97.

17. *New World*, 3.2.92.

18. Tariq Modood et al, 'Changing Ethnic Identities', in *Sociology: Selected Readings* Anthony Giddens (ed), Polity, Cambridge 1997, p213-217.

19. *Times*, 12.4.97. After the election the *Guardian*, put the figure at 7.5 billion, 26.3.97.

20. 'Blair Hails Britain's Super-Rich Asians', *Guardian*, 26.3.98.

21. Interview at 1990 Trust.

22. *Guardian*, 26.3.98.

23. Tariq Modood et al, *op.cit.*

24. *Ibid*, p217.

25. *Guardian*, 15.4.92.

26. Personal letter, dated 15 September 1997.

27. Telephone conversation, September 1997.

28. 'Fury at Labour's Party Whitewash' *Observer* 15.3.98.

29. 'Huttersley Urges Asian Successor', *Guardian* 1.2.96.

30. Personal interview.

31. Hilary Wainwright, *Labour: A Tale of Two Parties*, Hogarth Press, London 1987, p192.

32. 'Blacks "losing out" in Blair's new Britain', *Guardian* 22.7.97.

33. 'Blair breaks his race promise with £1m race cut"' *Independent on Sunday* 29.3.98.

34. 'A Beacon Burning Darkly', *Guardian* 2.19.97.

35. Public meeting, see note 15.

36. 'Children to be taught "the value of Britishness"', *Daily Mail*, 18.7.95.

37. Speech at community meeting, Southwark, quoted *Independent on Sunday* 29.3.98. Cf John Major's remark, 'I have always believed in a multiracial community. I grew up in a multiracial community, *Guardian*, 17.10.95.

38. *Daily Telegraph*, 8.10.97. These remarks extended Tebbit's notorious 1986 'cricket test' querying the sporting loyalties of immigrants.

39. *Independent*, 8.10.97.

40. *Telegraph*, 8.10.97.

41. *Telegraph*, 8.10.97.
42. Address by the Rt Hon J Enoch Powell MP to the annual conference of the Rotary Club of London at the Burlington Hotel, Eastbourne, 16 November 1968.
43. Dick Hebdige, *Subculture: The Meaning of Style*, Methuen, London 1979, p58.
44. Personal Interview at *Festival des Artefacts*, Strasbourg, France 5.9.97.
45. Personal interview at 1990 Trust, London August 1997.
46. Quoted in *Guardian*, 24.7.92.
47. 'Poppadam Preach', *Time Out*, 8.1.97.
48. Ceri Peach, *Ethnicity in the 1990 Census, vol 2: the ethnic minority populations of Great Britain*, HMSO, London 1996.
49. Modood et al, *Ethnic Minorities in Britain: Diversity and Disadvantage*, PSI, London 1997.
50. Public meeting, see note 15.

BLURRED VISION:
POP, POPULISM AND POLITICS

Jeremy Gilbert

New Labour is irrevocably identified with a project of political 'modernisation'. This term, though, like so much else in politics, is open to competing definitions. One definition suggests a determination to accommodate to the present without in any way challenging that present or its terms. To modernise is therefore to become more efficient and more successful under circumstances and according to criteria which are not only not of one's own choosing, but which there is no imagined possibility of changing. 'Modernisation' according to this definition means accommodating to modernity conceived as a fixed and permanent present. This account portrays modernity as characterised by the 'rational' centralisation of power and the regulation of groups and individuals.[1] A second definition of modernisation conceives it as a perpetual opening-up to modernity conceived as a constant, if uneven, process of change.[2] According to this account, the project of modernity is not the centralisation of power, but its diffusion through a permanent process of democratisation. This notion of 'modernisation' would involve a radical openness to the future and its possibilities. This version would embrace the modern not by trying to simply adapt to the present but by seeking to ride and to amplify those currents of change which might lead in progressive direction – to further, as Laclau and Mouffe (following de Tocqueville) would have it, the 'democratic revolution' of modernity.[3]

It's clear enough that new Labour is not characterised by an exclusive commitment to either of these definitions. The appeal to Middle England, the rhetoric of caution, the implicit social authoritarianism, the attacks on single parents and the centralisation of power within the party itself can all be seen as attempts to articulate a basically conservative modernity. On the other hand, the commitment to constitutional change, to some re-instatement of workers' rights and to an ethical internationalism can all be seen as elements of a democratising agenda.

Elements of both definitions can therefore be discerned as central to new Labour, but it may be that they can only co-exist for so long, and it may also be that it is the contradiction between them which will mark out the fault line of British political debate in the not-too-distant future. What is striking, and what the rest of this chapter will be concerned with, is the extent to which this fault-line can also be seen to run through important areas of contemporary culture. Consider, for instance, the interesting similarities between Blairism and that definitive cultural phenomenon of the mid 1990s, Britpop.

HANGING THE DJ

Britpop was a music discourse which emerged around 1993 and came to dominate large sections of the media for about three years. It was a set of bands, and their musical products, and a set of critical discourses which provided preferred understandings of the significance of the bands and their music; together with a set of media practices which privileged that music and those critical discourses. In naming itself as it did, in claiming to represent British pop as such, it aimed to some extent to define and delimit both British identity and the whole field of popular music. The bands in question all played music which self-consciously referenced a retroactively-imagined tradition of British white guitar pop, from The Beatles, Stones, Kinks, Who and Small Faces in the 1960s through to the Smiths and The Stone Roses in the 1980s. A particular notion of British cultural identity was therefore mobilised to which 'classic' guitar pop played by young white men on conventional rock instruments was central. This was effected through the articulation of some very specific 'chains of equivalence', both synchronically (guitar pop = Britishness = white masculinity) and diachronically (The Beatles – The Kinks – The Smiths – Blur/Oasis), in order both to articulate a coherent sense of 'Britishness' in the present and to define a number of moments from the past as constituting a tradition of which contemporary 'Britpop' was seen as being the latest manifestation.

The result was a definition of both British cultural identity and popular music which excluded an extraordinary range of people, sounds and experiences. According to this discourse, black music evidently had nothing to do with British pop. Forms which had ever allowed women more than marginal roles – from feminist punk to sweet soul – evidently had nothing to do with British pop. Traditionally gay-identified forms, like disco and Hi-NRG evidently had nothing to do with British pop. Most obviously, contemporary dance musics from house to jungle to trip-hop were implicitly defined as either not British, not pop, or both. Britpop, as several commentators suggested, was therefore a clearly reactionary response to a range of social and cultural changes which had dislodged the certainties of a previous generation of white men.[4] Job insecurity, the multiple effects of the women's movement, the increasing hybridisation of British culture, have all posed obvious threats to the normative hegemony of white masculinity. As divergent and disparate as these phenomena are, it's the observation that they can all be seen as converging in a process of radical cultural differentiation that has led so many commentators to try to name them as a totality ('postmodernity' for instance). It's this overall process of *differentiation*, with all of its democratising potential, that has undermined the cultural authority of a particular model of British identity and of cultural institutions which depend for their authority on an assumed cultural homogeneity. In the case of music culture, Radio One, *Top of the Pops*, *Smash Hits*, the indie press and the mainstream record industry had all suffered losses during the late 1980s and early 1990s in terms of unit sales, audience figures, and cultural prestige, as dance culture and the digital revolution gave rise to a proliferation of smaller specialist outlets.[5] It's perhaps not surprising, then, that these institutions should have given their enthusiastic support to a project which, in re-asserting a very traditional notion of British identity, tried to re-imagine just that condition of cultural homogeneity which they so missed.

THEY THINK IT'S ALL OVER

We can see this as a twofold reaction to distinct problems. On the one hand it was a reaction to the immediately dislocatory effect of Thatcherism and its deliberate disruption of stable notions of national community. 'Britpop' certainly wanted there to be such a thing as society, even if all that bound it together was a Union Jack motif and a love of the Beatles. But this was articulated with an underlying hostility to other cultural changes since the 1960s. It's no accident that 1966 was the moment to which both Britpop and much of 'New Lad' culture looked back as a Golden Age. The era of Alfie and the dolly bird, of silent wide-eyed girls on the back of bikes and scooters, was remembered with an unproblematic affection by the readers of *Loaded* and *Melody Maker* alike. It's not just that it was then that England won the World Cup; the moment immediately before women's liberation, the black civil rights' movement, Gay Pride, etc, was one which shook the self-confidence of normative white male heterosexuality and is an obvious point of reference for a group who no longer occupy quite the privileged place they once did. New Labour has likewise been characterised by a communitarian resistance to Thatcherism on the one hand and a tendency to authoritarian social conservatism (curfews for kids, compulsory workfare, the appointment of a 'Drug Czar' etc) on the other, not to mention a nostalgia for the Wilson era.

The convergence between Britpop and Blairism did not begin with Noel Gallagher's attendance at a No 10 soirée, or with his rather confused endorsement of Tony Blair's 1997 conference speech, or with Oasis's Alan McGee's substantial donation to Labour Party funds. Indeed, it was already sufficiently apparent six months before the election when the cover star of the Autumn 1996 edition of *New Labour New Britain* (the magazine for Labour Party members) was not the suited and smiling shadow-cabinet spokesperson one might have expected, but an enigmatically be-shaded Noel Gallagher. Not only was Oasis's guitarist/songwriter on the cover, but the centre-fold of the magazine was a feature co-written by Martin Moriarty and no less a person than the leader's press secretary, Alastair Campbell, entitled 'New Labour, New Britpop'. The article offered a brief account of Britpop which was remarkable at once for its precise and incisive analysis, and for its rather terrifying political implications.

Having dwelt on the previous year's much-hyped rivalry between indie bands Blur and Oasis, the piece concluded:

> But if the bands are very different, it might even be that it's what they share that so narks them. Neither of them could have happened without The Smiths in the 1980s (Damon inherited Morrissey's sense of theatre, Noel always wanted to play like guitarist Johnny Marr). And both of them are rooted in the 60s tradition of song-writing that includes the hummability of The Beatles, the alluringly rough edges of The Rolling Stones and the essentially English quirkiness of The Small Faces or The Kinks.
>
> And it's not just pop history that echoes down the decades. Thirty years ago the country was escaping from the stifling austerity of the Tory

1950s into the white heat of the technological revolution and Harold Wilson's 1960s Labour governments. After the first wave of Black American dance music (from Motown), it was British bands that provided the soundtrack for a generation as young people wanted an alternative to dancing away the blues, more rooted in their own experience of pet-shops, bus stops and pie and mash.

Thirty years on, after another wave of American-inspired dance music, (the house beats that dominated the charts from 1988 onwards) there's a demand for songs that couldn't have been written anywhere else but here, that Blur, Oasis and everybody else have shown themselves more than able to satisfy. Something has shifted, certainly. There's a new feeling on the streets. There's a desire for change. Britain is exporting pop music once again. Now all we need is a new government. [6]

Campbell and Moriarty were surely on to something. Consider just what the enormous success of Oasis has been based on. In uniting such a large, cross-generational audience after years of fragmentation – and in making themselves headline news in the process – Oasis brilliantly tapped into and helped to cohere a structure of feeling that was emerging in the country as Thatcher receded into memory, a structure of feeling that believed in just the vague, imprecise, often-reactionary, but nonetheless potent, sense of national community which Blair was trying to mobilise against residual Thatcherism. Big chords, big choruses, a self-consciously 'classical' sound which couldn't really offend anyone (although their public behaviour was a different matter); Oasis offered something remarkably similar to the vague inclusiveness of Blair's appeals to community, youth and virtue. But Blairism and Britpop share terms more specific than a commitment to vague inclusiveness, as Campbell and Moriarty themselves explained.

The historical elisions and inaccuracies in Campbell and Moriarty's article were less important than what it got right, amounting as it did to a clear articulation of new Labour's affinity with what they perceived as Britpop's claims to musical, cultural and national authenticity. The lazy chauvinism and explicit parochialism of their stated preference for British sounds over black dance music was frightening, if truthful. Their recognition of Britpop as a project which aimed to redeploy those versions of 1980s anti-Thatcherite indie discourse which were most hostile to other forms was perceptive indeed. Most importantly, Campbell and Moriarty recognised that the single most striking characteristic of Britpop was not its difference from the equally guitar-obsessed American rock which it sought to displace; rather, it was Britpop's radical difference from the techno-futurism of dance culture and the multiculturalism of the whole spectrum of black-dance-derived pop musics, not to mention the multicultural dance-pop-feminism of The Spice Girls. It was this difference between Britpop and a more international and multicultural tradition stretching from Motown to House that Moriarty and Campbell so astutely identified, and it is the continued centrality of white boy rock to British music culture – when in the early 1990s so many (Primal Scream's Bobby Gillespie and Prodigy's Liam Howlett to name but two) had declared it to have been displaced by house music – that is the marker of Britpop's lasting success as a project. What could be closer to new Labour's appeal to Middle England – marked as much as anything by the absence of any prominent black figure from its election campaign – than this cultural project of traditionalisation and homogenisation, this celebration of 'pet-shops, bus stops and pie and mash'?

Britpop wasn't just about ethnic identity, and its emergence at exactly the same time as 'New Lad' culture was equally significant. The New Lad was consumer culture's latest offer of a self-conscious subject position for men. He liked beer, football, birds and bacon sarnies, and seemed to regard the four entities as pretty much of a piece. He still seems to be prepared to pay for magazines like *Loaded*, *Stuff* and *FHM* to tell him about them (or at least show him pictures), and to be becoming increasingly avaricious in his appetites for culture-manuals which can guide him through his world of objects in a style free from intellectual pretension or political correctness. His actual age remains indeterminate, although his emotional age is still militantly retarded.

The New Lad, like new Labour, is a complex and at times contradictory response to recent changes in patterns of work, consumption and identity, in particular insofar as they have affected the position of young men. Like the rest of his generation, the New Lad identifies far more as a consumer than as a worker. This is partly because consumer culture offers more scope than it once did, but also because the New Lad is far less likely to have a secure and satisfying job than his father did. Even if he does, it will not confer the same status, and in particular the same authority over women, as it would have done in a time before young women were rapidly overtaking young men in the jobs market. Like most of his consumption-oriented generation, he values his personal freedom very highly. He has no desire to assume the traditional patriarchal responsibilities, to respect and care for women and children.

The New Lad is therefore a response to an anxious situation. The communitarian rhetoric of Family Values which new Labour has deployed in recent years has been a response to very much the same situation; the decline of traditional family structures and the distributions of power and authority that went with them. In a broader sense, new Labour's rhetoric of caution, its replacement of radicalism with a discourse on trust and safety, has been informed by a sense of foreboding at the immanence of the twenty-first century similar to that which leads the New Lad to seek refuge in infantile behaviour and retro culture. What's at stake in both cases is an evident anxiety about the place of men, especially young men, in the modern world. Men have increasingly lost their dominance over the workplace, and so look to other modes of expression for consolation and the articulation of identities. The continued public debate over the status of single parents is a clear symptom of this. Single mothers – like fatherless, street-wandering youths – are a constant source of anxiety within contemporary political discourse because their very existence threatens to undermine patriarchal power structures in quite obvious ways. The problem of what young men *are* when they are no longer breadwinners and fathers is one to which both new Labour and *Loaded* would like to offer answers.

Britpop offered an answer which wasn't much different. Having explicitly rejected Grunge – and with it Kurt Cobain's cross-dressing, his amazing public endorsement of archetypal British post-punk feminists The Raincoats, and the Riot Grrrl movement – Britpop's solution to the uncertainties of contemporary sexuality seemed to be largely one of regressive escapism. While some of its participants – notably Brett Anderson of Suede and a handful of female singers – experimented with androgyny, Damon Albarn of Blur publicly endorsed New Laddism while Liam and Noel went out of their way to resuscitate the image of the macho rock star. The beery blokeishness of Oasis' 'drunken pop anthems' (Noel Gallagher's words) was echoed in the pages of Lad mags as well as in the rhetoric of David Baddeil and Frank Skinner's appropriation of the newly resurgent football culture. 'Three Lions on Your Shirt' fitted Gallagher's self-deprecating description of his work better than any Oasis song. And of course, Chris Evans, the hero of Radio One during the peak of its association with Britpop, was and remains the definitive New Lad.

There's clearly a large amount of discursive common ground between Britpop, New Laddism, and the conservative modernity characteristic of at least one version of Blairism. On the other hand, the 'fit' between them is not perfect. Britpop's fascination with the 1960s, like New Lads' self-conscious relationship to consumer culture, is motivated by a clearly expressed commitment to hedonism. This is a far cry from the Puritanism informing Labour's work-compelling 'New Deal' for the young unemployed, and its ludicrous refusal to countenance a review of laws on drug prohibition. The Gallaghers' much-publicised drug habits and their hymn to *Cigarettes and Alcohol* didn't find much favour with the exponents of Family Values. What's more, the generally reactionary sexual politics of the New Lad are complicated somewhat by his apparent lack of interest in occupying traditional positions of patriarchal authority; husband, father or boss. The characters in *Men Behaving Badly*, the sit-com elevated to canonical status by *Loaded*, may shirk all responsibility, but they seem more than happy to cede all power to the women in their lives also, if that's the price to be paid for such freedom. It would be easy for this half-formed sensibility to develop into a full-blown anti-feminist reaction, but it isn't clear that that's happened yet.

SOCIALISING THE SOUNDTRACK

There are other areas of contemporary British culture which are far less ambiguous in their relationship to a closed and conservative account of political and cultural 'modernisation'. The various manifestations of dance culture which followed the Acid House revolution of 1988 have all manifested a commitment to forms of democratisation and hybridisation quite different from the versions of Britishness offered by Britpop, New Lad, or Family Values. The self-conscious futurity of musics which experiment with the latest in digital technologies is only one aspect of this tendency. Dance music has been a site of exchange between black and white cultures at least since rock'n'roll was born as a dance sound, and has continued as such throughout the history of soul, disco, house, reggae, jungle and hip-hop. And since the 1970s, dance forms – including House – have always been associated with gay cultures. Various critics have commented on the late twentieth-century dance floor as a site not just for the exercise of the male gaze but for autonomous self-expression on the part of young women excluded from street cultures and the officially-sanctioned public sphere. Dance culture's occupation of the centre-stage of British youth culture during the early 1990s therefore created unprecedented room for a proliferation of hybrid identities and a multiplication of shared cultural spaces, for an erosion of the homogeneous authority of white straight masculinity. The self-conscious mutant avant-gardism of Jungle – probably the most significant Black British music ever – and the ecstatic celebration of community and futurity in the most mainstream club anthems, and the resurgence of new forms of political engagement as the free party movement became articulated with eco-protest and campaigns around housing, were all part of this democratising modernity. Ecstasy culture gave rise to the re-definition of British night-clubs as places far safer for women and gays than the beer-soaked meat markets of old, places for collective experiments in non-phallocentric modes of experience, for the elaboration of new and more empathetic everyday ethics.

Perhaps the most important of these changes was this widely-commented on process of cultural 'feminisation'. Studies such as Helen Wilkinson's for Demos suggested that the shift in relative success and expectation between young men and women was leading to a cultural revaluation of traditionally-defined 'masculine' and 'feminine' values.[7] E-culture's communitarian pacifism certainly tended to manifest this kind of shift. As Maria Pini has suggested,

> despite women's relative absence at the levels of rave production and organisation, at other levels rave can be seen as indicating an important shift in sexual relations, and indeed might suggest (with its emphasis on dance, physicality, affection and unity) a general 'feminisation' of youth.[8]

Even the fiction of Chemical Generation hero Irvine Welsh – peopled as it is by lads, hard-men, schemies and casuals – almost always ends up endorsing a feminist/feminised perspective (a rapist is castrated, a casual dies for love, a chauvinist cafe customer gets a used tampon in his soup) while offering sophisticated and reflexive considerations of the status of post-industrial masculinity.[9] Indeed, Welsh's meditations on consumption, hedonism and contemporary masculinity ('I think I'll stick to drugs to get me through the long, dark night of late capitalism ... ' muses one character about his non-identification with socialist politics[10]) can be read almost as a counter-discourse to the simplicities of New Laddism. It's no accident that Welsh – who actually writes as much about soccer hooligans as about ecstasy – has been so firmly identified with rave culture.

But it isn't just in rave and post-rave that we've seen an assertion of the feminine, for this has been the era of Girl Power. The New Lass, or New Laddette, as she's been called, has emerged as the favourite model for young womanhood across a range of media, from magazines to music. Channel 4's infamous *Girlie Show*, *More!* magazine and its imitators, and of course the major industry that has been generated around the Spice Girls, have all been promoting an ideal of energetic, youthful, hedonistic and sexually aggressive femininity which has tended to provoke reactions at least as contradictory as those to the New Lad. On the one hand, she's been seen by some as the promised fruit of the sexual revolution; a lively, independent, confident young woman, comfortable with her sexuality, canny in her dealings with all forms of authority, especially masculine authority. On the other hand, it's been pointed out that – judging from the models she's presented with – this young woman must spend too much time doing her aerobics, making herself up, shopping for short skirts and queuing up outside night-clubs to really do anything useful with her much-vaunted independence. The emphasis on (specifically heterosexual) sexual activity in girls' magazines can be read as useful and liberating. It can also be read as simply encouraging young women to adopt a role of sexually-available man-pleaser which doesn't seem much different from the dolly-bird of the 1960s and 1970s.

The latter is an unnecessarily pessimistic reading, especially if we think through the status of the New Lass in terms of what she actually seems to want. She certainly doesn't want a return to traditional gender relationships. She wants autonomy *and* a re-articulated femininity, she wants a boyfriend not at the expense of her other relationships ('If you want to be my lover', the Spice Girls tell us, 'You've got to get with my friends'), she wants her place in the sun, not just the kitchen and the bedroom, she wants a job and a future. What's more, unlike the apathetic and frequently pessimistic New Lad, she thinks she can get it. It's this belief in the future which most specifically belongs to young women at the present time, and which is perhaps the most important element of that 'semi-structure of feeling' which Angela McRobbie has identified in the consumer culture of young women today.[11] All this has a lot to do with new Labour. Labour has traditionally suffered a massive poll deficit among women. It was a truism of British psephology until very recently that if this could be overcome then Labour would improve its position in a historic fashion. But in both 1992 and 1997 Labour's biggest lead over the Tories was among young women.

One of the great under-analysed fault lines in British politics is the gap between women over 35 who, like their mothers and grandmothers, have always voted Tory, and their Labour-voting daughters.[12]

People don't vote for sets of policies, or for personalities, or for media packages. They vote because of an overall resonance between their feelings about themselves and their place in the world with that expressed by the party they vote for. There's plenty of evidence that people in this country tend to vote for the left when they're feeling optimistic, open to the future, at least potentially radical. It's no accident that the party of the British right describes itself as nothing more specific than 'conservative'. The support of young women for Labour is hardly likely to be a result of their commitment to traditional shop-floor Labourism, seeing as that's a discourse from which they were largely excluded. There's no evidence that it's an expression of support for the authoritarian agenda of Jack Straw, seeing as it's a trend which began long before he started promising to reclaim the streets. The support of young women for Labour is an expression of their openness to the future, their social, cultural and political radicalism, their desire to live in a different and better world. All that is best about new Labour chimes with the needs and desires of young women in Britain today. It is support for a minimum wage, for a more pluralistic and democratic political culture, for investment in training, education and health. There's no better symbol of all that's best about it than the number of young women it has managed to get elected to parliament. At the same time, all that's worst about new Labour converges with all that's worst about New Laddism and Britpop; its rhetoric of social conservatism, its contempt for civil liberties and alternative culture, its hatred of all that's contemporary in contemporary youth culture, it's love affair with the past, specifically the past of thirty years ago.

So we see here a potential demarcation in both 'politics' and 'culture' between a conservative modernity and a radical one, a centralising force and a democratising one, feminism and anti-feminism. Even in terms of the issue of different *modes* of democratic participation, we can see our two cultural formations resonating with the poles of political debate. Consider the question of what modes of participation the two cultures offer. Britpop's return to the stadium concert and the traditional rock-icon mirror precisely Blair's turn to plebiscite democracy and centralised leadership. In both cases our participation is dependent on our support for the statements of a leader; we can all stand together at Knebworth, singing Noel's songs, we can all vote 'yes' to the new Clause Four, but that's the limit of our participation. The distinction between leaders and led is clear. Dance cultures, on the other hand, are notable for their de-stabilisation of traditional cults of personality, for their problematisation of the distinction between musicians, performers, and audiences on the dance floor (where DJs re-make other's music while the dancing 'audience' occupies centre-stage), for their DIY ethics. Autonomy, heterogeneity and participation are the watchwords, just as they might be in a participatively democratic party or movement.

BREAKING UP IS HARD TO DO

But these fault-lines have not yet emerged as clearly as they might, and it's worth considering what the *precise* points of commensurability and incommensurability between these different 'semi-structures of feeling' and our different accounts of modernity might be. There are two key issues here; the status of the libertarian hedonism which informs so much of contemporary youth culture, and the shape of gendered identities now and in the future.

There remains a great deal of convergence between the most conservative tendencies in new Labour and those underlying Britpop and Laddism. However, it will remain difficult to fully articulate New Laddism and Britpop with the most conservative tendencies of new Labour as long as they remain characterised by a commitment to libertarian hedonism and a refusal of the work ethic. Although the reported Death of Laddism and the musical substitution of the Verve and Radiohead for Blur and Oasis seem to be re-hegemonising a version of indie discourse which is positively puritanical in its joylessness, rock culture's attachment to liberal values is unlikely to disappear. This is what it continues to share with dance cultures, which remains more-or-less defined by a commitment to personal and (in a limited sense) collective freedom. The great weakness of the dispersed libertarianism of both rave culture and its offshoots remains, however, the relative absence of any notion of a coherent project. The strands of DIY culture have already unravelled as protest groups like Reclaim the Streets have gone back underground and free parties have become a historical memory for most people. Much of the rhetoric of rave culture has always been anti-political; 'change yourself to change the world'; 'It's not about politics, man; it's about having a good time ... ' A vague and uncritical notion of the importance of personal freedom informs most of contemporary youth culture, and while it could provide the basis for a strong resistance to new Labour's most authoritarian tendencies, it also harbours the potential for a very dangerous articulation with the terms of a conservative 'modernising' project. Just as the New Lad's self-conscious masculinity can easily turn into a reifying assertion of the unchangebility of traditional gender relationships, so rave hedonism can turn into an escape from problems which remain unsolved – poverty, job insecurity, powerlessness – because they seem unsolvable. The point at which both rave and Lad hedonisms can be articulated with a conservative discourse is the point at which hedonism becomes pessimism, libertarianism a disbelief in the possibility of collective action.

Secondly, and most importantly, it will remain utterly impossible to reconcile the conservative version of new Labour with the emergent culture of young women in Britain. If new Labour does persist in pursuing policy informed by the rhetoric of Family Values, it is difficult to imagine it retaining the support of this generation of women. The optimistic and democratic determination of this group to get what they want remains our best hope for a different hegemony. There is an implicit *politicality*, a willingness to expand the frontiers of possible change, inherent in the common-sense feminism of so many young women today which is not found in many other parts of the culture. Of course there is a danger that current forms of consumer culture will convince too many young women that wearing a short skirt is the extent of possible challenges to patriarchy. But if the prerequisite for change is a *desire* for change, then it is to this culture of young women and its tone of insistent demand that we should currently look for the brightest glimmers of radical hope.

Both of these key elements of contemporary structures of feeling – libertarian hedonism and implicit feminism – need to be taken into account when thinking through the possible shape of future left projects. There is a severe danger that new Labour communitarianism will continue to develop in authoritarian directions, and if this continues then the effect is likely to be either widespread alienation on the part of this generation or a resurgence of the libertarian right. There is nothing inherent in either of these sets of demands and desires that makes the solutions to them necessarily socialist; William Hague's liberalised and democratised Tory Party could all too easily become the vehicle for a feminism and hedonism cast entirely in the languages of individualist consumer culture. Campaigns around issues as diverse as union recognition and benefit reform need to keep in mind the centrality of these factors to contemporary youth culture if they are to have any popular and progressive resonance.

We saw both the possibilities and the dangers implicit in a politics informed by the concerns of indie rock discourse when, in March 1998 the *New Musical Express* published a special issue denouncing the Government. In an issue unusually dominated by white men even for that bastion of guitar culture, the *NME* accused new Labour of selling out its natural constituency in 'Cool Britannia'. The terms of their opposition to Blairism were revealing. Three issues attracted their particular attention: the ending of the principle of universal free access to higher education; the reform of the welfare system such that young claimants would be forced to undertake work or training, objected to on the grounds that many rock bands start out living on income support ('no dole, no rock 'n' roll', apparently); and the Government's refusal to consider decriminalising cannabis. We saw here on the one hand a clear-cut refusal of new Labour's puritanical tendencies, on the other an incredibly narrow understanding of the issues at stake. There was no indication that the writers had the slightest awareness of the rationale for reforming the system for funding higher education; that is, that the system it had funded was still one which overwhelmingly benefited the children of the middle classes and that the expansion of that system to make it available to a real majority of people required a totally different system of funding, means-tests and loans in order to make a living income available to all students during their time at university. One does not have to agree with this rationale or the policies which it has justified to believe that the continued expansion of higher education is as important a political issue as the question of whether or not employed professional graduates will have to pay back some of the costs of it. The *NME* showed not the slightest awareness that this had ever even been raised as an issue.

If the *NME*'s view of issues around higher education funding revealed a world-view as narrowly middle-class and nostalgic as its musical agendas, then this was nothing compared to their ludicrous claim that British rock culture depended on the ability of musicians to claim income support while working full-time on their music. If the writers had actually known anything about the working of the benefit system, they would have known that it had always been illegal to claim benefits while spending all your time messing about with guitars, and that it had for years been within the power of DSS officials to withdraw benefit to claimiants they deemed to be making insufficient efforts to find work or training. The idea that anyone could both survive and undertake a musical career on approximately £36.00 per week (the sum available to claimants under 25 in the early to mid 1990s), without help from family and friends with disposable incomes, use of their garages for rehearsal space, etc, etc, is a myth shared by middle-class bohemians for whom 'being on the dole' traditionally translates as 'living off one's parents'. If the *NME* had argued for a statutory basic income as a right for all citizens, or for widened access to facilities necessary for the development of creativity, then they would have had a sound argument. They didn't.[13]

Finally, the *NME* revealed the astonishingly narrow range of its political vision once again in its calls for the legalisation of cannabis. This is a perfectly sound policy to argue for, but to argue for it in isolation makes little sense in today's climate. Given that it is not cannabis – the continued criminalisation of which *is* a nonsense justifying a barbarity (people still get jailed for possession of it) – but Ecstasy which has transformed British culture, it is the entire concept of drug prohibition which today needs to be brought under the spotlight. But Ecstasy is the dance-culture drug, and the *NME* showed little interest in its legal status. Again, that paper's much-trumpeted political radicalism stood revealed as a woolly middle-class bohemianism with little imagination even in the application of its own libertarian principles.

There certainly was potential for a radical politics in the *NME's* gesture, but their arguments could all have been made by anyone from libertarian Conservatives to *Socialist Worker* sellers. What they do reveal is two things: first, a resistance to puritan discourse – anti-hedonism, pro-work – is ubiquitous across contemporary youth culture; second, indie rock culture remains dominated by the narrow concerns of middle-class white men. Thought in these terms, Cornershop's recent occupation of such Laddish spaces as the Chris Evans show and Oasis' US tour with their post-Asian, post-indie, militantly anti-Britpop version of what British pop could sound like is a remarkably hopeful sign, but the articulation of a problematised masculinity *with* rather than *against* a popular feminism remains a central task of democratisation. If we can do what we can to encourage such developments, then there may be a future for radical politics. If not, then we may as well go back to 1966 and start all over again.

NOTES

1. The notion of modernity as characterised by ever-increasing regulation goes back at least to the work of Max Weber, and also characterises that of Michel Foucault.

2. See, for instance, Marshall Berman, *All That is Solid Melts into Air*, Verso, London 1983.

3. Laclau and Mouffe, *Hegemony & Socialist Strategy*, Verso, London 1985, p186.

4. For example Mark Fisher, 'Indie Reactionaries', in *New Statesman and Society*, 7.7.95.

5. See Jason Toynbee, 'Policing Bohemia, pinning up Grunge' in *Popular Music* 12/2, pp289-300; Robert Burnett, *The Global Jukebox*, Routledge, London 1996; Keith Negus, *Producing Pop*, Edward Arnold, London 1992.

6. Campbell & Moriarty, 'New Labour, New Britpop', in *New Labour New Britain*, Autumn 1996.

7. Helen Wilkinson, *No Turning Back: generations and the genderquake*, Demos, London 1995.

8. Maria Pini, 'Cyborgs, Nomads and the Raving Feminine', in Helen Thomas (ed), *Dance in the City*, London 1997, p168.

9. Irvine Welsh, *Trainspotting*, Minerva, London 1993; *Marabou Stork Nightmares*, Jonathan Cape, London 1995; *Ecstasy*, Vintage, London 1997.

10. Irvine Welsh, *The Acid House*, Vintage, London 1995, p240.

11. Angela McRobbie, 'Pecs and Penises: The Meaning of Girlie Culture', in *Soundings* Summer 1997, Lawrence & Wishart, London, p159.

12. See any comprehensive breakdown of results form recent elections, e.g. MORI's.

13. Caroline Daniel made just this point in an excellent article in *New Statesman* 10.4.98.

SECTION THREE:
THE STATE WE'RE NOT IN

TOWARDS A RADICAL REFORMISM

Nina Fishman

The most convincing reason why the new Labour government is likely to initiate far-reaching constitutional change is that the status quo has little or no positive meaning for them. Since the 1960s, successive governments have taken office with sincere intentions of making necessary modernisations and modifications to the postwar settlement. Harold Wilson and Edward Heath were both committed to effecting major structural reforms in order to strengthen it. Mrs Thatcher nursed the clear ambition to replace it.

Similarly, when Tony Blair assumed office, he pronounced British parliamentary government to be riddled with outworn anachronisms. During his first year of office he has shown evident enthusiasm for carrying out his sentence of condemnation. The message tirelessly spun from Downing Street is that the youthful prime minister sees his mission as modernising the face of political Britain, infusing our institutions with fresh life and vigour. By the time he has completed his second term, the transformation will be so great that he will be known as The Moderniser, *sans pareil*.

It is evident that Blair's relish for sweeping aside outmoded ways is shared by a critical mass at Westminster. Support for replacing the old traditions has come not merely from the predictable sources of the scores of Labour MPs who are even younger than the Prime Minister himself, and the Liberal Democrats, whose programmatic commitment to constitutional reform is well known. Under William Hague's tutelage, the new Conservative Party has also shown faint but unmistakable modernising signs.

Hague is determined to be a Conservative of the Disraelian mode. He intends to lead the rump group of Tory backwoodsmen and wild people out of the ancestral wilderness into the same democratic future to which Blair has staked sole claim. Consequently, he has no interest in mounting last ditch actions to uphold the hallowed ground of *status quo*. Hague is pre-occupied with influencing the all important detail of the reforms rather than resisting the momentum towards them. The de facto Westminster consensus for constitutional change should give Blair ample room for manoeuvre. Barring last minute revolts from his own antediluvian backbenches, Blair should preside in deserved triumph over a new constitutional settlement during a second term. William Hague has removed Blair's most serious potential obstruction. If he should unexpectedly come from behind to beat Blair in 2002, Hague would gleefully emulate Disraeli in a neat manoeuvre to steal the new Labour reformers' clothes.

Though they are usually executed in 'the people's' name, political reforms are rarely the product of 'the people's will'. Unlike demands for basic social and economic reforms, pressure for political reform does not originate in the normal workings of civil society. Modern European and North American history shows that the motive force for fundamental political change resides inside the political establishment. This is hardly surprising since it is politicians' interests which are most immediately and thoroughly affected by political change.

NEW LABOUR'S REFORM AGENDA: WHIGGISH TENDENCIES V POPULISM

New Labour's reforming agenda, which by postwar standards is indeed radical, appears not merely progressive, but also sensible and timely. Informed opinion is convinced that new Labour's constitutional changes are desirable and deserve to be made.

There is, of course, a strong prejudice in favour of evolutionary change in British political culture. From the mid nineteenth century, the political establishment, led by the Whig grandees who had inherited the traditions of the Glorious Revolution, taught the British people that in order to conserve it was necessary to undertake periodic reforms. In this respect, Blair seems to be truly whiggish.

Two linked tenets lie at the heart of Blair's modernising project. It is argued that the current system of government, parliamentary sovereignty, is unsuited to current British society. New Labour aims to move Britain towards popular sovereignty. To do this, a written constitution is required. The reckoning is that a constitution will set out clearly the limits of parliamentary authority. The House of Commons will be subject to the rule of law administered by a separate judiciary. The assumption is that it will also be subordinate to an executive whose legitimacy derives from the constitution and ultimately from 'the people'.

It is wholly understandable that Blair's spinners and those reformers of passionate certitude should seek to magnify and hype the significance of the transition which new Labour is making between parliamentary and popular sovereignty. The transformation of Britain from being 'whig and paternal' to 'modern and democratic' has become one of the critical differences which new Labour sees between itself and old Labour.

A triumphant populist rationale underlies new Labour's rhetoric. The people's millennium dome, the people's parliament, the people's x, y and z, are denominated and intoned with the great solemnity and unctuous regularity. This same act of renaming has marked transformational political changes in European history since 1789. Most recently, it was the countries of east central Europe and Africa which invested their living spaces with new meaning by renaming them in the people's democracy mode.

In fact, the political system that the first majority Labour government inherited in 1945 from the wartime coalition government was neither wholly whig, paternal, nor sacrosanct. Absolute parliamentary sovereignty had ceased to function in Britain after 1832. The much-vaunted ancient unwritten constitution with parliamentary sovereignty at its core was regularly challenged in political conflict during the nineteenth century, and emerged from the fray modernised and more democratised. By 1910, it was abundantly clear to all concerned that Westminster's legitimacy was underpinned by popular sovereignty.

Since the Conservatives' galloping Europhobia has virtually destroyed public confidence in Westminster institutions, there is no longer a whiggish argument for keeping the appearances of parliamentary sovereignty intact. The new Labour project of legitimising popular sovereignty via a written constitution will provide a more realistic foundation for government. There will be an end of the tiresome conundrums in which wily political scientists and obfuscating retired colonels indulged about the unique longevity and inviolability of the

British political system. We won't have to think about British politics in worn-out terms which inadequately reflect the realities of Britain's place in the European Union or indeed the place of the English regions, not to mention Scotland, Wales and Northern Ireland within the United Kingdom.

Nevertheless, Blair's admirable reforms will not be sufficient in themselves to bring British society to the ultimate destination of political transformation in the reformers' vision. His reforms are formal changes which create the necessary pre-conditions for the restoration of a healthy, functional relationship between the government, parliament and the people. There is no guarantee that trust and good faith between government and the governed will follow inevitably from their enactment.

THE SUBSTANCE OF DEMOCRACY

At this *fin de siecle*, the stuff of functional democratic politics remains the maintenance of a concerted, ongoing and full dialogue between politicians and the people. Such a dialogue is time-consuming and often risky for politicians; they often end up adapting and revising their ideas about what should happen to take account of what they are hearing 'from below'. But the dialogue is also demanding for 'the people'. They have to apply their minds to the issues at hand, to understand the conflicts and ultimately resolve to accept a collective decision which cannot, by definition, please everyone. To keep this dialogue in good working order, both sides have to recognise and appreciate their different but mutually dependent roles.

Collective decisions, acts, and policies do not spring spontaneously from the serried ranks of any body politic, no matter how small – *pace* Rousseau.[1] A representative of any collective participates in a two-way process. Representatives must not merely listen to and interpret the gamut of responses from collective groups and individuals and interest groups, they must also provide a lead to these people using their knowledge and insights into the larger whole, the past, the future, and the myriad of constraints and special considerations just beyond the horizon of everyday life.

If the representative fails either to listen or to provide a lead, then there can be no progress towards a collective consensus. Without the input of active leadership from representatives, a democratic society will be unable to deal with social problems, political issues or provide for future contingencies. Anyone who has reflected seriously upon the relationship between politicians and the people (or experienced the stormy vicissitudes themselves, as a shop steward, councillor, school governor, trade union branch official, or any number of other representative functions in voluntary organisations) understands very well that there is no such thing as the people's will giving birth to a pristinely democratic political act.

Nevertheless, if representative democracy is to operate successfully, the people also have to exist in all their puzzling indeterminacy and rich complexity. 'The people' is a collective noun with no exact or social scientifically verifiable existence. In the real world, 'the people' is an aggregation of religions, ethnicities, sexualities, classes, genders, regional and national communities. The great achievement and virtue of Victorian and Edwardian politicians was their commitment to giving 'the people' a vibrant, healthy and constructive political persona on the historical stage. Looking backwards, it is impossible not to be impressed by the magnitude of the changes wrought by the intimate partnership between politicians and the people in that amazingly productive long nineteenth century, particularly from the 1890s.

There were significant countervailing conservative and outright reactionary forces which were successful in halting what they viewed as unacceptably modern developments. Yet this nineteenth century *fin de siecle* culture shows the same individualism, questioning of hierarchies and determination to make one's own decisions which modernisers regard as unique to our own time.

The architects of Blair's modernising project must work towards a pragmatic 'Heath-Robinson' compromise with our old political culture to fertilise and restore the relationship between government, parliament and the people. They should draw on the example of the Victorian and Edwardian political reforms, which adapted the older oligarchic culture and traditions and put them to good use in constructing new ways. Modernisers cannot dismiss the careworn old past out of hand. They must concede that parliamentary sovereignty with its grand old whiggish constitution and Bagehotian mysteries had palpable virtues.

Such modernising caution when approaching the past is prudent. There has never yet been a democratic political transformation which succeeded by throwing the baby out with the bath water and starting from some proverbial year zero. Enduring structural political reforms have to rely for their raw materials on the old ways. The art of effecting durable political change lies in knowing which parts of the old political culture and relationships are appropriate for adaptation and recycling.

It is not only the 'ancient' British state which has successfully and successively re-invented itself in this *ad hoc* way, utilising serviceable materials from the older institutions. European states with written constitutions and popular sovereignty at their core have routinely used old, often pre-democratic and apparently anachronistic survivals to buttress their new transformational projects. Analysis of the Federal Republic of Germany's postwar constitution shows that the foundations of the modern German state lie deep in the post-Napoleonic Prussian past, the Wilhelmine Reich's thorough-going federal structure, the 1914-18 total war economy, and the Weimar constitution arising from the 1918-19 revolution.[2]

The reflexive response of some reformers is to define a healthy, functional relationship between politicians and the people as being the exact opposite of the grand old traditions of whiggery and paternalism. This is both glib and dangerous, because the old ways contained an important core of sense, practicality, and good faith in their conception of how politicians should connect to their constituents.[3]

THE LIMITS OF 'THE PEOPLE'S' WILL

A currently fashionable reforming view is that democratic government means politicians doing what 'the people' want. The doughty people's government are mere servants, doing the people's will at every turn. It is interesting, and revealing of the date of the political socialisation of these partisans, that this view reflects the assumptions about the absolute good of democracy generated by the opposing sides in the Cold War.

Propagandists, theologians and thinkers in the postwar Soviet communist state and the American democratic republic were agreed that politicians' sacred trust was to implement the people's will. Of course, the opposing systems provided very different ways in which the people's will was determined. But both shared the assumption that it was the people who occupied the centre stage and played the heroic part in society.[4]

Blair should recognise the structural flaws and shortcomings in the

American populist model currently portrayed as the epitome of democracy by their friends in the White House and US think tanks. A perceptible gulf between the American people and the federal political establishment began to grow during the late 1960s. In the past thirty years, the gap has become profound and apparently unbridgeable in the current political climate. The low turnout in presidential elections in this period is clear evidence of citizens' alienation. At the last presidential election in 1996, only 48 per cent of registered voters used their vote. Moreover, voter registration is not compulsory. Only a minority of those eligible to register actually do so, probably just over 30 per cent.

The end of the Cold War in apparent victory for the US has precipitated a triumphal mood amongst American politicians and intellectuals, tending towards *hubris*. This mood is potentially dangerous and not only because it may lead US politicians into imprudence and lack of forethought in dealing with serious international issues. The features of the hothouse world of Washington DC bear a close resemblance to the Court of Versailles in the mid eighteenth century.

There are now only two connections between central government and the American people: the pork barrel of federal money for local projects and patronage; and the illusions and spectacle of television politics. There is no longer a serious representative polity in the United States capable of making the major democratic decisions that the USA will face in the early twenty-first century.

The appearance of post-Cold War triumphalism in the US should enjoin European politicians to adopt particular caution and tact in dealing with their American allies. There is also a pressing need for Europe to establish a discrete distance from the uncertain vicissitudes to which US politics are increasingly subject. Unfortunately, Blair's government and followers have eagerly fallen in step behind the Americans' self-regarding euphoria.

Instead of tactfully modifying our 'special relationship' with the US and repositioning the UK at the heart of an integrated European foreign policy, set out as a goal by the Maastricht Treaty, Blair has chosen to do the opposite.[5] He has trumpeted himself as the most recent embodiment of the mythical connection between English speaking peoples on both sides of the Atlantic. The currently potent American way, of seeing the world wholly through American-centred eyes, has evidently had an unsettling effect on the reasoning powers of new Labour.

Unthinking Americophilia involves grave risks in addition to those looming in the arena of international diplomacy. New Labour, especially Blair and his entourage, are emulating the corpus of American domestic political rhetoric. They apparently accept the superficial lesson of the end of the Cold War: American democracy has won. They are convinced that they will gain inspiration by creatively adapting the American way to British conditions. They will share in the aura of the USA's success and glory. Similarly, the American way of capitalism and flexible labour markets has brought prosperity. Hence, the Blair government's emphasis on the virtues of mega-corporate success and flexibility.

The abandonment of Americophilia certainly does not imply embracing its opposite, the Cold War anachronism of anti-Americanism. Instead, new Labour should arrive at a considered, sympathetic, and detached view of our most powerful ally. Sympathetic detachment will enable new Labour to judge our domestic political issues on their own merits rather than presume that the substance of their modernising project is to transform British parliamentary sovereignty to closely resemble American popular sovereignty.

DO MODERNISING PROJECTS REQUIRE MODERNISING PROBLEMS?

A central part of new Labour's modernising project has been to invest British society with modern problems. Modern problems require modern, up-to-date solutions. Highly fashionable politicians observe with regret the final passing of an integrated society and the onset of social disintegration. But British society has remained remarkably close-knit and cohesive despite the strong countervailing tendencies of individualism and the personal consumer culture. A real sense of living in a collective entity survives here, and has been of positive benefit to the political establishment. This collective identity has been a positive source of strength in enabling people to deal with the enormous social problems caused by the collapse of British industry.

In contrast to the United States, the apparatus of due political process, enabling a genuine two-way dialogue to proceed between politicians and the people, has also survived in Britain during the stresses and strains of the last thirty years. Owing to disuse, its workings have rusted over. But its machinery is long established, has been well maintained and periodically renewed since 1832. A hiatus of a mere half century has not destroyed its foundations in our political culture and collective memory.

The essential feature of a functional democracy is that the people and the political establishment recognise and fulfil obligations and duties towards each other. But both must also understand and accept that they can work productively and amicably together only when they recognise the higher claims of the polity's collective existence to their own narrow interests. A functional democracy is more than the sum of its aggregated parts.

British political culture contains ample space for the 'rank-and-file' of society to stand up for themselves, be counted and when necessary to rebuff those who are meant to lead them. There has always been an acknowledged place for leaders, and a ready acceptance of their obligation to provide a lead. But the political establishment also accepted the need for dealing openly and without condescension with the people.

British society retains an astonishing range of vigorous voluntary organisations – from charities and women's institutes to amateur music and dramatics, camera clubs, parent teacher associations and trade unions – which could play a valuable role in transmitting ordinary people's hopes, fears and demands to Blair's government. These disparate interest groups share an important characteristic: the habit of coming together, discussing, and arriving at a common position. Their members are accustomed to co-operating with each other and acting together.

Dialogue between the people and their government is only practical and constructive when civil society is organised into self-conscious and self-governing interest groups which recognise the need to subordinate their narrow interests for the common good. There are few 'win-win' scenarios in real life politics. But when citizens have trust in their government to mediate between conflicting interests and to treat them equally and fairly, there is acceptance that the needs of the collective polity mean that no interest group or individual should expect that their demands will be fully satisfied. A collective decision, taken by assembled representatives, contains the seeds of a myriad of compromises.

There are a whole range of new technology aids to democracy, such as electronic buttons on people's television sets or the internet, which will merit the attention of twenty-first century democrats. On their own, high tech gadgetry will not restore democracy. But coupled with serious intent on the part of the political establishment, information disseminators and gatherers would reinforce and enhance the due political process of arriving at agreed decisions between government and the citizenry.

THE RADICAL DUOPOLY

But new technology aids cannot tie 'the people' into accepting prob-lematic governmental decisions and co-operating with the state to implement them. We will be able to judge the government's intentions towards 'the people' by their conduct on two critical structural reforms. Will they extricate themselves from their refusal to take Britain into the single European currency until after 2002; and will they support the adoption of proportional representation for both the House of Commons and also for local government. If implemented, these two reforms will have profound long-term consequences. Together with the Government's major achievement in establishing the Scottish Parliament and the Welsh Assembly, they would restore the rough checks and balances between the people and government.

At first sight, they appear unrelated. The link between them is that they significantly undermine the anachronism of parliamentary sover-eignty *and* also enable civil society to regain its own voice in relation to the political establishment. They are the true litmus test for Blair's reforming intentions because, more than any other projected reforms, they involve the voluntary surrender of power by the central govern-ment. It is significant that they are the two reforms in Blair's constitu-tional agenda which William Hague has flatly refused to endorse.

LOSING THE POUND IN ORDER TO GAIN THE EURO AND A MODERN IDENTITY

A set of plausible economic reasons have been advanced publicly by the Treasury as to why they will not contemplate taking Britain into the European single currency until 2002. In fact, as the *Financial Times* leader columns and correspondents have tirelessly pointed out, they are all moveable feasts. Synchronising economic cycles, the strength of sterling and flexible labour markets would not and should not deter a government which was determined for political reasons to participate in Economic and Monetary Union (EMU). The manifestly weak economic positions of Italy and Portugal have not deterred their governments from insisting on their places in the first wave.[6]

The principal unspoken but perfectly clear reason for not participating in the first wave is that Blair has not yet reconciled himself to the loss of the trappings of British greatness, independence, sovereignty and – above all – the special relationship with the United States. In short, he has not yet accepted the radical structural adjustment to which Edward Heath committed the state when he piloted Britain into the European Economic Community in 1972. In this respect, Blair is indeed a fitting heir to Thatcher. The aspiration to bestride the world stage as key players is manifestly common to both.

Thatcher began her prime ministerial career as a rank pragmatist about Europe. A member of the Heath government in 1972, she was a strong supporter of the 'Yes' vote in the 1975 referendum on Britain's continued membership of the Common Market. Her conversion to Europhobia occurred when she realised that Britain could not dominate the EEC. She had bought into the neo-imperialist vision of Europe in which the British would be the Greeks controlling the Roman Empire.[7] She discovered instead that she would have to behave in a collegial manner towards the other European heads of state, and moreover that Germany, France and Italy knew their own minds very well and could not be led by the nose in the same way as her own backbenches.

Unlike his predecessor John Smith, who was a principled and enthusiastic European, Blair has never been, nor pretended to be, more than a Euro-pragmatist.[8] He evidently observed and carefully reflected upon Mrs Thatcher's conversion to Euro-scepticism. He concluded that though she had gone much too far, her reasoning was sound. Europe as a political economic entity remains a distant place for him. He is keen to lecture to it, to imprint his third way upon it, but not to behave in the required collegial manner. Britain must still be a player on the world stage in her own right, otherwise why would he bother to be prime minister?

Blair's lack of enthusiasm for EMU stems from his correct perception that it involves the further and significant pooling of political sovereignty by the member states. The eleven states who will participate in the first wave and adopt the single European currency are prepared for this pooling because they know it is in the long term interests of their electorates. EMU will guarantee Europe's continuing stability and prosperity in a unique way. There is no substitute for a single currency if the project of a European single market is to be completed.[9]

Political observers who had resisted the galloping Europhobia pervading Westminster were not surprised in May 1997 when the electorate decisively rejected the cataclysmic view of Brussels as a horde of conspirators and schemers attempting to deprive Albion of her free-born traditions and sausages. The people responded to the jeremiads of the Referendum Party and John Redwood with notable *sangfroid*. Despite the *Sun*'s strident xenophobia, voters refused to repudiate membership of a club which they recognised as their best guarantee of economic prosperity and political stability.

However, Blair's new Labour declined to fight a pro-European campaign, and did not challenge the basic assumptions of Major's claim that he was mounting a vital defence of British sovereignty by keeping us out of EMU and the single European currency. But neither did they play the Euro-sceptic card. They notably refrained from speaking the colloquial Europhobic rhetoric circulating inside Westminster out on the hustings.

The Prime Minister's spin-doctors let it be known that he feared the nationalist reaction of the British people if he took the UK into the Euro and shed the pound. This is a highly disingenuous line. There are certainly members of the political and economic elite who are keen on us retaining our American orientation. It is good for their transatlantic business interests and satisfies their self-image as keen participants in the mythical 'Anglo-Saxon' model of corporate governance and free-dom loving culture. But the British people are now pragmatic, if phleg-matic Europeans. They have undergone a genuine sea change since 1972 which most Westminster politicians have signally failed to observe.

The majority of Britons were visceral Euro-sceptics in the 1960s. They remained doggedly aloof from Heath's enthusiasm for the Common Market, but acquiesced provisionally in his decisive leader-ship when he took Britain into Europe. But this was only because they were in the habit of accepting that British governments acted for the best interests of the country, not because they were optimistic about the prospect of joining the Common Market.[10]

The British view of themselves and of Europe changed gradually over twenty-five years. The cumulative effect of this gradual change has been dramatic. Developments in our domestic economy, the international market and global politics confirmed that Heath's redirection of Britain into Europe had been sensible. The majority of the British people are now pragmatic Europeans. Their commitment to the European Union has ceased being provisional and is now part of their basic orientation to the rest of the world.

By committing Britain to participating in EMU at the earliest possible moment, Tony Blair would inflict a simultaneous blow at two of our political culture's most enduring illusions: firstly, that Britain can still bestride the international stage as a power in her own right. And secondly, that Britain is still a parliamentary sovereignty. His action would be popular, since the majority of the British people hold neither view. Not surprisingly, it is mainly particular sections of the political establishment who still cling tightly to these Westminster-centric myths.

Britain's early adoption of the single European currency would also be a vital safeguard for the people that our current standards of living will be protected and secure. Unlike multi-national businesspeople, we cannot move our very human resources to the most profitable part of the global market. Our fate and fortunes remain in the UK, and unless the UK goes into the Euro, our economic future will be bleak indeed.

THE CARDINAL VIRTUES OF PROPORTIONAL REPRESENTATION

The essential defence of parliamentary, i.e. House of Commons, sovereignty, is that the Commons has been the principal bulwark of British liberties since the Glorious Revolution in 1688. This line of defence was mounted by Michael Foot and Enoch Powell in their successful battle to stop Harold Wilson's government reforming the House of Lords in 1968.[11] As a rearguard action, this duo fought brilliantly to preserve the *status quo*. However, the object of their crusade, the independent and freedom-loving House of Commons, was long gone.

The days when the House of Commons enjoyed autonomous power in its own right had vanished even before the first world war – the date when most conventional histories place the unstoppable shift in power away from the floor of the House of Commons to the government. In fact, it is highly likely that historians of the twenty-first century will date the Commons' critical loss of power and initiative in 1910 when the Liberal Government, led by Lloyd George, made a radical appeal to the British people against the unelected House of Lords. It was not the House of Commons which stood up for the people against the Lords, but the people themselves who were incited by Lloyd George to deploy their power through the ballot box.

The fiction of parliamentary sovereignty was a highly convenient fig leaf to mask the accretion of power by the central government. Whilst successive observers from the parliamentary benches, like Arthur Balfour or Michael Foot, might enthuse about the excellence of a free and independent House of Commons, they were content to use the strong, vice-like mechanisms of the central state to curtail that freedom and independence in practice.

In itself, a strong central state is not inimical to a democratic political system. As the current political impasse in the United States illustrates so vividly, a weak central executive may be an obstacle to democracy. The much-vaunted checks and balances built into the American constitution in 1783 in emulation of the 1688 British constitutional settlement have proved durable, but positively troublesome for democracy.

Instead of addressing and connecting with civil society, the American central state in the shape of the President is constantly engaged in turf wars with the American Congress. Whilst such disputation certainly resembles British politics of the early eighteenth century, it does not provide civil society with a serious voice in the affairs of state. Instead of due political process, there are a succession of skirmishes between these two arms of the state, which apparently see each other all too frequently as opponents.

In the twenty-first century, the most effective check against an overweeningly strong and potentially tyrannous central state will be 'the people'. The central state has learned over the past century how to effectively circumvent, outflank and flannel the legislature to which it is nominally responsible. If that legislature is to act as a real check against the central executive, its voice must be strongly reinforced by and connected to the popular will. It is through voting that 'the people' can exert the most effective power over their politicians. A government elected through universal suffrage and proportional representation will resemble the profile of the people's wishes and concerns most closely. Proportional representation ensures that there are no institutional obstacles to popular choice.

It is easy to see why Tony Blair is playing his hand in this matter so close to his chest. His government has a majority of 179 seats in the

House of Commons. However, Labour won only 44.4 per cent of the popular vote in May 1997, yet gained 65.2 per cent of the seats. New Labour is glorying in the enormous power and unchallenged hegemony in parliament bestowed by their large, but unearned majority.

A proportional voting system for the House of Commons would have three truly radical effects on British politics. Firstly, it would give everyone who voted the assurance that their vote actually counted. Today there is widespread understanding and consequent disillusion that most votes do not count, and are worthless in determining the result of the general election.

Secondly, a proportional voting system would routinely produce results in which no one party could command a parliamentary majority. Coalition government would consequently become the norm. It would render obsolete the old fashioned, unmodern adversarial politics which underlies the House of Commons gladiatorial culture. Coalition government would enforce the goal of central government as consensus seeking amongst the complex, variegated interests which make up 'the people'.

And thirdly, a proportional voting system would abolish the rotten boroughs of the late twentieth century – old, and new Labour's safe seats in the North of England, Wales and Scotland as well as the Conservatives' remaining safe seats in so much of England south of the Humber. The essence of safe seats is that their incumbents can always sleep easily in their beds, knowing that however dramatic the swing in the general election, they at least will keep their fiefdoms. A glance at the current new Labour cabinet reveals just how many officeholders are also rotten borough barons and baronesses.[12]

It is, however, local government that remains the principal bastion of rotten boroughs. The operation of the majoritarian, first-past-the-post voting system in local government has produced permanent Labour majorities in councils up and down the country. The predictable by-product of Labour's permanent rule has been that these local councils exhibit the same corruption and imperviousness to local needs as notorious one-party regimes elsewhere. The only reliable way to end this lamentable, indefensible situation is to institute proportional representation for local government.

Because of the tireless campaigning of the Liberal Democrats, a growing number of local councils are already coalition governments. Liberal Democrats have persuasively convinced Labour supporters to vote tactically and elect Liberal Democrats to provide an effective check against Labour dictatorship. After all, the point of a democracy is to allow the expressions and representation of many points of view.

The new Labour government has loudly proclaimed its intention of dealing summarily and firmly with Labour councils and councillors who are corrupt. But the most effective way to stop corruption is to end one-party rule. Most councils with coalition administrations have proved innovative and notable successes. Their achievements could be reproduced and extended if the Blair government enacted a system of proportional representation for local government. A proportional voting system for local government would also pre-empt the socialisation of budding politicians in a rotten borough mode.

TOWARDS A DEMOCRATIC MODERNISATION

The crucial criterion of whether a democracy is working in practice is to find out if both the people and their government are conscientiously honouring mutual obligations through the observance of a due political process. Due political process enables serious dialogue between the people and the political establishment. Each side must act in good faith, without having either pre-conditions or a pre-determined outcome.

The way in which Blair's modernisers are using opinion poll and focus group results pre-empts any possibility of serious dialogue. The political establishment typically tell 'the people' what we are feeling and demanding. They have ceased to play their part in due political process by listening to us. Social scientific research has already informed them more accurately what we really think.

The adaptation of market research methods to politics has had profoundly negative consequences. The impact of politicians' message is social scientifically measured by opinion polling. There is test marketing of politicians' programmes through the use of focus groups. The only conclusion can be that under the modernisers' rubric political dialogue will be replaced by political consumerism.

Market research methods are useful aids for politicians anxious to know what their constituents are thinking. But when they are used to replace dialogue, they become not only counter-productive but also anti-democratic. In order to bind 'we the people' into a solution to a difficult political problem, we must be consulted by our representatives. We are willing to set aside the attainment of short-term self interests, but only if our points of view have been listened to, pondered and then finally taken into account in arriving at a way forward.

A balance between the people and politicians enables a dialogue of equals to be conducted between them within which potential conflict and disintegrating influences can be resolved and overcome. In an unpredictable world, the only realistic expectation is that there will be periods of comparative calm and times of increased tension. In emergency situations, a functional democracy's virtues are manifest, enabling a society to pull together and make temporary sacrifices and accept substantial disruptions to individual routines in order to salvage and safeguard the collective whole.

If Blair's government decides to revitalise a functioning democracy, they must find not only energy and will but also humility to play their part in genuine dialogue with the people. A cardinal virtue of Britain's Victorian and Edwardian politicians was their keen awareness of the autonomy of civil society. However, a section of the political establishment were convinced by utilitarian social engineers that civil society could and should be controlled for its own good. The utilitarians' enthusiasm for social control was comparable to our current modernisers' embrace of market research. Both impulses contain within them the seeds of a strong authoritarian attitude towards civil society.

Fortunately, in Victorian Britain, utilitarians made only limited progress. The dominant view of the political establishment remained that politicians must take care to treat the various orders, classes and interest groups comprising civil society with courtesy and attention, as independent agents who loyally observed their obligations to the state. Britain retained a remarkably free society in which civil servants and politicians were reluctant to interfere too openly.

New Labour have the chance to construct a durable political culture comparable to that created in Britain during the nineteenth and early twentieth centuries when politicians believed they had to come to terms with democracy or perish. It is possible that new Labour will merely adopt American populist politics and then claim that they have modernised and transformed British politics. The terrible attraction for Blair is that American populism appears modern but entails no substantial loss of power by the political establishment.

A prime motivation of new Labour is to retain the overwhelming weight in the balance of political power in the government's hands. Having embraced the rhetoric of popular sovereignty, the Blair government hopes to avoid the further steps required to revive a serious two-way dialogue between leaders and led. They have decided that they would find it too risky, emotionally demanding and time consuming to routinely move outside parliamentary institutions and engage in meaningful collective dialogue with the citizenry.

Popular disillusion and disappointment are the most likely results if new Labour persists in equating modernisation with Americanisation. The British people have a famously long collective memory. There is a reflexive recollection of the need to ensure equality between politicians and the people by means of an open political culture and due political process. Popular recognition of the cumulative erosion of the people's place in British politics under Thatcher underlay the euphoric response to new Labour's stunning election victory. It will be only fitting if nemesis greets Blair's government if they abandon their democratic pledges.

Given the opportunity, 'the people' will respond wholeheartedly and sensibly to the responsibility of resuming a full role in taking political decisions. 'The people' are regarded by too many contemporary politicians and their fashionable spinners as mere vessels into which they may pour pre-digested opinions and attitudes.

If new Labour gives them the chance to share the centre stage of British politics again, their performance is likely to be memorable. Both 'the people' and Tony Blair will earn their places in the twenty-first century history books.

NOTES

1. Jean-Jacques Rousseau (1712-1778) was born in Geneva, at that time a self-governing city state. He used his memories of thepolitics and morals of his birthplace as a model for his arguments in favour of republicanism. See Maurice Cranston, *Jean-Jacques. The Early Life and Work of Jean-Jacques Rousseau 1712-1754*, Allen Lane,1983, chapter 16, particularly p318.

2. See *Politics and Government in the Federal Republic of Germany, Basic Documents*, edited by Carl-Christoph Schweitzer *et al*, Berg Publishers, 1984. Useful background can be found in Gordon A. Craig, *The Germans*, Pelican, 1984.

3. See, for example, Anthony Barnett, *This Time. Our Constitutional Revolution*, Vintage, 1997, chapter 8, pp251-81, and Tony Wright, *Citizens and Subjects*, Routledge, 1994.

4. In the postwar Soviet Union, the Leninist conception of the vanguard party was subtly and pragmatically altered to emphasise that it was 'the people' who

occupied the centre stage in the socialist Soviet Union and the people's democracies of east central Europe. The postwar American political establishment confirmed their belief in the sacred trinity: government of the people, by the people and for the people. 'Of, by, for' became a theological dogma which could not be reflected upon rationally or examined without occasioning accusations of Communist subversiveness. It was literally political heresy to question this mystically inseparable trinity.

The underlying commonality between the political positioning of America and the Soviet Union is less surprising than it appears. The Cold War was a global political contest, but its principal protagonists were these two states. The USA and the USSR engaged in the conflict with serious intentions to wound and if possible destroy the other's political system. Engagement at this political level is impossible unless there are definite points of the coincidence of ideas. Conflict arises from differences in interpretation of the shared corpus of ideas. Western Europe did not wage the same war of political principle with the Soviet Union. Western Europe's differences with the USSR were actually about the balance of power on the continent.

5. The treaty's provisions are summarised in the background report, *The 1996 Intergovernmental Conference (First Report)* issued by the European Commission, No. B/9/95. The structure established by the Maastricht Treaty provided for 'three pillars but with a single institutional framework ... The second pillar deals with Common Foreign and Security Policy (CFSP) ... '(p4). 'Title V of the Maastricht Treaty provides for two instruments that can be adopted by Member States. Firstly common positions (article J.2) in order to co-ordinate the co-operation between the Member States. Secondly, joint actions (article J.3) financed by both national and Community budget. Both instruments require unanimity and do not commit Member States. However joint actions that have been agreed can be put into practice by qualified majority.' (p8)

6. An excellent, concise analysis of the economic issues involved in Britain's participation in EMU is *Restating the case for EMU – Reflections from the Left*, by Dan Corry, IPPR, 1996. Also useful are *One Money for Europe? The economics and politics of EMU*, by Malcolm Crawford, Macmillan, 1998, and *The Political Economy of Monetary Union. Towards the Euro*, by Francesco Giordano and Sharda Persaud, Routledge, 1998.

7. George Brown provides a candid statement of this approach in his autobiography. 'I have always quarrelled with Dean Acheson's much-repeated remark about Britain's having lost an empire and not found a role. We have a role: our role is to lead Europe ... It may be that Britain is destined to become the leader of Europe, of Western Europe in the first place, and of as much of Europe as

will come together later on ... It is our business to provide political leadership, to provide the stability that for so long has eluded the democracies of the mainland of Europe'. (Lord George-Brown, *In My Way*, Penguin,1972, p202.)

8. Paul Anderson and Nyta Mann describe Smith as 'a long-standing pro-European who had defied a three-line whip to vote for entry into the European Community in October 1971'. (*Safety First, The Making of New Labour*, Granta, 1997, p70).

9. It is notable that the single European currency will present a significant challenge to the dollar's premier position as international reserve currency. If the Euro becomes a reserve currency to rival the dollar it will benefit Europeans' standard of living, but could also create political tension between the EU and the USA.

10. The movement of British opinion on Europe has been routinely monitored since 1972 by the European Commission. See their regular reports, *Eurobarometer. Public Opinion in the European Union.* For an academic discussion of these issues see Andrew Gamble, 'The European Issue in British Politics', in David Baker and David Seawright (eds), *Britain For and Against Europe: British Politics and the Question of European Integration*, Clarendon Press, 1998.

11. A brief, colourful description of this unholy alliance is in Kenneth O. Morgan, *The People's Peace, British History 1945-1990*, Oxford University Press, 1992, pp305-6. 'Hereditary peerages would now be replaced by a two-tier system of appointments, while all peers entitled to vote would be appointed by the Prime Minister' (p305).

12. Cabinet members holding very safe seats in the North of England include the Prime Minister, the Deputy Prime Minister and the Home Secretary. Others in the Cabinet are Mo Mowlam and Jack Cunningham. Margaret Beckett holds a very safe seat in the East Midlands. From Scotland, we find the Chancellor of the Exchequer and Alistair Darling. From Wales, there are Kim Howells and Peter Hain.

CALEDONIAN DREAMING: THE CHALLENGE TO SCOTTISH LABOUR

Gerry Hassan

The majority of people in the United Kingdom, namely the English, see Scotland as an afterthought or addition to an English perspective on the world; Scotland is not a place in the forefront of their minds because it has no direct impact on their lives. The exact opposite is true for how most Scots see England, because no matter what view they hold, there is no avoiding the fact that for Scots their relationship with England still defines a large part of how they see themselves and the wider world. This is the asymmetrical relationship of two nations in the Union: an England which regularly ignores and misunderstands Scotland, and a Scotland that spends much time examining itself and how others see it, particularly the English.

Scottish politics can be seen through these two very different geographical and political perspectives: the Scottish dominated agenda of the Scots media and press, and the Westminster obsessed agenda, where Scottish politicians often play walk-on parts in major British political dramas.[1] These two perspectives influence the shape of Scottish politics and the strategies of the major political parties.

The discourses of Scottish politics do not exist entirely separately, but are mediated and influenced by what is British politics, and in turn influence it. The extent of Scottish *autonomy* and *difference* – the two are not necessarily the same – is constantly changing and moving and being continually renegotiated, as Scottish and British agencies respond to the social views, opinions and pressures of various agents and institutions. The expression of Scottish *autonomy* has at differing points encouraged homogenisation when it has been seen as in the interests of Scotland as a regional player in the United Kingdom. An example of this is at the time of the high point of the British welfare state circa 1945-64. At other times this has been expressed as the advocating of *difference*, when national economic growth slowed down from the 1960s onward and post-1979 as the British state was associated with Thatcherism.

What has never been in doubt within the paradigm of modern Scottish politics is that it has always operated within a framework of 'managed' and 'partial' 'autonomy'.[2] For all the debates in Scotland post-1979 about the assimilation of Scotland into the UK, the reality of modern Scottish politics has always been an acknowledgement and understanding of a spectrum of differing degrees of autonomy for Scotland within the Union.

James Kellas has argued that the concept of a 'Scottish political system' 'does justice to the scale and nature of the phenomena which are found in Scottish politics.'[3] Kellas is not prepared to see Scotland reduced to the level of a sub-system of the British political system. Midwinter puts the opposite case: 'There is a British political system which is periodically under stress in Scotland ... The Scottish environment and civil society places specific demands on British government, which is forced to produce responses which may be differentiated yet which maintain the integrity of the British system as a whole.'[4] Others, including Richard Rose, have used such concepts as 'Scottish input to the British political system', 'policy networks' and 'Scottish policy making community' – which all attempt to analyse the degree of autonomy Scottish agencies can institutionalise for themselves in the British political system.[5]

Scottish political parties have historically had to address both Scottish and British interests at the same time: a delicate and constant process of 'bridge building.'[6] The most successful Scottish political parties – the Liberals in the nineteenth century, the Conservatives from the 1920s to 1950s, and Labour in the 1960s – did this: defending Scottish interests at Westminster and selling the merits of the British nation for Scotland back home. This careful balancing act was one reason for their electoral success, but it was also an implicitly Scottish nationalist agenda of standing up for Scottish interests at Westminster while articulating a basically pragmatic and instrumental sense of Britishness, and this eventually caused their downfall.

When this strategy began to fall apart and failed to deliver the goods for Scotland as economic growth slowed down from the mid-1960s onwards, the British parties left themselves open to the arrival of the Scottish National Party (SNP) promising a new, better Scotland.[7] The SNP has since then unsettled the potential of both major British parties to carry out this balancing act: witness Labour's unease over Scotland in the 1970s, Thatcher and Major's English Conservatism, and new Labour's problems with Scotland prior to the 1997 election. It remains open to question whether this 'pork barrel' approach to politics, where Scottish political parties acted as a lobby for Scottish interests, can survive in a political environment shaped by the twin pressures of a broad based Scottish nationalism with an appeal far beyond the SNP, and the post-Thatcherite realpolitik of new Labour.

THE DOCTRINE AND ETHOS OF SCOTTISH LABOUR

Scottish Labour's self-image emphasises its uniqueness and special place in both Scottish politics and British Labour. Scottish Labour sees itself as a party which is radical, popular and Scottish, and from this springs its view of itself and its place in the world.[8] These beliefs coalesce into an over-arching sense by Scottish Labour of what Drucker differentiates in Labour's ideology as 'doctrine and ethos'. Doctrine is defined as 'a more or less elaborate set of ideas about the character of (in this case) social, economic and political reality' which 'lead to a programme of action.'[9] Ethos represents 'sets of values which spring from the experience of the British working class' and 'a shared past, a series of folk memories of shared exploitation, common struggle and gradually increasing power.'[10]

Scottish Labour's doctrine has always been shaped from, and by, the left, with Annual Conferences consistently taking positions which have outflanked the British party. Issues chosen were often of a radical symbolism, with Scottish Labour councils in the 1980s supporting CND and twinning with Palestinian towns, but not addressing issues where it had real local power and responsibility, such as decentralising services, consulting tenants and promoting equal opportunities.

This kind of posture politics allows Scottish Labour to define itself as politically pure in relation to new Labour. At the 1998 Scottish Labour conference, for example, there was the ritual politics of voting against Trident, and also, more damagingly, condemning the Labour Government's welfare reforms as 'economically inept, morally bankrupt and spiritually bereft.'[11] Scottish Labour's politics of posture and maximalism infects its parts, and has in this case hung an albatross around the party's neck, which will be quoted by its opponents time and again, in the long run-in to the Scottish Parliament elections by its opponents.

Scottish Labour's ethos has simultaneously faced two ways: it proclaims its radical heritage – the legacy of the Highland Clearances, Crofters' radicalism, the anti-temperance movement, Gladstonian home rule and Red Clydeside – while presiding over an insular, inward-looking view of the world. Its outlook is conservative and it is resistant to any attempt to change the Scottish status quo, or to threaten Labour's position as the political establishment. Scottish Labour's ethos has defined and shaped Labour's doctrine, allowing the party to talk with a radical voice, while acting locally and nationally as the upholder of a conservative social and political order. Gordon Brown, Chancellor of the Exchequer, and author of much of the modernising project, exemplifies this approach, combining a reverence for Labour's past with a Christian moralism.[12]

The welfare debate at the 1998 Scottish Labour conference gave an example of the extent of which Scottish Labour is imbued with, and pays homage to, its history. Anne McGuire, MP for Stirling and PPS to Donald Dewar, defended the Government in a barn-storming and well received speech which supported the Government's welfare reforms in relation to the labour movement's heroes. McGuire invoked Keir Hardie, John Maxton and John Wheatley for the cause of welfare reform, claiming that none of them 'campaigned for benefits, but for the dignity to work.'[13] The conference lapped it up, but still chose to ignore her and support the stinging indictment of welfare reform.

What such language reveals is the widespread conservatism and inward-looking nature of Scottish Labour: whether you are a moderniser or an old Labourite, homage to the history and pioneers of the movement is the framework within which all discussion has to take place. Scottish Labour has to be constantly treated with due respect and praise, and its special place in the history of Scotland and British Labour honoured.

THE CHARACTERISTICS OF SCOTTISH LABOUR

A range of Scottish Labour organisational and institutional practices from membership to local government and Parliamentary representation show the conservative nature of the party.

Membership

Scottish Labour membership is comparatively low compared to the

British average. The Scottish party has 8 per cent of party members while providing 13 per cent of the Parliamentary Labour Party (PLP). The Blairisation of Labour which saw UK membership rise from 264,000 to 405,000, saw Scottish Labour gain, proportionately, the same increase, rising from 19,321 to 30,371.[14] The average size of a Scottish Labour constituency party is currently 422 members in contrast to a British average of 632; Scottish constituencies are 33 per cent smaller than the British average. Membership remains relatively low in the West of Scotland, with some Glasgow constituency memberships restricted to a local network of extended family and friends.[15]

Of its current 56 seats, Scottish Labour has held 40 continuously, throughout the entire Thatcher-Major years, and these have become, along with other similar seats across Britain, part of the Heartlands Project. The aim of this is to bring the drive and professionalism of Operation Victory to safe Labour seats, to address low voter turnout and party inactivity. It wishes to tackle 'the big city constituency where a small group of activists is long accustomed to running the local authority and has a vested interest in making newcomers unwelcome. The Heartlands Project is directly relevant to the drive against corruption and cliqueism in Labour town halls.'[16] Such an approach is long overdue in Scottish Labour's one-party local states.

Labour local government

Scottish Labour controls 20 out of the 32 local authorities; this includes most of the nation's population and all four major cities.[17] During 18 years of Conservative rule, Scottish Labour strengthened its hold on local government to near monopoly status, and this acquired a greater significance for Labour as Tory rule continued, since it gave it some semblance of power.

Local government has also fulfilled a different role in Scotland from that in the rest of the UK under the Conservatives. Strathclyde Region was the largest local authority in the EU until its abolition in 1996, and acted as a surrogate Scottish Parliament – undermining Westminster by a variety of devices. Strathclyde had the audacity to by-pass Westminster and deal directly with Europe, and held a referendum on water privatisation producing, on a 72 per cent turnout, 97 per cent opposition to selling off water.

It is perhaps no coincidence that Scottish Labour hit a pile of scandals in the West of Scotland after Strathclyde Region was abolished, in the same way that the abolition of the Greater London Council (GLC) produced the scare of 'loony left' corruption and mismanagement stories in 1986-87 about Labour London boroughs. Strathclyde and the GLC were large scale authorities with political and financial clout, and their respective abolition increased the degree of scrutiny of local authorities left behind. They were also strategic authorities able to engage with civil society by producing ambitious social and cultural strategies, and, without the municipal responsibility for housing, free to develop new ideas of community participation. It was no accident that the abolition of Strathclyde Region coincided with the end of Glasgow's recent cultural renaissance.

Scottish Labour representation

The calibre of Scottish Labour MPs beyond the Government front-bench is varied to say the least. Labour currently has 56 MPs and throughout the lean years of opposition its star names – Gordon Brown, Robin Cook, Donald Dewar and others – continued to attract plaudits. These senior politicians, with the exception of Dewar, did not contribute directly to the development of Scottish Labour in the opposition years, but had their eye on bigger things. They were also the exception in the party, with a vast chasm in quality between them and most Scottish Labour backbenchers who did not aspire to any rank at Westminster.

A large proportion of Scottish Labour MPs, and most of those from the West of Scotland, have previously been councillors. This is most obviously the case in Glasgow where 7 out of the 10 Labour MPs are ex-councillors and have followed an established pattern – they are male, have a manual occupation or working class background, a local government record and, on becoming an MP, remain in obscurity and inactivity. The public profile of most of Glasgow's post-war Labour MPs has been low to non-existent, while only two of them have ever served in the Cabinet or been elected to the Shadow Cabinet: Bruce Millan and Donald Dewar.[18]

Scottish Labour elected just three women MPs in 1992, the same number as in 1945. This dramatically increased at the 1997 election to nine women out of 56 Labour MPs, due to women-only shortlists imposed by the British party.

THE RED FLAG AND THE SALTIRE: SCOTTISH LABOUR AND NATIONALISM

Scottish Labour and nationalism have always had an historically uneasy relationship.[19] In its early years, the party was a champion of home rule, inheriting this from the Gladstonian Liberal Party as one of the defining characteristics of Scottish radicalism; but this support sat uneasily alongside the British context of support for state planning and centralisation. From 1922, when Labour became first the official opposition party and then the party of government, Scottish Labour still formally supported devolution, but became more and more lukewarm, and ultimately sceptical, about it.

Under the Churchill wartime coalition and the Attlee government, the Scottish party become steadily more anti-devolution, until in 1958 it officially adopted an anti-devolution stand which remained policy throughout the 1964-70 Labour government and the period of the first wave of the SNP. Scottish Labour's evidence to the Kilbrandon Commission on the Constitution opposed devolution.[20] It only changed back to a pro-devolution policy in 1974 under the threat of the second wave of the SNP, and pressure from Harold Wilson.

Yet this is not the way the party chooses to present and understand its history, either internally or to the outside world. Scottish Labour has always seen itself as the unflinching advocate of home rule, with an unbroken lineage from Keir Hardie to the present day. Tony Blair, for example, has said 'all Labour leaders to differing degrees supported devolution',[21] ignoring the Attlee-Gaitskell years of centralism. Labour home rule supporters opposing the referendum U-turn in the summer of 1996 presented their argument in the context of the ethos of Labour history: 'After a century of campaigning our movement is on the brink of delivering our promise to establish a Scottish Parliament, finish the unfinished business.'[22]

This reinterpretation and representation of Labour history is possible and plausible because of the position of home rule in Labour's culture. Home rule has from the outset of Scottish Labour been a defining part of the movement's ethos.[23] It has been a crucial factor in Scottish Labour's romanticising of its self and its past, and in preserving its uniqueness and specialness, connecting it to the movement's original heroes and pioneers. This has been the case irrespective of whether devolution was party policy or part of its formal doctrine. Thus, even when Labour adopted an anti-devolution policy as it did during the 1950s and 1960s, the ideal of home rule as an aspiration has always remained part of the movement.

The distinct influences of class and nation as agencies of change have influenced the Scottish party at different times, but, given the extent to which both are deeply embedded in the party's ethos, one has never completely achieved long lasting dominance over the other. For most of its existence, the party has had the luxury of seeing class and nation as mutually reinforcing: of Labour as the party of the working class in Scotland and also as the national party of Scotland and self-government. This balancing act has continued throughout Scottish Labour's history, and was given impetus by the period of Conservative rule from 1979-97. The conjuncture of new Labour and the establishment of a Scottish Parliament will put this process under severe scrutiny and tension.

Scottish Labour in the 1980s saw itself as increasingly autonomous and Scottish: a pivotal point here being the 1987 general election when the Conservatives were returned at a UK level but humiliated in Scotland – 'the Doomsday scenario.'[24] Labour had to respond to several different agendas here: one was a seemingly increasingly confident Scotland which wanted home rule and centre-left policies; another, that Scottish Labour kept winning elections while English Labour kept losing them; and, finally, England was written off as lost to Thatcherism and dominated by the South East.

Donald Dewar, then Shadow Secretary of State for Scotland, writing after the 1987 election, highlighted the problems in the scale of Scottish Labour's success, in words which, luckily, did not come back to haunt him:

> The political problem is very real. The Nationalists have been quick to accept the scale of Labour's Scottish victory and to lay down the challenge. Can Labour deliver? Can 50 MPs protect Scotland from Mrs. Thatcher? Can the Poll Tax be stopped? Can Labour set up the Assembly? If the answers are in the negative the Nationalists will be there to draw some very uncomfortable conclusions.[25]

This was an uncomfortable period for Scottish Labour and it got through it, in part, because of its twin supports of class and nation, which correspond with the defining discourses of Scottish public life. However, the cost to the party in surviving and prospering in this difficult period was a deliberate avoidance on Labour's part of asking tough questions about itself and Scotland, and instead opting for going with the grain of received wisdom and consensus, an approach that was to store up problems for later.

New Labour has in some ways shifted Scottish Labour back towards re-emphasising a new Unionist, British perspective: how else can remarks such as Tony Blair's 'sovereignty resides with me' comment during the 1997 election campaign be interpreted? However, many in Scottish Labour remain driven by the twin pillars of class and nation, and still see Labour as the party of the Scottish working class and the national party. They do not care to take lessons in political strategy from someone they consider a political chameleon, and as operating on the self-same agenda as Thatcherism.

Scottish Labour is defined by the twin pressures of British new Labour and old Scottish Labour, a position which is crowding out the potential for a creative Labour politics towards the Parliament. It has always been a mistake to see Scottish Labour as either entirely Unionist or Scottish nationalist at any point in its history; all through its history it has been a mixture of both, and any successful modernisation strategy must acknowledge this.

THE BRITISH ROAD TO DEVOLUTION

Scottish Labour in the 1980s developed an oppositional politics around devolution and the politics of nationalism. Its success was coupled with a sense of powerlessness, due to Labour's losing at a British level, and anger at the imposition of Thatcherism. The 1980s were a strangely reassuring one for Scottish Labour – because it was easy for it to define what it stood for by what it was against – the imposition of Thatcherism and its 'alien' politics. Unlike British Labour, the Scottish party did not go through any painful rethinking and redefining of itself.

The Kinnock leadership aided this process. Kinnock was opposed to, or at the very least sceptical, about Scottish devolution. A legendary example of his indifference came after his speech to the 1988 Scottish Labour Annual Conference, in which he did not mention devolution. Asked afterwards about this omission, Kinnock replied that he had not addressed several subjects in his speech such as 'environmental conditions in the Himalayas'.[26] He cared about it so little during his nine years as party leader that he virtually allowed the Scottish party an opt-out from the British party on this subject – granting it a large degree of autonomy and discretion on home rule – the end result of which was Labour's historic involvement in the Constitutional Convention.[27]

The Scottish opt-out from British Labour policy-making fuelled unrealistic Scottish expectations which built up future trouble. Blair's various conflicts with the Scottish party have stemmed from this: a legacy from the compromises of the Kinnock years. New Labour set out soon after Blair's election on a review of all policy commitments. With devolution this focused on how it could be progressed at a British level: an area which had been left unexamined by the mixture of detailed Scottish work and the romantic notions of the Convention.[28] This process resulted in the announcement of the two-question referendum in June 1996 – a policy change which broke many delusions in Scottish Labour about the degree of autonomy Scottish Labour had over policy-making in relation to a Scottish Parliament.[29]

SCOTLAND UNITED? THE 1997 SCOTTISH GENERAL ELECTION

The 1997 general election campaign exposed painfully and in detail the tensions between Blair's Unionist strategy and the Scottish Labour approach of popular sovereignty which sprang from Labour MPs signing 'A Claim of Right for Scotland'.

At the launch of the Scottish Labour manifesto, Tony Blair (asked if once a Scottish Parliament was established his Sedgefield constituents might not find the realities of the West Lothian Question unfair) said, 'I don't believe so because I will say to them we have devolved these matters to the Scottish Parliament but, as far as we are concerned, sovereignty resides with me as an English MP and that's the way it will stay.' Questioned about a Scottish Parliament's tax raising powers Blair replied, 'the Scottish Labour Party has no plans to raise income tax and, once the power is given, it's like any parish council, it's got the right to exercise it.'[30]

All of this touched deep Scottish Labour nerves about how Blair and new Labour were seen in Scotland. A party document, drawn from System Three focus-groups of uncommitted voters and leaked to the press in December 1996, showed the extent of this unease. The paper was unequivocal about the problem: 'Tony Blair is perceived to be English, and his identity or image is associated with that of a Southerner.' It went on: 'There has been serious damage to the trust that voters have in new Labour's promises with regard to Scotland.'[31]

The paper concluded: 'Tony's easy smile arouses suspicion in the dour Scots. At worst this tends to be described as 'smarmy'. The Blairs are perceived to be emulating the Clintons.'[32]

The System Three findings pinpointed four main concerns amongst voters about Blair and new Labour: little difference was seen between new Labour and the Tories; Blair was seen as middle class and shifting Labour rightward, with the loss of John Smith still felt; George Robertson was perceived as acting on London orders; and the disadvantaged were perceived as having lost Labour as a voice.[33]

This background, combined with Blair's remarks, created a fertile atmosphere of nervousness and concern in Scottish Labour during the election campaign. The party became even more uneasy and defensive on the national question. Brian Wilson raised the prospect of a 'glass ceiling'[34] to stop a devolved Parliament moving to independence: 'If you're talking about legislation which broke up the UK, then that is clearly a matter for the United Kingdom Parliament because whether it is right or wrong, it certainly affects the whole of the United Kingdom.'[35]

George Robertson, then Shadow Scottish Secretary, speaking at the STUC, continued in this vein: 'There is no way that the Scottish Parliament could, or should be able to turn itself into an independent state.'[36] On the same day a journalist asked Jack McConnell, then Scottish Labour General Secretary, about the chances of the SNP winning a Parliamentary majority. 'Why worry? Isn't the electoral system designed to prevent the SNP getting power?, asked the journalist. To which McConnell replied 'Correct', and was forced to issue an immediate clarification.[37]

Against this backdrop, Scottish Labour won a resounding victory, achieving 45.6 per cent of the vote – its highest since 1966 – and 56 out of 72 seats – an all-time record.[38] How can this be squared with the obvious tensions of the time? First, Scottish Labour was fighting an election where the choice of government was between Labour and Conservatives, and the latter were seen by a majority of Scots as English and extremist. Second, in terms of seats, the competitive four party system has given Labour a disproportionate bonus in the electoral system, which has become more and more pronounced.

However, deeper factors were at work. A crucial element is that political parties mean different things in different parts of a system and voters interpret the same messages in different ways. In this sense, there is no such thing as a homogeneous party which implements in an unaltered fashion the dictates of a centralist strategy. Scottish Labour is a prime example of this, with a large part of its vote in 1997 not made up of people voting for new Labour or Tony Blair, but responding to a very old Labour message. Both perspectives could be contained within the umbrella of the Scottish Labour coalition.

A second factor is that most of Scottish Labour's difficulties arose on the constitutional issue, but this was not the most salient issue at the election. Scottish voters had exactly the same priority as British voters, putting their top priorities as: health (46%) and education (31%), with a Scottish Parliament ranked eighth with 10%, down 2% from 1992.[39]Thus Scottish voters saw Labour's social agenda as the most salient issues in the campaign and this, combined with the continued low ranking of the constitutional question, offers some explanation for Scottish Labour's election victory.

SCOTLAND FORWARD?: THE 1997 DEVOLUTION REFERENDUM

Donald Dewar's appointment as Scottish Secretary was received with relief and optimism within Scottish Labour and beyond. Dewar's nine years as Shadow Scottish Secretary coincided with Kinnock's leadership, which had allowed him a fair degree of autonomy. He had navigated Labour through some very difficult circumstances, such as the 1987 'Doomsday scenario' and the uncharted water of Labour's involvement in the cross-party Scottish Constitutional Convention, to a positive outcome.

The government White Paper on devolution, *Scotland's Parliament*, was published on 24 July 1997 to near universal acclaim in Scotland.[40] It retained the central pillars of the 1995 Convention document *Scotland's Parliament, Scotland's Right:* a Scottish legislative Parliament, with tax raising powers and 129 seats, elected by proportional representation. It went beyond and improved on the Convention by taking the simpler, but more radical, option of listing the powers retained at Westminster, rather than delegated to Scotland – the Governance of Ireland Act 1920 option rather than the Scotland Act 1978.

The White Paper appeared at a time when many people in Scotland were unsure of the direction of the Labour government in relation to devolution. That it was such a progressive and coherent document is partly due to the strength of the Scottish home rule consensus. It was this consensus, with its faults and failings, which via the detailed work of the Scottish Constitutional Convention and its dominance of political discourse, was the driving force behind the White Paper. The Labour Party was part of that consensus, but it followed, rather than led it. As Marquand commented: 'Labour's plans were, in short, made for it as much as by it.'[41]

The extent to which the White Paper was rooted in the Convention shows the influence of the Scottish home rule consensus over the Scottish Labour Party; and, while it created the possibility of such a White Paper, it may store up problems in the future, preventing Labour from asking tough questions. Popular Scottish opinion had expected the worst because of British Labour's narrow vision on devolution. This was seen in the reservations of Westminster absolutists like Jack Straw, and Unionist traps like the 'glass ceiling' argument. The overcoming of these meant that the road was open to devise a broad, inclusive home rule campaign for the referendum involving the three main pro-devolution parties under the banner of the umbrella organisation, 'Scotland Forward'.

The ghosts of the 1979 referendum campaign, when there was no single devolution campaign because of Labour-SNP distrust, and where years of activity and ferment produced not a decisive victory, but indecision and a constitutional impasse, had for too long shaped Scottish political discourses.

Post-1979, the SNP, weary and suspicious, having supported an unenthusiastic Labour government's flawed devolution plans for five years and seen them come to nil, drew the lesson that it could not trust Westminster British plans. But, under Alex Salmond's leadership, the SNP had slowly moved away from this fundamentalist cul-de-sac, to the point where they were willing partners with Labour in the referendum, on the condition that the White Paper did not attempt to limit self-government by 'glass ceilings'.

Labour had in many ways moved far from 1979. One of the great problems of 1979 had been the failure of the home rule parties to work together, and this was by design not accident. Helen Liddell, then Scottish Labour General Secretary, ruled out such umbrella organisations when she sent out a memo which declared in the age-old voice of Labour chauvinism: 'First, the Labour Party is the only party in Scotland which believes in devolution ... Second, the achievement of an Assembly for Scotland will be ours and it would be wrong to allow our consistent opponents – including those who helped to destroy the last

Bill – to claim credit for this constitutional advance.'[42] This attitude seemed far removed from the Scottish Labour spirit of the 1997 referendum when it needed the SNP to win a decisive majority for change; but it returned soon after, as Scottish Labour tried to stamp its own seal of approval and legitimacy on the result.

The referendum campaign was lifeless and unengaging. Old home rule questions were fought out with little passion. The 'No' campaign was composed of the remains of the Scots Tories and Tam Dalyell, the ghost of 79, representing a very old, discredited, male and Protestant Scotland. In spite of, rather than because of, the campaign, Scottish voters turned out to support emphatically – 74 per cent to 26 per cent – a Parliament, and, by 64 per cent to 36 per cent, tax raising powers.[43]

The 1997 referendum victory raised as many questions as it answered. What was the nature of the 'Yes' vote? Why had Scotland so decisively voted for change? And in what ways had it changed so dramatically since 1979? At one level, the 'Yes, Yes' triumph was a vindication of the Scottish status quo of social democracy, anti-Thatcherism, and the continuation of the political settlement of stasis and inertia that characterises much of Scottish public life.

What the result did underline is the conservatism of the 'Yes, Yes' vote as the articulation of John Smith's 'settled will of the Scottish people' in all the multiple meanings of the phrase. The Scots had made up their minds many years ago about home rule, but were also voting for not disrupting a political and social order they knew and felt comfortable with. The articulation of this in the campaign was concerned with winning the widest coalition of support, and by necessity this meant avoiding tough and radical choices, thus further entrenching the already existing conservatism. The nature of a 'Yes, Yes' vote, and the question of what kind of future Scotland people were voting for, had to remain ambiguous to keep together such a varied popular front of home rule, which spanned from old and new Labour to SNP, Liberal Democrats and the far-left Scottish Socialist Alliance. Clarity and tough choices about Scotland's future would have produced numerous fissures and faultlines in a nervous and sensitive coalition that was a new experience for all the participants.

The 'Yes, Yes' campaign was able to invoke the *connection* between Scottish identity, pride, self-confidence and a growing desire for Scotland's government to come home to where it belonged and better economic prospects and public services. The governance-instrumental-ity dichotomy – 'the thistle in your kilt versus the pound in your pocket' – can be seen in governance issues driving the 'Yes' votes and economic issues the 'No' votes. The double 'Yes' votes represented a perception of a Parliament that would lead to better health and education services, by a majority of 81 per cent, and better government, by 75 per cent.[44]

In 1997, many of the fears of 1979 had become less powerful. Central Belt dominance and Labour rule from Edinburgh had been significant issues in 1979 in mobilising the 'No' vote, but this was no longer the case in 1997, with only 29 per cent seeing a Parliament as dominated by the Central Belt and 37 per cent by the Labour Party.[45] Many of the possible negatives, for example over-government and breaking up the Union, still existed, but they had lost their salience due to the experience of Tory rule. People wished to express disapproval and anger at the eighteen years of Tory minority rule, and make sure that such a situation never happened again. The 'No, No' side on the other hand was seen by most people as synonymous with the Tories and Thatcherism, and with such major disadvantages it was never going to be able to mount a convincing campaign.

The referendum result ended one part of Scottish political history, the campaign for a Scottish Parliament and the period of constitutional stalemate between 1979-97, and opened up a new one, where the vision and policy of different future Scotlands would be the main issue.

THE WEST OF SCOTLAND LABOUR QUESTION

A much more potent political issue than the arcane West Lothian question is the West of Scotland Labour question, which, unlike Tam Dalyell's infamous dilemma, can be answered and addressed: namely, the shameful record and quality of many of Labour's representatives in its one-party fiefdoms in the West of Scotland.

Central to the West of Scotland Labour question are the characteristics of the West of Scotland Labour councillor – drawn narrowly from certain sections of Scottish society.[46] The local authority in which such councillors operate is overwhelmingly Labour in seats, if not votes, with the opposition parties barely represented. Labour's rule has often lasted uninterrupted for thirty years or more, allowing the patronage of party and local state to interweave to an incestuous extent.

Decisions taken at committee meetings often have no opposition representation, are held in secret, and have actually been taken in some unaccountable party cabal.

The West of Scotland Labour fiefdoms are a kind of semi-quangocracy with minimal public accountability, and are as deformed and corrupt as the Tory quangos of the last eighteen years. Monklands District Council allegations about a 'Catholic mafia' running the Labour council, with jobs for the boys and discrimination in council spending in favour of Catholic Coatbridge and against Protestant Airdrie, haunted Labour for several years, prompting a party enquiry and action;[47] it did not help the party that the council covered the seats of John Smith, the then Labour leader, and Tom Clarke, at the time Shadow Scottish Secretary.[48]

The Glasgow City Council junkets for votes scandal exploded when Bob Gould, council leader, made public allegations to the press at a time when the local council proposed a 22 per cent council tax rise, the highest in Scotland, while imposing massive cuts in services. Labour quickly announced an internal party inquiry to attempt to diffuse the issue before the general election, and this reported in September 1997. As a result of the report, nine Labour councillors were suspended, including Gould and the Lord Provost Pat Lally, for actions ranging from factionalism and corruption to inappropriate behaviour including bullying, intimidation and violence.[49] Lally and some of the others then took the party to court, and six months later the party abandoned its plans to expel him and the other Glasgow Labour councillors in what can only be described as a shambles which aided Labour's opponents.[50]

The West of Scotland Labour question involves not only local councillors, but every level of the party from the grass roots to national representatives. Mohammed Sarwar, MP for Glasgow Govan, who has known political controversy from the outset of his national political career, defeated Mike Watson, MP for Glasgow Central, in a two ballot contest.[51] Sarwar was elected on 1 May 1997 with a much reduced majority; eighteen days later his political ambitions were all but over when the *News of the World* ran a front page story about Sarwar bribing an election opponent. Other allegations arose about electoral registration inaccuracies and election expense irregularities, and Sarwar was suspended from the Parliamentary Party for 'action grossly detrimental to the party' and 'unbecoming and totally inappropriate for a Labour MP.'[52] Seven months after the election, Sarwar was charged as a result of a police investigation, and his future as a Labour MP looked set to draw to a close.[53]

Gordon McMaster's suicide, three months after the general election, drew public attention to the cesspit of Renfrew politics. McMaster, MP for Paisley South, and Irene Adams, MP for Paisley North, had been elected in simultaneous 1990 by-elections. They had created local enemies by their tireless anti-drug campaigning, while Tommy Graham, MP for the neighbouring Renfrewshire West, had begun recruiting party members in Adams's seat because of uncertainty caused by boundary redistribution.[54] It has been alleged that Graham engaged in a campaign of rumour and discrediting of McMaster including malicious gossip about his sexuality;[55] Graham was suspended by the party. McMaster's suicide and Graham's suspension also led to the focusing of media attention on Renfrew Council and the degree of intimidation and corruption within it, from which neither Labour or the SNP emerged with any credit. It prompted yet another party investigation and suspension of local councillors.

Labour rightly made political capital out of Tory sleaze in the run-up to the 1997 election; yet after 1 May at one point it found itself simultaneously conducting four separate party inquiries into malpractice of some kind or another, all within a few miles in the West of Scotland. Labour has to address this problem by more than reactive politics and firefighting. The basic roots of party misconduct are not being addressed nor new ways of working suggested.

Glasgow City Council showed some possible hope of party renewal with the election of Frank McAveety as council leader,[56] and he has set a high priority on cleaning up local politics and engaging in a dialogue with opposition parties. A commission on standards for local councillors has been established, which has set a precedent by its composition of five Labour and four opposition councillors, with three outside observers.[57] Other possibilities include considering the way local government relates to local communities by looking at such processes as citizens juries, provost elections and local referenda.

The endemic nature of corruption in West of Scotland Labour results from more deep-seated factors than simply individual weaknesses or duplicity. The extent of corruption and malpractice and, more widely, poor services and lack of responsiveness to public needs is the direct result of Scottish Labour's uncontested control of the West of Scotland – where it controls 31 out of 32 MPs and 11 out of 12 local authorities – the exception in both cases being the geographically peripheral Argyll and Bute.

As Labour's dominance of local government grew throughout the

1980s, two factors occurred which have aided the current crisis. First, Scottish Labour had no widespread infusion of new left 'local socialism' beyond brief experiments in Edinburgh and Stirling, so the traditional Labour centre-right model of the local council has remained relatively intact. Second, for a variety of reasons, most notably Conservative restrictions on local government powers, many imaginative Labour councillors wanting to make a difference to their local communities withdrew from local politics in the 1980s, leaving an even less representative and unskilled group of Labour representatives to manage councils under increasingly difficult conditions.

Scottish Labour has made some attempt to address the West of Scotland problem, through its selection procedures at a local and parliamentary level. Selection processes have been established for approving prospective Scottish Labour Parliament candidates (with a British Labour input which aroused fears of a Blairite rout of old Labour). These processes include a 'person specification' which sets out a list of abilities would-be MPs should have: creative skills, strategic thinking and action, advocacy skills, interpersonal skills, leadership and teamwork, communication skills and campaigning skills.[58] Such a formal process and criterion has advantages from an equal opportunities perspective, opening up the party to new talent and discriminating against the old boys networks.

The Scottish party needs to facilitate a new style of politics from the grass roots up, encouraging new members into the party and aiding them to be active and involved. Local constituency parties need to be revitalised and to become centres of discussion, debate, campaigns, political education, fundraising and socialising, and from this Labour needs to develop quality thresholds for candidate selection which open up Labour representation to a more diverse range of opinions and people, rather than relying on the 'old labour movement' networks which have been tried in Scotland and have failed.

THE CHALLENGE OF NEW LABOUR

Scottish Labour's dominant view of itself during eighteen years of Conservative rule was of a party rooted in local communities and Scottish society and winning elections because of this. Its view of new Labour is shaped by this experience: why try to change Scottish Labour's record of electoral success which shows the appeal of traditional socialism in Scotland. John McAllion, Labour MP for Dundee East, expressed this when he said: 'Old Labour was never unelectable in Scotland. Even at the high tide of Thatcherism in 1983, Michael Foot's Labour won a majority of seats in Scotland. In 1987, Scottish Labour recorded its best ever result.'[59]

The new Labour perspective, encouraged and reinforced by the recent spate of West of Scotland Labour scandals, sees Scottish Labour's politics as a culture of paternalism and traditionalism built on a monopoly of political power at a local and parliamentary level. It has increasingly reacted to this by adopting an interventionist policing strategy into the processes of Scottish Labour, imposing a degree of external control and discipline on the party. The problem with this is that these interventions are not advancing a positive politics of change, but a reactive politics of damage limitation. Scottish Labour is thus currently caught between the twin pillars of British new Labour and Scottish old Labour, between a centralising controlling view of politics and a crumbling closed order from which a genuine Scottish modernisation cannot find the room to grow.

The role of the Blairite Scottish Labour Forum, previously known as the network, associated with such newly elected Labour MPs as Jim Murphy, MP for Eastwood, and Rosemary McKenna, MP for Cumbernauld and Kilsyth, has been limited. Its greatest achievement so far was the sweeping away of an array of Labour left-wingers and home-rulers on the Scottish Labour executive at the March 1997 Annual Conference and their replacement by pro-Blairites.[60] This is an example of the Blairite limited agenda – of preventing the Scottish party causing problems – and thus far this group has contributed little towards a positive politics of remaking Scottish Labour.

Another alarming sign in terms of developing innovative policy and campaigning ideas has been the winding up of Scottish Labour Action, the dissident left group on the nationalist wing of the party. This group has been a constant thorn in the leadership's side for ten years, but it has also undertaken the constructive role of providing a forum for floating what were at the time unfashionable ideas – such as cross-party co-operation in the Convention and electoral reform for the Scottish Parliament – which were later taken up by the leadership.

British Labour's modernisation has affected all the major actors in Scottish politics. The Scottish political environment is characterised by a highly conservative four party system where all the parties operate within the same paradigm of the Scottish economic and social status quo. There are no major currents of the radical left or right with parties differentiating themselves in the area of constitutional reform and the Union. This conservative consensus has tended to see new Labour as English intruders similar to the supporters of Thatcherism, to be resisted at all costs.

New Labour's emergence has given an opportunity to the SNP to emphasise its identity as a social democratic party and the upholder of the Scottish status quo, and its most fervent defender against the advances of the proto-Thatcherite new Labour. This strategy places the SNP on firmly old Labour ground, advocating tax and spend policies and a substantial degree of redistribution, mass support for which would only be possible with the failure of the new Labour project on a scale comparable with previous Labour governments.

There are a number of problems in SNP thinking here. First, its approach, for a radical party of independence, is actually one of conservatism and caution and of upholding the internal Scottish political settlement. Second, it is naive to assume that the failure of the new Labour project upon which all its strategy is predicated will lead to a swing to an old Labour style SNP; it could just as easily lead to a post-nationalist politics or a new Unionism of the centre-right.

The establishment of a Scottish Parliament will challenge this political order which is already fraying and falling apart. However, whether the Parliament can actually succeed in defeating the old political consensus and open up opportunities to the new Scotland depends on what choices the people of Scotland take. One of Scottish Labour's core concerns is home rule, and yet the developments of the last few years have disorientated it in the extreme; while the Scottish Conservatives' fundamental Unionism has been proven electorally unpalatable. The politics of a Parliament will demand that the political parties begin differentiating themselves on economic and social terms and, hopefully, will spell the beginning of the end for the conservative consensus.

A SCOTTISH MODERNISATION: 'THE FREE ECONOMY AND THE SCOTTISH STATE'

A new vision of Scottish Labour has to break this stand-off between new Labour's limited agenda of Scottish politics based on damage limitation and old Scottish Labour's view of the Blairites as the equivalent of a Thatcherite Southern English alien force. It has also to develop a 'new politics' agenda which is about more than constitutional arrangements and structures of a Parliament, and begins to address ways in which that body can facilitate new ways of working and of changing society.

Any coherent modernisation has to begin by being based in an analysis of Scottish politics and society, and must be drawn up and advocated by Scottish party members responding to Scottish circumstances and imbued with a new vision of Scotland. It cannot be dictated by a Blair leadership from London, nor, equally, can it be imposed in a top-down manner by a Scottish leadership – as Michael Forsyth attempted with his 'new Unionist' rebranding of Scottish Conservatism.

A radical modernising strategy has to take on board two major problems. First, the campaign for Scottish self-government has looked almost exclusively at ways of achieving a Parliament to the detriment of what difference the Parliament can actually make. Second, the strength of the Scottish home rule consensus has hindered any detailed policy work because it has been automatically assumed that a Parliament will be an expression of this consensus.

Three social policy scenarios for the Parliament have been identified by Richard Parry: 'professionally based stasis' where the Scots professional classes use their influence to maintain their advantaged position; 'innovative social policy' with flexibility and client-led policies; and 'conflict-ridden social policy' based on differences between expectations of a Parliament and its actual policy agenda.[61] This has to be seen in the context of the Scottish left's defensiveness and blanket opposition to a Thatcherite agenda post-1979, while at the same time the English left has responded to the crisis of the left and traditional models by developing new notions of citizenship and civil society.[62]

The administration of the Scottish status quo, or disillusionment of the hopes of the Parliament, can only be challenged by thinking anew about the policy agenda of the Parliament and the environment it will be situated in. This requires acknowledging the changes that Thatcherism aided and encouraged post-1979, such as limited government, low taxation, increased labour market flexibility and wider personal choice, and working within this framework to develop policies on greater opportunities and for the attacking of social inequalities. The parameters of any Scottish Labour modernisation would combine a post-Thatcherite economics with a nationalist dimension or, to paraphrase Andrew Gamble, 'the free economy and the Scottish state.'

A Scottish Parliament cannot put the clock back to some mythical golden age before 1979, and has to operate within the terrain of what has been called, borrowing from Will Hutton's analysis of contemporary Britain, 'the three Scotlands': the settled, insecure and excluded Scotlands.[63] These social realities are similar to those found across the Western world, but there has been a tendency for the Scottish consensus to assume that Scotland is immune from such change, or could be made so by the power of active government. This rationale is unfortunately still the motivating force behind some of the Scottish left's support, within and outwith the Labour Party, for a Scottish Parliament.

The modernisation of the Scottish Labour Party will require a fundamental shift in the balance of forces within it given the strength of old Labour.[64] This can be seen in the way in which the Blair/Brown divide has developed at the heart of new Labour.

The differences between Tony Blair and Gordon Brown are not on paper very much, being more about style and presentation than substance and policy. However, this is to read the situation superficially, because the issues of style and substance, where they differ, reflect differing types of political languages and philosophies of the world. An example of this was provided by the 1998 Scottish Labour conference in Perth – its first gathering since the general election triumph. Blair, in marked contrast to the style of the Wilson-Callaghan years, spoke and acted in his usual public manner: the need for modernisation of party and nation, 'tough choices' and 'a third way'. Gordon Brown, on the other hand, consistently followed the time-honoured Labour leadership route of talking radically to internal party audiences – reassuring them that the flame of 'Red Clydeside' still burns brightly – and then reassuring City and business audiences that new Labour is the genuine article which has completely shed its socialist beliefs.

At the conference the extent to which Scottish Labour was sceptical about the Blair approach, and felt comfortable and familiar with the Brown style was clear. It was very telling that the biggest applause in Blair's speech was directed at his mention of Mick McGahey, the former Scottish miners' leader and Communist, who Blair invoked in support of his 'third way'. Never mind the details, the audience loved the sentimentality and confirmation of its own world view in this. Gordon Brown gave them this in abundance. In a speech where he never mentioned 'New Labour' once, he gave his audience a sense of the moral mission and crusade he thought should underpin every action of the Labour government, and the conference judged him one of their own.

Another obstacle to Scottish Labour modernisation is the party's constantly changing attitude towards the SNP. To the British and Scottish leaderships, Labour got too close to the SNP during the 'Yes, Yes' referendum campaign, and by the time of the 1998 Scottish Labour conference, the time had come to reclaim that historic victory as Labour's alone and open up 'clear tartan water' between practical reformist Labour and the separatist Nationalists.

The intemperate language of the Labour leadership used to open up this distance was no accident; it was a knee-jerk response in place of a political strategy. George Robertson, Defence Secretary, labelled the SNP 'snake oil peddlers', while Donald Dewar called them 'wreckers' and 'dishonest'.[65] This masks the massive similarities between Labour and the SNP and, in particular, the over-lap in agendas and profiles of Labour and SNP voters. A large number of Labour voters list the SNP as their second preference, while the polls for a Scottish Parliament show that 10 per cent of Labour's vote for Westminster switches to the SNP for Scottish elections. (Robin Cook, Foreign Secretary, was surprisingly off-message after the conference – he acknowledged the possibilities of a 'consensus for policy changes' and the degree of 'common social objectives' between Labour and SNP.[66]) One month later, shocked by the SNP drawing level with Labour in polls on voting intentions to the Scottish Parliament, Labour's confrontational approach was hurriedly ditched with a party strategist admitting they had 'blundered last month by launching bad-tempered attacks on the SNP'. One Labour source promised: 'From now on, it's positive, positive, positive.'[67]

The pseudo-anger displayed by the Scottish Labour leadership towards the SNP misreads Scottish politics and Labour's needs. It is because Labour and SNP agendas and voters are so similar that the Labour leadership feels the need to use such language to differentiate itself from the SNP. Instead of this tribalist language of hatred, Labour needs to develop a positive and realisable agenda for the Parliament, which focuses on what it can deliver in contrast to the unrealisable wishlist of the SNP. A coherent modernisation strategy has to break with old Labour notions of talking in one manner and acting in another, and has to work within the economic realities and nationalist dimension of Scottish politics.

The future of Scotland beyond Blair and Brown

Scottish politics is currently awaiting the biggest series of changes and challenges it has ever witnessed in contemporary times: the establishment of a Scottish Parliament. This will create shockwaves across Scottish society and politics which could develop in multiple different directions. The Scottish home rule consensus has got us through some difficult times and aided us through the terrible experience of Thatcherism, but it is not equipped for the new politics of the new Scotland.

The current dominant perspective of Scottish politics and the home rule consensus is defined by two characteristics: a social democratic outlook and a nationalist dimension. This means that within this framework four possible paradigms are possible:

a social democratic Britishness: this is a very old Labour strategy from the halcyon days of Attlee and Gaitskell and not a runner today

a post-social democratic Britishness: the Blair strategy for the UK but would cause problems in Scotland on the national question

a social democratic Scottish nationalism: this is the approach of old Labour and the SNP: the politics of the Scottish status quo

a post-social democratic Scottish nationalism: this is the potential ground for a Scottish Labour strategy of modernisation and renewal.

What are the obstacles to this fourth road emerging? Firstly, the Scottish political consensus has, both in terms of public opinion and institutional support, embedded a social democratic consensus across most of Scottish public life and civil society. Secondly, the home rule expression of this political consensus perceives a Parliament as maintaining and reinforcing this tradition, while a significant section of the Scottish left support a Parliament which returns politics to an agenda where Thatcherism never existed and issues like globalisation do not need to be dealt with.

Thirdly, in a four party system, in which all the political parties operate in this social democratic framework, change is difficult. With old Labour and the SNP the leaders of this social democratic nationalism, and the Blair project perceived by many as English and a threat to the existing order of things, it is difficult to see the political space and opportunities that could open up.

Scottish Labour has little room for manouvre. There is a possibility that it is so wedded to an old model of political development that it cannot change. Past patterns do not augur well here: previous strategies of modernisation, such as that of the Bennite period of 1979-81, or the 'local socialism' new left of the mid-1980s, had little impact on Scottish Labour. Whereas British Labour, post-1979, first veered to the left, and then, post-1983, shifted slowly and gradually back to the centre ground, throughout this period Scottish Labour has stood still. This has provided Scottish Labour with strengths, such as a sense of certainty about its place and identity; but it also has weaknesses, in that the party has not had to undertake the cathartic journey of rethinking and reappraising itself which the English party has been through.

As far as linking a modernising agenda to a national politics is concerned, although the current paradigm of the nationalist question is a conservative social democratic one, this does not prohibit the articulation and influence of other expressions of nationalist discourse. There is the potential in Scotland for a new kind of post-social democratic nationalist politics which embraces pluralism and diversity.

The future of Scottish progressive politics lies in developing this post-social democratic way, between the old Unionism and nationalism with their static, fixed identities of nation, identity and class. This has be centred in an acknowledgement of the political failure of the old models, from Labour councils to fundamentalist nationalism in one nation, and an acknowledgement of the economic and social realities and uncertainties of the new Scotland.

This requires the gradual development of a new political agenda which, via electoral reform and gender equality, could open up the possibilities of weakening the old models and supplanting them with new, diverse practice. Such processes have been an intrinsic part of the Labour-Liberal Democrat Convention package and part of the home rule consensus, but they also offer opportunities to open up and shift Scottish politics. A new kind of politics is required, a politics which allows Scotland to rid itself of its inbuilt and gigantic Labour majorities, base its local government on PR and break up of its Labour city states. The Scottish Labour Party would be greatly strengthened by a vision of a new kind of devolution, not of the old labourist kind, but one based on new forms of democracy and participation, which would make Scotland an exciting and unpredictable place.

A new politics also needs a sense of Scottish identity that is pluralist and diverse. Scottish national identity played a key part in Scottish opposition to Thatcherism and in the 1997 referendum, but its current conservative expression is ill-equipped to make the transition from an oppositionalist identity to one that aims shape and define a new social order. Ideas about Scottish national identity need to move into the modern world, instead of reflecting an – often essentialist – backward-looking romanticisation of heroes and villains. Scottish identity needs a new song, new heroes and a new set of myths.

To the English left, the Scottish home rule project as we stand at the end of the century is a radical, liberating and victorious cause. This is a moment for new avenues and routes at a Scottish and UK level. However, a Scottish perspective on these same changes will offer an entirely different view: Scotland's home rule consensus is in fact 'the settled will', and 'unfinished business' – an expression of conservatism and caution more than radicalism, and linked to the political expression of a very non-radical Scottish identity. In this version, Scottish home rule could change very little in Scotland and the UK, bar introducing another layer of politicians in Scotland with large salaries and egos.

In the early years of the Scottish parliament, particularly under a Labour government in London with much of its political capital invested in making devolution work, there will be a strong pressure on both British and Scottish Labour to make this happen. They will need to prove that the new structures can work effectively and harmoniously with other bodies in Scotland and the UK, and bring about change in Scottish society. The onus will be on minimalising conflict and achieving agreement by compromise, and this will maintain the Scottish political consensus. Realistically this means that the parliament's early years will be a time of conservatism and caution, and of small, achievable, incremental change, rather than big bangs.

In the short term, a Scottish parliament may change very little, and could reinforce a Scottish political settlement long past its sell-by date. However, in the medium and long-term, a Scottish parliament elected by PR holds out many possibilities of exploration and discovery – of a reborn Unionism, a post-nationalist sense of Scottishness, and, on new Labour's terrain, a post-social democracy of Scottish sensibilities.

A Scottish parliament elected under PR with no automatic Labour majority will at some point elect an anti-Labour governing majority. This will have several profound consequences: first, it will lead to the dismantling of the already crumbling old Labour order in Scotland, and second, it will force the issue of a new Scottish Labour politics onto the agenda, a politics made not in Blair or Brown's image, but by the Scottish people.

Either way, change is coming for Scotland and Scottish Labour: the challenge for the Scottish party over the next few years is to decide whether it wants to drive this process of change, or be driven by others.

NOTES:

1. Examples of English misrepresentation and misunderstanding of Scottish politics and the nature of the United KIngdom are of particular significance here. A recent example was *The Guardian*'s coverage of the publication of the Scotland Bill with a chart showing which powers would be devolved to a Scottish Parliament and which retained by the English Parliament – when they clearly meant the British Parliament. Such a view shows a complete ignorance of the basis of the Union and the United Kingdom. *The Guardian*, 19 December 1997.
2. Lindsay Paterson, *The Autonomy of Modern Scotland*, Edinburgh University Press, Edinburgh 1994, pp 9, 180-82.
3. James G. Kellas, *The Scottish Political System*, Cambridge University Press, Cambridge (4th edn.) 1989, pp 4, 17.
4. Arthur Midwinter, Michael Keating and James Mitchell, *Politics and Public Policy in Scotland*, Macmillan, London 1991, p. 199.
5. Richard Rose, *Understanding the United Kingdom*, Longman, London 1982; Michael Keating and Arthur Midwinter, *The Government of Scotland*, Mainstream, Edinburgh 1983.
6. Alice Brown, David McCrone and Lindsay Paterson, *Politics and Society in Modern Scotland*, Macmillan, London 1996, p 117.
7. It is no accident that the crisis of British social democracy coincided with the rise of contemporary Scottish nationalism as measured by the popularity of the SNP. Labour's grandiose National Plan was destroyed on the altar of Wilson's delayed devaluation in autumn 1967: the SNP won the previously safe Labour seat of Hamilton – turning a 16,576 Labour majority into a 1,799 SNP majority – on 2 November 1967, in a climate where the Labour government's deflationary politics were being widely attacked within the Labour Party and elsewhere and the option of devaluation was a matter of public debate.
8. Gerry Hassan, 'New Labour and the Politics of New Scotland', in Mark Perryman (ed), *The Blair Agenda*, Lawrence and Wishart, London 1996, pp171-173.
9. H. M. Drucker, *Doctrine and Ethos in the Labour Party*, Allen and Unwin, London 1979, p8.
10. *Ibid*, pp9, 31.
11. *Scotland on Sunday*, 8 March 1998.

12. Gordon Brown's first speech to a Labour Conference as Chancellor of the Exchequer is a good example of his approach. He places the modernising project within the context of the Labour movement's heroes: 'It was because a century ago Keir Hardie looked at the world as it was and saw what a new world could be that he broke with the old order, set politics a new modern path and founded the Labour Party. It was because fifty years ago Aneurin Bevan looked at the old world of disease and deprivation, and saw what a new world could be, that he broke with the private health care of the past and established a National Health Service that still serves us today. And so now for our time, let the message go out. We govern and we seek to serve as a new political gener-ation.' This approach claims Keir Hardie and Nye Bevan as pioneers of new Labour. Quoted in Paul Routledge, *Gordon Brown: The Biography*, Simon and Schuster, London 1998, p316.

13. 1998 Scottish Labour conference, Perth, author's own notes.

14. Labour Party and Scottish Labour Party information.

15. One of the most interesting measurements of Labour Party membership is its ratio to the Labour vote. This ratio is 2.3 members to voters in Scotland, compared to 3.0 across the UK, according to 1997 Labour Party membership figures.

16. John Williams, 'Keeping the Heartlands Happy', *New Statesman*, 6 March 1998.

17. Scottish Labour's dominance of local government – 20 out of 32 Scottish local authorities (62.5% of all councils) – hides different distortions at a local and parliamentary level. The four main parties' votes and seats at the 1995 local elections were:

	% Vote	% Seats	Seats/Votes Diff. 1995	Seats/Votes Diff. 1997
Labour	43.8	53.0	+ 9.2	+32.2
SNP	26.2	15.6	-10.6	-13.8
Con.	11.3	7.1	- 4.2	-17.5
Lib Dem	9.7	10.4	+ 0.7	+ 0.9
Others	9.0	13.9	+ 4.9	- 1.2
Sum of Moduli			29.6	65.6
Deviation from Proport-ionality			14.8	32.8

Source: local government results from David Denver and Hugh Bochel, 'Catastrophe for the Conservatives: The Council Elections of 1995', *Scottish Affairs*, No. 13, Winter 1995, pp34, 36.

The degree of proportionality of local government was 14.8% in 1995, the lowest it had been for twenty years, while the 32.8% figure for the 1997 general election was the highest ever recorded. The reasons for these differences include: Labour's winning bonus in seats being 9.2% in local elections, but 32.2% in national elections; the SNP and Conservatives doing better in local elections; and the presence of a sizeable bloc of Independents at local level.

18. Michael Keating, Roger Levy, Jack Geekie and Jack Brand, *Labour Elites in Glasgow*, Strathclyde Papers on Government and Politics No. 61, University of Strathclyde 1989.

19. For the best accounts of the history of Scottish Labour and nationalism, and the campaign for Scottish devolution, see Michael Keating and David Bleiman, *Labour and Scottish Nationalism*, Macmillan, London 1979; Robert McLean, 'Scottish Labour and Home Rule: Part One: Mid-Lanark to Majority Government: 1888-1945', *Scottish Labour Action* n.d. 1990; and 'Part Two: Unionist Complacency to Crisis Management: 1945-1988' *Scottish Labour Action* n.d. 1991.

20. Royal Commission on the Constitution, *Minutes of Evidence: Volume Four: Scotland*, HMSO 1971, p23.

21. Tony Blair interview, BBC2, 21 November 1996.

22. Margaret Curran, Bill Spiers, Ian Smart and Bob Thomson, 'The Case for a Single Question', unpublished paper, 23 August 1996, p10.

23. Keating and Bleiman defined home rule as part of 'the radical heritage' of Scottish Labour which it inherited from the Liberals, along with disestablishment, temperance and land reform. Scottish Labour began to shift in its emphasis on home rule in the 1920s: 'Home rule was no longer as important and 'live' a demand as in the 1880s, and remained part of the policy of Labour in Scotland mainly because of the radical heritage, and the fact that Labour tended to follow Liberal party policy in the issue. Keating and Bleiman, *op. cit.*, pp27-29, 58.

24. The Doomsday Scenario was a term originally devised prior to the 1987 election by the pro-home rule magazine *Radical Scotland*, to describe the election of a Conservative government on English votes while Labour won in Scotland.

25. Donald Dewar, 'Scotland: the Way Forward', in Jeremy Beecham et al, *Labour's Next Moves Forward*, Fabian Society, London 1987, p15.

26. Susan Deacon, 'Adopting Conventional Wisdom: Labour's Response to the National Question', in Alice Brown and Richard Parry (eds), *The Scottish Government Yearbook 1990*, Unit for the Study of Government in Scotland, Edinburgh 1990, p67.

27. For a summary of the Convention's work see Peter Lynch, 'The Scottish

Constitutional Convention 1992-95', *Scottish Affairs*, No. 15, Spring 1996, pp1-16.

28. Peter Jones, 'Labour's Referendum Plan: Sell-out or Act of Faith'?, *Scottish Affairs*, No. 18,Winter 1997, pp1-18; Paul Anderson and Nyta Mann, *Safety First: The Making of New Labour*, Granta Books, London 1997, pp271-289. Anderson and Mann's text is a rare example of an analysis of British Labour which deals in a detailed and informed way about the politics of Scottish Labour. Most other accounts of British Labour are accounts of Westminster Labour.

29. Labour's change of policy on the referendum involved three different policies in just over two months between June-September 1996: first, the no referendum status quo of 17 years, then Blair's two question referendum, followed by Mohammed Sarwar's three vote referendum, requiring another vote on tax-raising powers before a Parliament could enact these powers – which briefly became party policy after a Scottish Labour executive vote – and finally, six days later, the return to the two vote question, a unilateral decision by Tony Blair.

30. *The Scotsman*, 5 April 1997.

31. *The Herald*, 5 December 1996.

32. 'The Views of Scottish Floating Voters', *System Three*, October 1996, p8.

33. *Ibid.*

34. The 'glass ceiling' argument was put forward by Scottish Labour spokespeople during the election, and afterwards by Jack Straw and Peter Mandelson. It states that a Scottish Parliament with a majority for independence cannot achieve Scottish independence because it is a subordinate body to the sovereign Westminster Parliament.

35. *Sunday Times*, 27 April 1997.

36. *The Scotsman*, 23 April 1997.

37. *Ibid.*

38. On the Scottish general election see David Denver, 'The 1997 General Election in Scotland: An Analysis', *Scottish Affairs*, No. 20, Summer 1997, pp17-33; Alice Brown, 'Scotland: Paving the Way for Devolution?', *Parliamentary Affairs*, Vol. 50 No. 4, pp658-71; Iain McLean, 'The Semi-Detached Election: Scotland', in Anthony King et al, *New Labour Triumphs: Britain at the Polls*, Chatham House, London 1997, pp145-175; James Mitchell, 'The Battle for Britain?: Constitutional Reform and the Election', in Andrew Geddes and Jonathan Tonge (eds), *Labour's Landslide: The British General Election 1997*, Manchester University Press, Manchester 1997, pp134-145.

39. *The Scotsman*, 17 March 1997.

40. Gerry Hassan, 'Towards A New Territorial Settlement: Labour's

Devolution Plans for Scotland', *Renewal*, Vol. 5 Nos. 3 & 4, 1997, pp 43-51.

41. David Marquand, 'Half-way to Citizenship: The Labour Party and Constitutional Reform', in Martin J. Smith and Joanna Spear (eds), *The Changing Labour Party*, Routledge, London 1992, p53.

42. Allan Macartney, 'The Protagonists', in John Bochel, David Denver and Allan Macartney (eds), *The Referendum Experience: Scotland 1979*, Aberdeen University Press, Aberdeen 1981, p17. Helen Liddell's memo was dated January 27 1978 and endorsed at the Scottish Labour Annual Conference in March 1978. For such an anti-Scottish nationalist and deeply sectarian document it includes the following revisionism of Scottish Labour history: 'The history of Labour's fight for devolution, both for Scotland and for people in general, precedes by a century the rise of the separatists.'

43. *The Scotsman*, 13 September 1997.

44. *Political Context Report on Scottish Devolution for Partnership for a Parliament*, December 1996, pp. 5-6.

45. *Ibid.*

46. See 'Portrait: The West of Scotland Councillor: The Durable Dinosaur', *The Scotsman*, August 23 1997.

47. *The Guardian*, 25 January 1993.

48. The extent of the Monklands factor in terms of damage to Labour can be measured by the parliamentary by-election caused by the death of John Smith, MP for Monklands East. Given that at the time, June 1994, Labour was riding high in the polls after Smith's death, Monklands East saw Labour's majority slashed from 15,712 to 1,640 in a campaign dominated by the conduct of the council and religious issues. See Graham Walker, *Intimate Strangers: Political and Cultural Interaction Between Scotland and Ulster in Modern Times*, John Donald, Edinburgh 1995, pp. 180-84.

49. *The Scotsman*, 23 September 1997; Euan McColm, Jason Allardyce and Graeme Stewart, 'A city's shamed leaders vow: we'll not go quietly', *The Scotsman*, 24 September 1997.

50. *The Scotsman*, 25 March 1998; 26 March 1998.

51. *The Herald*, 15 December 1995; 25 June 1996.

52. *The Scotsman*, 17 June 1997.

53. *The Scotsman*, 18 December 1997.

54. Ken Symon, Julie Smyth and Joanne Robertson, 'Suicide by Poison', *Sunday Times*, 3 August 1997; Jason Allardyce, 'Paisley Pattern Politics', *The Scotsman*, 9 August 1997; Ken Symon, Tim Kelsey and Joanne Robertson, 'Rotten Burgh', *Sunday Times*, 10 August 1997.

55. Brian Deer, 'The Public Life and Death of a Political Man', *New Statesman*, 14 November 1997.

56. *Scottish Labour Party Specification for Scottish Parliament Member*, Scottish Labour Party 1998.

57. The *Scotsman*, 26 March 1998.

58. *The Herald*, 11 October 1997.

59. John McAllion, 'Blair's modernisers want a party of the people. But up here, the people want a party of the Left', *The Observer*, 22 March 1998.

60. *The Herald*, 8 March 1997.

61. Richard Parry, 'The Scottish Parliament and Social Policy', *Scottish Affairs* No. 20, Summer 1997, pp45-46.

62. Lindsay Paterson, 'Scottish Autonomy and the Future of the Welfare State,' *Scottish Affairs* No. 19 ,Spring 1997, pp62, 68.

63. James McCormick and Graham Leicester, *Three Nations: Social Exclusion in Scotland*, Scottish Council Foundation, Edinburgh 1998.

64. Gerry Hassan, 'Labour Adrift In Tartan Water', *New Statesman*, 27 March 1998.

65. *Scotland on Sunday*, 8 March 1998.

66. *The Scotsman*, 9 March 1998.

67. *Sunday Times*, 12 April 1998.

RETROLUTION:
CULTURE AND HERITAGE IN
A YOUNG COUNTRY

Andrew Blake

Britain increasingly depends on brain not brawn. The dominant and rising companies are related to communications, entertainment, education and leisure. These are industries of growing global value; all can generate benefit to economy and society alike; all depend on the creative instinct that is fed by the artistic imagination; and all have great benefit for Britain.

'The Creative Economy in the Twenty-First Century', Tony Blair's speech to the British Screen Advisory Council, 3.2.97.

Tony Blair's Labour government came to power as 'the people's', soundbiting that last vestige of the discourse of socialism into every press release and public appearance. The conflation of a traditional appeal to the mass of the population, part of Labour's heritage, with the techniques of contemporary political management, exemplifies the moderniser's dilemma in a culture which since 1945, apart from an occasional burst of optimism in the 1960s, has seemed happier with the past than the future. When Britain, grown cynical under the vague leadership of post-Thatcherite Conservatism, welcomed in new Labour, its leaders had to envisage a modernisation which conserved rather than destroyed – a reinvention of culture rather than a revolution.

The ability to do so was tested early in the new regime. Responding with speed and discretion to the crisis of August 1997, in which the death of Princess Diana released an outbreak of public disquiet over the place of the royal family in public life, new Labour presided over the reworking of that institution into a modernising, Mayday monarchy. Gearing himself up as a latter-day Disraeli, Tony Blair fawned openly before the Queen on the occasion of her golden wedding anniversary –

yet behind this apparent sycophancy he was rewriting the rules of the monarchy-public relationship, by parading anecdotally aspects of a relationship which had previously been outside the public sphere. His speech was part of the formation of a new constitutional contract, opening up to public scrutiny the institutional relationship between monarchy and legislature. It was delivered at an event which brought some of 'the people' together with their Queen – not, as the monarch had usually met them, behind the closed gates of the Buckingham Palace garden party, but at a televised 'people's lunch', whose very existence changed the ways in which the monarchy could be seen and understood as public spectacle and public symbol. This new contract between the absolute centre of 'heritage culture' and the prophets of the modern forms a significant aspect of a wider attempt to rethink the relation between state and culture, which – as with so much of new Labour's project – tries to negotiate seemingly incremental changes with existing aspects of British life in such a way as to prepare them for genuine transformation.

This process, helping in the reinvention of a constitutional centre which still echoes feudal privilege, could be read as simply regressive, a way of living with the past which denies contestation and avoids the genuine change which would achieve a genuine *future* rather than mere continuity. Another view, however, would be that what new Labour is trying to achieve through this shift is *retrolution*: disguising the future as the past in order to present it as palatable, and in this instance using 'heritage culture' while shifting its terms of operation. The monarchy would remain, if modernised into a more accountable, tax-paying constituent of the nation, while the final vestiges of hereditary power in the House of Lords would be removed. Behind the symbols of tradition lurked modernity.

The idea of retrolution provides an important way of seeing new Labour's renegotiation of the cultural sphere. The pre-election new Labour website, for example, was itself retrolutionary, a hi-tech communications instrument in which images of Union Flags and red roses predominated, while the text appeared against a grained, yellowy background – an electronic parchment, in other words.[1] In the document itself, alongside appeals to 'heal the fractured society', the information technology future was welcomed – and, significantly, welcomed as a future which business and government would co-operate to realise. One idea promulgated in this electronic document was to cable up all schools, through a British Telecom-government partnership, to the information superhighway. This revealed starkly the ways in which new Labour sees the future of both culture and the state: a key policy decision, one crucial aspect of its resounding election focus on 'education, education, education', is to be brought into being through a partnership with businesses – which will remain in control of the technologies through which both education and entertainment are to be disseminated.

THE INTELLECTUAL ORIGINS OF THE RETROLUTION

The term 'culture' is so weighed down with non-commercial meanings that it is not currently possible to assign it simply to the realm of the exchange of commodities. Indeed, one way through which new Labour tried to see the cultural sphere was as a realm of popular expression, as a 'people's culture', in which products like pop music and fashion would feed into the work of the culture industries from the bottom up rather than from the top down. Similarly the millennium celebration was reidentified by Labour firstly as a 'people's festival', a participatory rather than professionally provided event; and secondly as a way of reviving the culture industries, through an imagined synergy between the popular and the commercial.

It is a highly optimistic vision, partly because we have to see this two-pronged suggestion in the 'Middle England' frame within which new Labour successfully campaigned for election victory. Middle England has expectations, but it looks for leadership in culture as in politics – it is happy, nay enthusiastic, to be represented by champions: to flock to Milton Keynes to see Oasis or to Wembley to see the England football team; or to watch with approving complacency while Tony Blair leads the nation without raising income tax. New Labour, in encouraging the culture industries, is necessarily interested in reproducing will and leadership in sport and the arts. This is one important version of the individual enterprise which Labour now acknowledges; yet it suggests a 'people's' culture in which some do, while most watch, and indeed pay to do so.

In formulating the new cultural settlement, the tendency is to work with a mix of the attitudes of the 1940s and 1980s. This combines firstly the elitism of supposedly meritocratic subsidy, an idea dependent on the notion that the best in the arts can be identified by experts, and made available by subsidy to all the people. Secondly, and existing cheek by jowl with it, is the extreme commodification of organisations such as the British Phonograph Industry – whose fundamental assumption is that the market will find the best in the arts, and big business will offer the results for sale. There is not much room for mass social participation in either model, however the two components are balanced. And yet there *is* an attempted mass cultural politics in the new Labour project. One clear sign of this kind of engagement was the renaming of the Department for Heritage as the Department for Culture, Media and Sport.

THE MAN FROM THE NEW MINISTRY

Largely the creation of onetime Tory minister, opera lover, Chelsea fan and wannabe New Lad David Mellor, the notion of a Department for Heritage sat within the post-Thatcherite attempt to revitalise a Conservatism whose populist hegemony had been shattered by the impact of the Poll Tax. The Department represented a culture driven by two motors: a sense of its own past as the centre of its identity, and the successful commodification of that collective memory – of the type dismissed by highbrow critics as 'heritage culture'.[2] Mellor presided over such manifestations of this tendency as the Imperial War Museum's provision of 'the Blitz Experience' – a fairground ride through a moment of the past still of personal importance to people over 60 (the majority of whom were Conservative voters) which owed as much to Disney as to the careful historical scholarship for which the Museum had been known – and the Victoria and Albert Museum's departure from an equally scholarly reputation with the advertising slogan 'an ace caff with quite a nice museum attached'.

Meanwhile the Department maintained a traditional 'hands-off' relationship with the elitist subsidy distributor, the Arts Council – though it re-emphasised the growing sense of Britain's fragmentary composition by renaming the Arts Council of Great Britain the Arts Council for England, and strengthening the role of the Welsh and Scottish Arts Councils, in 1994. Yet the level of public funding available for the arts was gradually reduced. To address this problem, typical of this post-Thatcherite moment was the formation of the National Lottery, through which the Conservatives sought to recapture the ideological hegemony they had achieved during the brief boom engineered by Chancellor of the Exchequer Nigel Lawson. The idea was both to address once again the fantasies of individual wealth which were so common in the late 1980s (identified as a 'feel-good factor'), and to provide a new source of funds for the support of what were euphemistically called 'good causes', including the arts and sport.

Early distribution of Lottery funds to the Churchill family and to the Royal Opera House damaged this populist attempt, which Prime Minister John Major's plan to form an Australian-style national centre for sporting excellence did little to repair beyond re-emphasising the importance of sport to the national culture. New Labour's decision to rename the Department in order to underline the coexistence of the arts and sport as, equally, aspects of 'culture' had therefore been prepared by the establishment of the Lottery. Details of the membership of the Cabinet had hardly been released before Chris Smith, the new Minister for Culture, called in the administrative leaders of the Lottery, who had been paying themselves large bonuses on a contractually agreed formula. While Smith blustered about greed, he counterposed an idea of a 'people's lottery' – proposing among other things a change in the game's rules which had been signalled in 'The Creative Economy in the Twenty-First Century', Tony Blair's pre-election speech on cultural policy quoted at the head of this chapter. Money would be allocated to endowment funds for the young and talented in science and the arts, in a parallel scheme to the proposed academy for sporting excellence, rather than spending arts funding on capital projects which shifted builders away from unemployment statistics, but which did not create new cultural products beyond architecture. Smith set up a Departmental advisory think-tank of creative talent – including fashion designers, record company executives and film-makers, each of whom argued that the Arts Council should move away from subsidy of theatre, classical music and the like, and should instead fund their particular pet industries – fashion, film, and popular music. He then went to the Cannes film festival and, basking in the reflective glow of yet another mini-revival in the British film industry, announced a new Lottery fund for film-makers.

Labour's strategy continued to take shape during renegotiations over the Lottery Arts Fund's biggest and least popular distribution, to the Royal Opera House, which closed for Lottery-funded rebuilding in 1997. London's other full-time opera house, the less unpopular English National Opera, lobbied in its turn for rebuilding funds, proposing a move to a purpose-built house near the new British Library: precisely the kind of national cultural investment which has transfigured Paris under Mitterrand's Presidency, but to which Britain has historically been resistant. And so it continued: Smith personally intervened to advise the two institutions to perform, along with the Royal Ballet, alternately in the one refurbished Covent Garden building. When the new Royal Opera chairman, former EMI chairman Sir Colin Southgate, reinforced the snobbery of his institution by remarking that 'we mustn't downgrade the opera house. I don't want to sit next to somebody in a singlet, a pair of shorts and a smelly pair of trainers', Smith, without questioning the accepted financial practices of the genre (the payment of huge sums to artists and producers and their agents), merely countered that more seats should be made available at affordable prices.[3] This would-be populism did not begin to address the question of what a genuinely popular subsidised arts regime might be: instead it conceded the existing, class-laden notions still operating through an Arts Council which had been run largely to support professional performances of work enjoyed by its officials, and whose most 'progressive' moment, under Labour minister Jennie Lee in the 1960s, allowed the subsidy of self-indulgent work by younger elitist artists and performers – avant-gardism such as Newton Harrison's public execution of various catfish (1969).[4]

Such a position was not inherent in the original Arts Council idea, but in the way in which it has always operated. Though the original 1947 brief was somewhat like Labour's 1997 'people's' approach, emphasising the support of amateur as well as professional events, the Council was soon dominated by its first chair, the economist John Maynard Keynes, who knocked back the amateurism in favour of subsidy for middle-class professionals. This is how Keynes envisioned the Arts Council:

> The purpose of the Arts Council of Great Britain is to create an environment, to breed a spirit, to cultivate an opinion, to offer a stimulus to such purpose that the artist and the public can each sustain and live on the other in that union which has occasionally existed in the past at the great ages of a communal civilised life.[5]

Taking it for granted both that a past organic society of mutual interest had existed, and that the division between the professional artist and the public is an absolute, Keynes's Council helped to create a new public sphere for the creation and performance of hyper-individualised, personal work which was unaccountable to public taste.

Laudably far removed from the closed forms of 'socialist realism' and its fascist equivalents, this process nevertheless tended towards the creation of a culture of dependency among artists, and to an apparently profound aesthetic as well as economic gulf between the subsidised – such as classical music performance – and the commercial, such as pop music, which remained resolutely outside the frame of public support. Some artists, musicians, and actors were publicly funded in much the same way as East European athletes, while paradoxically British sport was consigned either to the commercial sphere or to the genuinely amateur, and public financial support through the Sports Council remained at a far lower level than for the arts – which was, arguably, reflected in relatively poor British performance at the Olympics and the various sports World Championships.

CULTURE, COMMODITY AND COMMERCE

The naming of a ministry of culture and sport, replacing 'heritage', has to be seen as a positive intervention – but the 'heritage' mix of dirigisme and elitism remains, despite the massive changes in the public and economic profile of the arts since the formation of the Arts Council. The economic transformation of the market in contemporary art – driven by speculative collectors such as Charles Saatchi – has remade art as a commodity whose most successful practitioners, such as Damien Hirst, can achieve pop star status and income. The parallel commodification of classical music, from the opera boom of the late 1980s through the 1990s success of the commercial radio station Classic FM, with its knock-on effects on BBC broadcasting, has transformed the status of many performers, though much less so the contemporary composers, in what had been routinely a heavily subsidised form. The result has been an increase in wealth for a super-elite of performers, while for the rest – including the prestigious but costly orchestras in London and the provinces – subsidies declined along with audiences, and debts mounted.[6]

This star-centred commodification has happened in all the cultural professions; while in the parallel world of sport, most notably in professional football and rugby union, a small super-elite has risen at the expense of those who play and follow the game. At the same time another tendency in all the arts paralleled the league tables of competitive sports. The arts were hierarchised during the 1980s and 1990s not through the quiet opinions of literary reviews or academic journals, but through the much more public and openly competitive arena of prizes and their shortlisting processes. Arts prizes such as the Booker and Whitbread, for literature, the Turner, for art, and the Brits and Mercury awards, for music, have constructed a new place for commercial institutional producers such as publishers and record labels as sources of authority in aesthetic judgement. While the new hierarchies appear less elitist than those produced by academic critics, it is hard, in this new commercialisation of taste, to discern 'the people' as arbiters.

Meanwhile these new processes have constituted new creative elites. There are obvious dangers here of the emergence of a set of mutually-serving promoters, their products uncannily emerging onto shortlists despite the width of fields of entry – there seems to be a Bookerocracy in literature, and a Mercurockracy in music.[7] Yet it is hard to argue that this culture of prize-giving is, of itself, a bad thing. It can signal cultural change and the acceptance of new forms as easily as it can support conservative artistic principles. The success of a particular set of tendencies within music in Bristol, signalled by Mercury Prize success for both Portishead in 1995 and Roni Size and Reprazent with the aptly named *New Forms* in 1997, is one of the strongest signs yet of the potential for a reinvention of British culture within a positive vision of multiculturalism. It is one of the profound failures of new Labour that its symbolic representations of 'Cool Britannia' have tended to stress the more nostalgic, monocultural Britpop at the expense of such genuinely new forms.

This commodification of contest has also been carried into television, which broadcasts the prize-giving ceremonies in a parody of the sportscast. Television itself, however, rapidly changed its place in the national culture during the 1990s – and is increasingly in a position to subvert any national culture altogether, denying certain events, shared over the previous thirty years, to those who cannot pay for them. The cosy 1950s-1980s settlement between the state-supported BBC and advertising-driven ITV has been interrupted by the satellite broadcasters B Sky B, who have purchased popular events in order to increase subscriptions. The populist elitism of Sky's appropriation of major sport, through massive cash injections, has made the English football Premier League into one of the finest in Europe, while the highly convenient success of the most popular team, Manchester United, has made it a more sellable product at home and abroad. This is a sign of something which is commonly feared by governments: of the deconstruction of the state and national representation and its replacement by a globalised 'information economy' dominated by the owners of information carriers: newspapers, broadcasting channels, telephone lines and internet access. Tony Blair's pre-election rapprochement with Sky's multi-media owner Rupert Murdoch both helped to produce favourable election coverage for his party and seemed to concede the growing importance of such multinational business organisations to a state whose control will in future operate through franchising and validation rather than through direct ownership. The attempt to provide internet links with all schools in collaboration with BT, a company which, though based in Britain, aspires to the global, is another example of this tendency.

It is hard to reconcile this desperate desire for partnership with quasi-monopolistic providers of the apparatus of cultural diffusion with new Labour's equally urgent wish to encourage a popular culture whose origins are from 'the people'. Looking through the refracting glass of the millennium, the party seemed caught inside this paradox. It proposed a millennial peoples' festival 'with thousands of local initiatives and community celebrations embraced within a national strategy focused on expanding access and participation at all levels of society ... popularising our cultural heritage, giving new momentum to our cultural industries'.

Yet again, the culture industries are crucial to the agenda, and there's more at stake than mass participation in a festival: 'Art, sport and leisure industries are vital to our quality of life and the renewal of our economy. They are significant earners for Britain. They employ hundreds of thousands of people'.[8] Quality of life, national culture and that most important generator of the feel-good factor, sporting success, plus the publicly demonstrated freedom of a number of relatively successful small businesses to flout popular proposed legal changes, are all part of an endeavour to produce a culture in which a Labour-friendly business class can operate in an agreed national interest: a new Labourite hegemony of corporate governance with the consent of business.

SLIGHTLY FOXED

Meanwhile outside the state, and outside the pure commodity fetishism of Classic FM et al, there remain forms of popular engagement, production and resistance in which cultural practices are still the site of fierce contestation. A 1997 Private Member's Bill to ban a relatively popular participant sport, hunting with dogs, was strongly opposed by many of the semi-rural bourgeoisie who had helped to procure the Labour landslide – and who, for social or sadistic reasons, like to hunt. Therefore it was not given Government time, despite the measure's massive support in both Parliament and the country.

Resistance to the Bill, much of it centred around notions of heritage culture – the traditional 'Englishness' of death-dealing country sports – was both articulate and visible, centring on the largest mass demonstrations seen in London since the CND campaigns of the early 1980s, and promising an unpoliceable Act resisted by the unspeakable. Wishing to avoid highly televisable but un-soundbite-friendly confrontations of the type apparently enjoyed by Thatcherites (such as the miners' strike or Poll Tax riots), ministers opted for a quiet life. Hegemony cannot be seen to operate where brute force is employed. Similarly quiescent responses followed farmers' protests against beef imports, and rural dwellers' objections to housebuilding plans. The new government's reluctance to sanction new road building, likewise, can be seen as a response to public anger which has manifested itself in very visible protests of a sort which can be identified as a rather different kind of heritage culture – inherited from the politics of the fourteenth century Peasants' Revolt, the seventeenth century Levellers and Diggers, the Luddite movement of the early industrial revolution, or the Suffragettes' campaign for votes for women which was at its height a century ago.

The law still operates in the cultural sphere. Despite the trumpeting of 'young Britain', much of youth culture remains beyond the pale of cultural policy and part of the criminal law. New Labour's decision to appoint a 'drugs czar', and shocked official responses to any suggestion of the relaxation of laws regarding the possession and use of drugs for personal pleasure, reveals a continuing reluctance to face the truth of the commodity culture at the heart of the experience of many young people. For all the Mercury Prize success of Roni Size and Reprazent, and for all new Labour's positive vision of the importance of the creative arts to an imagined 'young Britain' or 'Cool Britannia', this routine aspect of people's lives, part of a dance/club culture which has been massively popular since the late 1980s, is denied and driven to the murky periphery of illegal trading. No hegemony there, or partnership with business; repression is the order of the day, as it has been in British drugs policy through most of the twentieth century.[9] Drugs are often characterised as threatening the mental integrity of their users; clearly, however, they are a source of such a strong psychic threat to those who do not use them that their legalisation cannot be discussed, perhaps not even imagined. The result is the nominal criminalisation of many, perhaps most Britons in the 16-25 age range.

This attitude consorts aptly with the place of the musics associated most directly with the drug cultures of the 1990s. Here the threat is to the orthodox workings of capital within cultural production. Musics which rely on short-life product made with cheap high-technology instruments, and techniques only vestigially associated with traditional notions of musicianship, are in the vanguard of a digital democratisation through which the hyper-individuated forms of production associated not only with ideas of high art, but with most commercial popular culture, have come under threat. Dance music is based not on the primacy of an 'authentic' performer or creator, but on the continuous reinvention of the sample and the remix. It therefore stands for the ways in which digital technologies problematise the stable mutualities implied in most agreed notions of 'culture' – which tend to hark back, as did John Maynard Keynes, to a golden age of communal stability and mutuality, but take for granted a set of resolutely modern, individualised copyright relationships through which creative work can be rewarded. On this rock intellectual property and its exploitation stand. The drum'n'bass of Roni Size is one among many unstable dance-music genres built not on rock but on the shifting sands which produce silicon microchips, and on which the financial settlements necessary for the corporate exploitation of creative work – so important to Tony Blair's vision of a nation driven by successful culture industries – becomes highly problematic.

New Labour, Old Guitar: An Empty Vessel?

It is perhaps unsurprising, then, that new Labour, with its eager team of besuited young white men researching, advising and writing speeches, incorporates an orthodox, rock-oriented, musicality. Party spin-doctors symbolised Blairite modernity through pictures of the new Prime Minister's Fender Stratocaster guitar being taken in through the front door of No 10, Downing Street, and via the massive publicity given to the meetings he had there with entertainment-business stars such as Liam and Noel Gallagher, of Oasis. As Jeremy Gilbert argues elsewhere in this volume, the rise of new Labour had an uncanny parallel in the fate of the national pop music radio station, BBC Radio One, which in the mid 1990s reinvented itself for (it proclaimed) the under-24s, paradoxically by increasing the airtime given to guitar pop. The 'Britpop' phenomenon – the product of a music industry anxious about its future in the digital age – is, like Blair's guitar, a hark-back to the 1960s. Whether retrolution or pure regression, the guitar pop phenomenon is at the heart of the moderniser's dilemma. While it reproduces orthodox economic relationships of copyright-based capitalism, it feeds a new fantasy of a golden age to succeed Keynes's vision. Modernism in a postmodern world, in which the music of the 1960s is recycled by people too young to have heard it the first time around, guitar pop changes the terms of 'heritage culture' from an obsession with country houses and the second world war to one with the Swinging London of the mid-1960s, meanwhile casting 'young Britain' as yet again making a future from an obsession with the past.

All of which leads naturally enough back through those imagined 1960s to that icon of 1950s modernism, the Millennium Dome. An empty vessel 320 metres in diameter, suspended in mid-air by a series of twelve 100 metre steel masts, dominating a festival site of 130 acres of land poisoned by industrial use, the building signifies the emergence of Britain from its manufacturing past. It also incorporates utterly contemporary technologies, but in a way which, unlike its 1851 Great Exhibition forebear, the genuinely revolutionary Crystal Palace, relies almost wholly on the past for its design image. The building is a retrolutionary Dan Dare science fiction fantasy, its masts echoing the Skylon, the rocket-shaped sculpture which dominated the 1951 Festival of Britain. But the major legacy of that event was not the ephemeral Skylon but the immensely solid Festival Hall, centre of the arts complex on the South Bank of the Thames; an institution which has since the 1970s been trying to modernise itself and find new audiences, as the classical music on which it relies gradually loses public interest and public funding.

The Millennium Dome is, however, no mere signifier. It is physically and financially very much part of the political modernisation of Britain. Both building and festival are caught in the immensely complex webs of financial responsibility-avoidance which have marked the transition from a semi-nationalised Britain to a semi-privatised government. The site was once owned by British Gas, who transferred its ownership to a wholly-government-owned company which cleansed the heavily polluted site at public expense, before handing it on to another nominally government-owned company with a single share, held as of January 1998 by then Minister without Portfolio Peter Mandelson. Debates about the festival's site, about the materials used in the construction of the Dome, about the content of the exhibitions to be held inside it, and about the nature and extent of sponsorship, indicate the extent to which new Labour is a post-Thatcherite project. Its renegotiation of the changing terms of ownership, of private and public space, of experience, and of the new role of government as franchiser are complex, and will only be resolved as the celebration takes its course. The event, in this new and profoundly symbolic national space, may well crystallise the new relationship between government and business, and this may in turn help to produce the technologically-supported cultural industries which new Labour foresees. Though, as I argued above, this would be based on an imagined synergy between the commercial and the popular, such an emergent formation would be hard to see in terms of the proposed 'people's festival'; it would confirm the emergence of an aesthetics patrolled by business, replacing the snobberies still on show at the opera with the new elitism of cool-Britannic commodities.

NOTES

1. The Labour Party's web site can be found at http://www.labour.org.uk
2. The moment is dissected admirably in John Corner and Sylvia Harvey (eds), *Enterprise and Heritage. Crosscurrents of National Culture*, Routledge, London 1991.
3. See Rosemary Bechler, 'The Frowning Version', *New Times*, 31.1.1998, pp6-7.
4. See Andrew Blake, *The Land Without Music*, Manchester University Press, Manchester 1997, pp57-61; and compare the orthodox Andrew Sinclair, *Arts and Culture: The History of the Fifty Years of the Arts Council*, Sinclair-Stevenson, London 1995, with the enjoyably scurrilous Richard Witts, *Artist Unknown: an Alternative History of the Arts Council*, Little, Brown, London 1998.
5. R.F. Harrod, *The Life of John Maynard Keynes*, Harmondsworth, Penguin 1972, p619.
6. For a polemical view of the 'crisis' in classical music, see Norman Lebrecht,

When the Music Stops. Managers, Maestros and the Corporate Murder of Classical Music, Simon and Schuster, London 1996.

7. The following acts were shortlisted twice in the first six years of the Mercury Prize, 1992-7: John Tavener, Primal Scream, P.J. Harvey, Suede, Pulp, Prodigy; 12 of the 60 shortlisted acts. This could be taken as one sign of an emerging Mercurockracy. Oddly, each of the two centres of Britpop rivalry in 1995, Blur and Oasis, were listed once only in this period.

8. This was on the Labour web site cited above, in April 1997, under the title 'Healing our Fractured Society: Rights and Responsibilities together'. A revised version appeared in the party's Manifesto.

9. For aspects of the prehistory of these current discontents see Marek Kohn, *Dope Girls: The Birth of the British Drug Underground*, Lawrence and Wishart 1992; Andrew Blake, 'Foreign Devils and Moral Panics: Britain, Asia and the Opium Trade', in Bill Schwarz (ed), *The Expansion of England: Race, Ethnicity and Cultural History*, Routledge, London 1996.

FROM REALISM TO CREATIVITY:
GRAMSCI, BLAIR AND US

Anne Showstack Sassoon

To understand what is modern as opposed to new is, for politicians, a way of seeing how the shape of the man-made world can make a stronger, fairer, healthier and wealthier society. Or it could be.

Jonathan Glancey, *Guardian*, 17.11.97

Not everything that is new is modern. And not everything that is old is old-fashioned. Jonathan Glancey was criticising the assumption that Canary Wharf Tower, Tony Blair's choice for a meeting with Jacques Chirac and Lionel Jospin, was the best example of a forward-looking, modern, New Britain. He argues that,

> Throughout Britain, and up until the eighties, local councils, education authorities, universities and other public or publicly minded bodies fused Modern architecture to Modern ideologies ... not simply to create the shiny and new, but to modernise class-divided, low-wage Britain ... New Labour has inherited (the) Thatcherite penchant for fancy dress and has yet to separate in its mind the New from the Modern. The former is all about fashion; the latter about the health of the body wearing the latest clothes.[1]

Glancey's argument about modern architecture extends beyond the built environment to the architecture of society more generally. It reflects both the widespread scepticism about new Labour amongst sectors of the population, and the broadly felt need to modernise. It is striking, however, how Glancey defines objectives, 'a stronger, fairer, healthier and wealthier society', which Blair and his government would claim to share:

> Without social justice, without modernisation, without mutuality and solidarity there will be no prosperity ... A high level of social cohesion is not just urgent in itself; it is essential for an efficient and prosperous economy, which is why we have to bring together a drive for economic efficiency with that for social justice.[2']

Holding Blair to account for his modernising vocation implies sharing many of his objectives while reserving the right to criticise the means chosen to achieve them. This enlightened if sharply critical engagement with new Labour links to wider issues. A deep-seated and highly conservative cynicism about the possibility of change for the better is reinforced by the fear that what is put forward as new and exciting merely represents repetition of old, oppressive power relations in new guises. At the same time, the desire to modernise and to escape from the fateful consequences of an increasingly polarised society reflects the conviction that there is no returning to pre-1979, that restoration is not an option.

Whatever our reservations, the thrust of new Labour represents a necessary political shift to the future. As the Commission on Social Justice Report argued in 1994,

> Our world is so different from that which William Beveridge addressed fifty years ago, and it is now changing so fast, that there is no way in which the prescriptions that suited an earlier time can merely be renewed, however much goodwill, money or technical sophistication one might hope to call up in their support.[3]

But will change be for the better? If we cannot go back to the past, can we look forward to a fairer, more inclusive, less polarised society?

FACING THE FUTURE: REALISM OR FATALISM?

For all that the future rather than the past is on the agenda, most of our present concerns share points in common with urgent questions which were being posed many years ago. Many of the dilemmas facing political leaders at the end of the twentieth century were described by the Italian Marxist writer Antonio Gramsci in a fascist prison in the 1930s as he thought about the problems facing the left in his time. Claims by a wide range of public figures, from Mussolini and Hitler, through Roosevelt, to Stalin, to represent the 'future' were a challenge to anyone committed to forward-looking, progressive politics.[4] Throughout Europe, North America and elsewhere political, economic, and social projects were launched during the 1920s and 1930s to modernise productive systems and infrastructures, to respond to popular pressures for a better life, and to create a 'new' generation of men and women better suited to the demands of a modern society. Grand reclamation projects, public building and art schemes employing modernist architects and artists, and education and social welfare policies were presented as forward-looking.[5] Then, as now, political legitimacy and political commitment were reinforced by arguments that what was being created was 'rational' and 'needed'. Debates raged about what policies were the best response to the need to modernise. At the same time opposition came from both left and right to pressures for change.

As Gramsci re-thought left politics, he reflected on an urgent issue: how to avoid passive resignation to seemingly overwhelming historical trends without resorting to schema which were utopian because they had very little basis in reality and therefore little chance of success. The question, he wrote,

> ... is one ... of seeing whether 'what ought to be' is arbitrary or necessary; whether it is concrete will on the one hand or idle fancy, yearning, daydream on the other. The active politician is a creator, an initiator; but he neither creates from nothing nor does he move in the turbid void of his own desires and dreams. He bases himself on effective reality, but what is this effective reality? Is it something static and immobile, or is it not rather a relation of forces in continuous motion and shift of equilibrium?[6]

In posing this question Gramsci was building on a long tradition of political thinking from Machiavelli to Marx. In *The Prince* Machiavelli described the capacities, or 'virtù', which a leader needed to develop in order to grapple with 'fortuna', or fate, and to be able to achieve a united Italy. Marx argued that human beings make history, but not in

conditions of their choosing.[7] Just as no one can choose their biologi-
cal parents, we cannot choose our historical context, but neither do we
simply have to face the future fatalistically.

POLITICAL LEADERSHIP AND POLITICAL RENEWAL

Gramsci was struggling with issues which are still central to today's
politics. Any project which aims at creating a better society must take
account realistically of things as they are in order to help to create what
might be. Change is inevitable but the forms which it can take vary, and
are amenable, within certain bounds, to political intervention. The
question therefore is not *whether* to reform but *which* reform. Politics
and policy choices matter but so does effective reality. The challenge is
to analyse this reality as a dynamic, with constantly shifting relationships between different social, economic, and political forces.
Moreover, it is clear that deep-seated social and economic trends in all
their complexity can never simply be reduced to the aims of politicians
or policy-makers. Outcomes are often unintended. Social creativity
exists *despite* what governments do. The only thing to be taken for
granted is that no historical transition can be understood as all good or
all bad. If we are to avoid cynicism, resignation and pessimism, or
utopian wishful thinking, it is important both to seek out the spaces for
inventive political practice and to take the measure of the constraints
which impinge on progressive outcomes.

Of course, much of Gramsci is superseded, and certainly care must
be taken before we recast Blair into a contemporary Gramscian
Modern Prince – and in any case, as Gramsci argued, a 'modern prince'
in twentieth century circumstances has to be much more than a charismatic leader and implies a transformation of parties and politics more
generally.[8] While we, and Blair himself, might speak of a modernising
'project', a term which *The Economist* has attributed to a Gramscian
influence,[9] it would be wrong to see this as a pre-constituted, finite
objective. A 'project', as those impatient to see the 'big picture' may
perceive, can imply something unfinished, in the making, to which
many different actresses and actors not only may, but, must contribute,
rather than 'a cold utopia' or merely 'learned theorising'.[10]

Today's use of the term 'project' rather than the more dirigiste and
ideological 'programme' is therefore significant. 'Programme' comes
from the political language of the past and can imply that final destina-

tions may be determined from on high, with little regard to the process of arriving at them, or to whether they reflect widespread social needs. In contrast, given the increasing complexity of society, any serious reform can only be realised through harnessing the diverse energies, skills, and different kinds of knowledge in the wider population.

Although the word 'project' goes beyond Gramsci's own terminology, it nonetheless captures something significant in his approach to politics.[11] He argued that politics in the modern period entails constructing widespread consent around alternatives which are in part 'created from scratch' but which also reflect 'historical necessity'.[12] Political leadership, according to Gramsci, required a sense of direction, goals, a conviction that society can be different, and a strategy to unite disparate groups into a 'collective will'.[13] This requires an intellectual, moral, and cultural reform which in turn must be rooted in economic change.[14] Widespread and active consent around social and economic reforms is the precondition for creating an alternative society. Gramsci described this process as the establishment of an alternative hegemony.[15]

Such an alternative hegemony, or widespread support for a different project for society, is not, however, easily constructed. Building and maintaining popular support for fundamental change will only be possible, given the inertia of society, if reforms correspond to real needs and are justified by changes in the way millions of people live rather than reflect 'idle fancy' or 'daydreams'.[16] Adequate knowledge of societal change, however, requires more than 'learned theorising'. Information from the widest sectors of society is necessary to ground any hegemonic reform. Hegemonic leadership, therefore, cannot be based on a party which is cut off from the wider society.[17] Effective leadership, and Gramsci argued this was true even in the constrained conditions of clandestinity, requires both expert knowledge and a web of connections to the wider society which can teach party members and therefore the leadership what they need to know to keep up with rapid change.[18] This is connected with his description of the party as 'a school of state life', which develops leadership skills but is also an exemplar, for better or worse, of politics more generally.[19]

Long term, modern, progressive outcomes are only possible by attempting to shape historical change that is already underway, deep rooted, and that cannot be reversed. Politics which goes with the grain of change does not mean endorsing the forms which it has taken hitherto. If it succeeds in connecting with and influencing the way that institutions, cultures, people, develop and interact with trends and tendencies that we cannot control, it operates on the 'terrain of effective reality' to create and initiate rather than simply to reinforce a status quo.[20]

EARLIER PARALLELS TO TODAY'S CHALLENGES

The possibility of creative political intervention which was realistic yet progressive was sharply posed by the debates about modernisation and rationalisation in Europe in the 1920s and 1930s,[21] as it was after the second world war. Cataclysmic destruction, the Russian revolution, waves of popular militancy, and the emergence of the United States as a world power and cultural model, contributed to the desire to reconstruct not as things were in the past but in new, modern, better ways which reflected the needs of the mass of the population rather than those of tired, and often displaced elites. This applied as much to the social and economic structures of society as to the physical fabric.[22] Today the need for reconstruction and popular support for reforms may not appear as urgent as in the aftermath of the devastation and dislocation of the two world wars. But few would doubt that ecological dangers and globalisation pose enormous challenges. Naturally, as the century draws to a close, we have to update our thinking to take account of new developments which no thinkers from earlier periods could have analysed, least of all Gramsci; but we can still *also* learn from the past, from the insights of thinkers contemplating previous challenges even when we recognise their limitations.

Certainly Gramsci's notes on Americanism and Fordism have particular resonance for debates today about what it means to promote a progressive form of modernisation.[23] And if we think laterally, these notes can provide useful perspectives on the contemporary phenomenon of globalisation. In particular, they help us to consider whether varied outcomes could result from different political responses to the pressures and possibilities coming from such a major historical transition.[24] Gramsci was fascinated with the multiple dimensions of this major push towards modernisation and rationalisation of production, and of society more generally, in the 1920s and 1930s. Americanism and Fordism took its name from the United States and Henry Ford's mass produced Model T Ford, and marked a new era internationally, which no political force and no regime could ignore, and indeed many embraced. So-called scientific management and assembly-line production for a mass market involved both brutal discipline and high wages for sectors of workers. Gramsci noted that '… it was relatively easy to rationalise production and labour by a skilful combination of force (destruction of working-class trade unionism on a territorial basis) and persuasion (high wages, various social benefits, extremely subtle ideological and political propaganda)'.[25] These developments also signalled the advance of mass retailing and important changes in popular cultural production and consumption, and in gender roles, as policies to create different kinds of workers resulted in interference in even the most intimate details of private life.[26]

Large scale mass production also provided a model for social provision as political compromises were struck between the representatives of business, labour and other social forces, in the context of serious economic and political crises. In the face of the fear of a repetition of the Russian revolution and the spread of fascism, progressive social and economic policies emerged in a number of countries, for example, guarantees of paid holidays, legal recognition of trade unions, and other social provision. At the same time, an expanded role for the state could serve a variety of ends depending on the political project and the forces in the field. Nazi Germany, fascist Italy, and the Soviet Union were only some examples of increased state activity. There were also widespread calls for more active state intervention to rescue society from the effects of the depression, for example in Popular Front France, New Deal America, Social Democratic Sweden, and, in Britain, by Lloyd George, the young Macmillan, and, of course, Keynes. The responses to economic and political challenges shared many features, but the specific outcomes derived from specific factors, above all from the political aims and capacities of different groups and individuals.

Gramsci was as interested in the varied reactions to these developments as in analysing the complexity of what was a major historical transition: 'The reaction of Europe to Americanism merits … careful examination. From its analysis can be derived more than one element necessary for the understanding of the present situation of a number of states in the old world and the political events of the post-war period.'[27] 'The problem,' he wrote, 'is rather this; whether America, through the implacable weight of its economic production (and therefore indirectly), will compel or is already compelling Europe to overturn its excessively antiquated economic and social basis.'[28]

The dilemma facing the left concerned what attitude to take towards Americanism and Fordism. At one and the same time as capitalism faced its most dramatic economic crisis ever, new wealth was created amongst sectors of the working class as well as the population more generally. Yet such developments also devalued old skills and led to working conditions which in many ways could be much worse than those they replaced. The trends which undermined so many of the dearly held assumptions of the traditional, skilled working class of the day, and defeated the opposition of trade unions until new organising strategies were pursued (for example industrial unionism), also served to undermine old economic and social elites.[29] Moreover these trends were portrayed as the height of modernisation, and the irresistible way of the future, not only by those whose economic interests were immediately involved, or by sectors of Italian fascism,[30] but also by the Bolsheviks, who greatly admired the increased productivity and dynamism of this American model.

CREATIVE RESPONSES IN TIMES OF TRANSITION

What Gramsci managed to contribute in his dense and difficult notes was the argument that such trends, while they could not be reversed, could be shaped by those who understood what was potentially progressive within them. He pointed out that skilled workers in Italy were not against innovation *per se*.[31] Technical, scientific, and managerial change could also become the basis for social and political renewal – but with a proviso. The model could not simply be adopted as it was but had to be transformed within a different political project 'to turn into "freedom" what is today "necessity".'[32] A precondition for this to be possible, however, was a fundamental transformation in the relationship between the management of such a transition and changes in the knowledge and skills of the population which implied much more than management from on high, whether promoted by Mussolini, Stalin, or Roosevelt.[33]

Gramsci's vision rejected the assumption, held across most of the political spectrum in a wide range of countries, that the expansion of state activity was by definition progressive. This was no mean achievement on the left in the 1930s, but, perhaps not surprising given the activities of the fascist state. The danger was, and is, that management of change from on high may supplant active contribution to renewal from below, so that progressive outcomes are undermined at the same time as many popular demands are being addressed, in a more or less authoritarian, populist, or corporatist manner. Gramsci called this passive revolution, or, another term he used, revolution-restoration, ultimately a conservative strategy of managing change which both transforms society in important ways and conserves many traditional hierarchies, as it responds to certain popular demands while pre-empting popular participation.[34] Gramsci acknowledged that recognising that 'every epoch characterised by historical upheavals' might result in a passive revolution could lead to defeatism and fatalism.[35] That was why it was all the more important to develop an alternative strategy capable of gaining active consent rather than to rely on largely passive acquiescence. A pre-condition for building such an alternative hegemony was to base it on 'necessary conditions' and 'actual reality'.[36]

Creative yet effective political intervention required negotiating the line between resigned pessimism and unrealistic optimism. Reading contemporary reality as preventing progressive political intervention leads to resignation. Such hyper-realism denies that there is anything potentially positive in contemporary challenges, and is consequently unable to develop a strategy of politically creative intervention to achieve different, more progressive, outcomes. Gramsci writes that, 'Too much' (therefore superficial and mechanical) political realism often leads to the assertion that a statesman should only work within the limits of 'effective reality'; that he should not interest himself in what 'ought to be' but only in what 'is'. This would mean that he should not look farther than the end of his own nose.[37]

The alternative, however, is not unrealistic optimism:

> If one applies one's will to the creation of a new equilibrium among the forces which really exist and are operative ... one still moves on the terrain of effective reality, but does so in order to dominate and transcend it (or to contribute to this). What 'ought to be' is therefore concrete ... [38]

Rather than remain trapped in generic opposition, the real challenge was to understand the contradictory dynamics of a complex process, which was neither a given nor a reality which could be ignored but was itself the product of policies and interventions by many different actors and organisations. Gramsci was perhaps thinking of his own role in prison when he wrote of Machiavelli that his aim was to show 'concretely how the historical forces ought to have acted in order to be effective'.[39]

A HEGEMONIC POLITICS FOR OUR TIMES?

Gramsci's courage in challenging many of the political orthodoxies of his own day was remarkable. Tony Blair's attempt to remake Britain poses similar questions to those put forward by Gramsci, about the role of political leadership and the new kind of politics and political party appropriate for the twenty-first century. Certainly Gramsci has been appropriated by such a wide range of interpreters that mere citation is no proof of his relevance today, let alone comparisons to Blair. *The Economist*'s link between the bold heterodoxy of Blair's thinking and Gramsci's, via the influence of the think-tank Demos, one of whose founding members was Martin Jacques, formerly editor of *Marxism Today* is, however, not completely fanciful.[40] Whatever its derivation, a strategy which attempts to expand the basis of consent to a project of renewal has the potential of becoming, and remaining, hegemonic over a wide field of allies.

Of course, if Gramsci's ideas are to be meaningful today, they have to be developed to take account of contemporary realities. Appeals to identify with a new, modern project for Britain are one aspect of the attempt at hegemonic politics. The goal of tackling social exclusion while improving the quality of universal provision of services like health and education is a fundamental part of broadening who 'we' are, certainly beyond a self-defining 'left', in order to link those who are now excluded, marginalised, and poor to the vast majority of the population who all depend on public services. This is in fact, if not in words, a politics of expanding the basis of hegemony, to create and strengthen consent, in order to found what Gramsci would have called a new collective will.[41] The desire for broadly based support should not surprise us. Gramsci argued that the need to maintain and broaden consent to reconstruct society went hand in hand with undercutting the potential appeal of the opposition. At the same time, Gramsci was quite clear that the success of a progressive strategy required both a moral and intellectual revolution and the development of concrete policies which, if they corresponded to real needs, would bind the population to the national project.[42]

There are even points of contact between Gramsci and new Labour on much more specific aspects of policy, for example, education. The objective of raising the education level of the widest possible majority of the population was one that he would have strongly supported. Indeed, we might even be reminded of Gramsci's criticism of those who pretend that learning is easy on the grounds that they fail to validate the experience of those children from less privileged backgrounds who find it anything but.

> Many even think that the difficulties of learning are artificial, since they are accustomed to think only of manual work as sweat and toil ... This is why many people think that the difficulty of study conceals some 'trick' which handicaps them – that is, when they do not simply believe that they are stupid by nature. They see the 'gentlemen' – and for many, especially in the country, 'gentlemen' means intellectual – complete, speedily and with apparent ease, work which costs their (children) tears and blood, and they think there is a 'trick'. In the future, these questions may become extremely acute and it will be necessary to resist the tendency to render easy that which cannot become easy without being distorted. If our aim is to produce a new stratum of intellectuals, including those capable of the highest degree of specialisation, from a social group which has not traditionally developed the appropriate attitudes, then we have unprecedented difficulties to overcome.[43]

Gramsci was thinking about a very different society, but his engagement with the concrete problems of his own day including the harnessing of the intellectual potential of wide sectors of the society could not be more relevant today.

THE ART OF POLITICS

It may not be easy to recognise a compact, articulated pre-constituted hegemonic project in new Labour in day to day coverage in the media of government activity and political debate scattered though indications are of an overall vision in speeches, documents and policies.[44] There is nevertheless preliminary evidence of an awareness that for democratic politics to regain the confidence of the population new channels of communication and of opinion research are needed. Testing the ground through focus groups or by other means, careful reflection on what works and does not, enhancing the roles of people who have a great deal of knowledge and skills to offer as well as needs and desires, for example through citizens' juries, acknowledging the functions of organisations in local communities and civil society more broadly – all these could amount to the beginning of a different kind of politics which implies that no single political party or group of policy-makers has all the answers. Behind it all, according to Michael Kenny,[45] may indeed be the attempt by Blair to construct a new social coalition, or what Gramsci would have called an historic bloc,[46] around a wide set of social issues, to underpin the Labour Party in a much longer term sense than people often imagine. After all it was Gramsci who thought of blocs as porous and multi-faceted and who drew out the implication that, in the modern period of mass politics, the consent of diverse groups had to be earned and maintained through compromises and concrete reforms.

The new political language, and the refusal to consign to the right many issues of concern to a wide sector of the population, could be a sign of aiming to create the basis for a radical restructuring of British democracy rather than a passive revolution. Indeed, Gramsci developed his concept of hegemony as a recognition of the changing nature of political power in the twentieth century and the *political* significance of civil society. Analysed rather than idealised, the attributes of civil society were an indicator of the democratic nature of a society. If its democratic, pluralistic potential develops, coercive aspects of the state could diminish.[47] New Labour policy seems, in fact, to struggle to find the balance between enhancing the democratic potential of civil society by facilitating local, community responses to major social challenges and assuming a prescriptive leadership role with regard to institutional and private activity. What is undoubtedly true, and Gramsci helps us to be sensitive to this, is that the nature of politics is in large part defined by the changing and tangled relationship between state and civil society in different countries in different periods.

No one thinker, however brilliant, can absolve us of doing the thinking we need to do for ourselves. And Gramsci was someone, who for all his theoretical insights, underestimated the threat of nazism and fascism to world peace, did not specify how fundamental human rights are for progressive politics, and did not use gender as a category. His view of the party as a protagonist of change is in large part superseded. Yet, as Stuart Hall demonstrated, applied sensitively to new questions, with political and analytical intelligence, Gramsci remains a precious intellectual resource.[48]

Gramsci is a remarkable source of inspiration for anyone trying to embrace change, but also trying to think and act politically to shape it for progressive ends. Much of Gramsci's originality came from a courageous recognition of the part which the failure of the left had played in the victory of reactionary forces, and in the inadequacy of traditional understanding to grasp the theoretical and political require-ments of a progressive politics in the twentieth century. His insistence on the significance of ideas, his interest in how they are constructed, and how they contain within themselves diverse and often contradic-tory elements; his conviction that people do not simply absorb, but reject or work with, ideas thrown at them; and his understanding of the democratic potential of civil society; all these are reasons for thinking that his ideas are still relevant today. Not least, he helps us to be aware of the real danger that the potentially progressive features of the contemporary historical transition may rapidly dissolve into a passive revolution. With new Labour now in power, it is easy for politics once more to be defined in narrow Westminster terms.

Yet while scepticism about the likelihood of progressive outcomes of new Labour's political project is perfectly understandable, above all in the period before many concrete results are there to be analysed, we should be careful not to be close-minded. New possibilities open up with reforms which break through old logics. Slowly, the way people view themselves and the world is unsettled, and new spaces are created for new exchanges between ideas, cultures and structures. Should reforms as significant as the institution of NHS – for example, good quality childcare which begins to be taken for granted, or lifelong learning – become a reality rather than a slogan, this could help raise the aspirations of the British to what might appear the heavens today. British common sense could shift in profound and deep-seated ways. Bolstered by constitutional change, a new social consensus – or in Gramsci's terms, hegemony – would become more difficult to under-mine even with a different government. At the same time, elements of proportional representation in the Scottish, Welsh, and Northern Irish assemblies, and in elections for the European Parliament, all mean that more than ever consent will have to be earned. An intellectual and moral reform is both a precondition and a result of such change. It will never be the mere reflection of the wisdom of experts. For example, as it becomes integrated into the national psyche, and accepted as integral to children's experience, socially provided childcare could be a factor in bringing about still further change in women and men's views of their roles with regard to both professional and parental responsibilities, and it could also help to place children's needs on the political agenda. Beginning to provide some of the conditions which are necessary to enhance the abilities of people with diverse special needs could initiate a process of rethinking paid work and social provision on the road to creating a more people-friendly society.

Yet at the very moment when change is possible, and the talents and skills of creative and innovative people are so needed, many feel betrayed, offended, and bypassed because the terms of debate are so altered and new allies are courted. We have to grieve if we have a sense of loss and then move on, to go beyond expecting parental figures to be perfect, to recognise the positive and the negative, to assume our own adult responsibilities, to analyse what is missing and needed, and to consider how it can be supplied. The implication is, of course, that we are also treated as adults by Blair and company. The danger, as Peter Hennessy has written, is that scepticism, ' ... the necessary intellectual condition for improvement' gives way to cynicism.[49] Those who are unable to contribute to radical renewal with good will but with critical faculties intact will be left behind. At the same time the forces for change must be open to hearing those voices who offer constructive criticism. Most dominant left traditions find it remarkably difficult to acknowledge that such openness is not an option but a necessity for social renewal. Gramsci helps us to understand that building an alternative hegemony requires leadership which resembles conducting an orchestra rather than commanding an army.[50] All are stronger for having to meet the challenge of co-operation between diverse talents. All are weaker without it.

NOTES

1. Jonathan Glancey, 'Who would live in a world like this?', *Guardian*, 17.11.97.
2. Tony Blair, 'Introduction: My Vision for Britain', in Giles Radice (ed), *What Needs to Change. New Visions for Britain*, HarperCollins, London 1996, pp3-4. These themes run through the election manifesto, *Because Britain Deserves Better*, and Blair's 1997 conference speech. They are threads in speeches going back many years. See Tony Blair, *New Britain*, Fourth Estate, London 1996.
3. Commission on Social Justice, *Social Justice. Strategies for National Renewal*, Vintage, London 1994, p16.
4. Upon return from a visit to the Soviet Union in the early 1930s, the American radcical journalist Lincoln Steffens claimed that he had 'seen the future, and it works'. There was also, of course, the important, mainly Italian, cultural movement known as the Futurists.

5. See Dawn Ades *et al, Art and Power: Europe Under the Dictators. 1930-1945*, Hayward Gallery, London 1995, the catalogue for the exhibit of art and architecture in Paris, Madrid, Berlin and Moscow in that period. This is not, of course, to deny the complex relationship with the past, and in particular with pre-industrial traditions of the different political forces, also evident in this volume.

6. Antonio Gramsci, *Selections from the Prison Notebooks*, Lawrence and Wishart, London 1971, p172. It should be noted that the gender of the subject of verbs, e.g. 'he', is not necesseraly specified in Italian as it is in English.

7. ' ... I think it may be true that fortune is the ruler of half our actions, but that she allows the other half or thereabouts to be governed by us.' Niccolò Machiavelli, Ch. XXV, 'How Much Fortune Can Do in Human Affairs and How It May Be Opposed', The Prince, from *The Prince and the Discourses*, The Modern Library, New York 1950, p91. 'Men make their own history, but not of their own free will; not under circumstances they themselves have chosen but under the given and inherited circumstance with which they are directly confronted.' Karl Marx, *The Eighteenth Brumaire of Louis Bonaparte*, in *Surveys from Exile. Political Writings*, Volume 2, Penguin Books, London 1973, p146.

8. Antonio Gramsci, *op.cit.*, p129. It should be emhasised that only some of his writing on the political party is still relevant today and in any case requires lateral thinking if we are to appropriate his insights for a very different context.

9. See 'New Labour's gurus. The apostles of modernity' and 'New Labour, new language', in *The* Economist, 25.10.97.

10. Gramsci, *op.cit.*, p130.

11. Gramsci in fact uses traditional language and refers to 'party programme', *op.cit.*, I have developed this argument more fully in 'Postcript. The People, Intellectuals, and Specialised Knowledge' in Anne Showstack Sassoon, *Gramsci's Politics, op.cit.*.

12. Gramsci, *op.cit.*, p130.

13. Gramsci, *Ibid*, p125ff.

14. Gramsci, *Ibid*, p129.

15. There is an enormous literature and debate about Gramsci's concept of hegemony. A brief introduction can be found in my entry, 'egemony', in Tom Bottomore, *et.al.*, *A Dictionary of Marxist's Thought*, Blackwell Publishers, Oxford 1991, pp229-231.

16. Gramsci, *op.cit.*, p172.

17. See, for example, Antonio Gramsci, *op cit.*, p418.

18. See, for example, Antonio Gramsci, *op.cit.*, pp188-190, p211. See also Anne Showstack Sassoon, *op.cit.*, p162ff, pp249-284.

19. Antonio Gramsci, *op.cit.*, p268.

20. *Ibid*, p172.

21. Gramsci's notes on what he calls Americanism and Fordism are an intervention in these debates. Gramsci, op.*cit.*, pp270-318.

22. Glancy, *op.cit.*

23. Gramsci, *op.cit.*, pp279-318.

24. See Linda Weiss, 'Globalisation and the Myth of the Powerless State', in *New Left Review*, September/October, 1997; and Anne Showstack Sassoon, 'The Space for Politics: Gramsci and the Debate on Globalization', in Johannes Dragsbaek Schmidt and Jacques Hersh (eds), *Globalisation and Social Change*, Routledge, London forthcoming.

25. Antonio Gramsci, *op.cit.*, p285. Also see p310-313. There is an interesting parallel with Gramsci's definition of the state as 'hegemony protected by the armour of coercion', *op.cit.*, p263. Gramsci's concept of the state is a vast topic. For an introduction, see Anne Showstack Sassoon, *Gramsci's Politics*, second edition, Unwin Hyman, London, University of Minnesota Press, Minneapolis 1987.

26. See notes on 'Some Aspects of the Sexual Question', 'Feminism and "Masculinism"', and '"Animality" and Industrialism', Antonio Gramsci, *op.cit.*, pp294-301. While some of his comments can be queried, his interest in these areas must have been reinforced by parallels with attempts in the Soviet Union and elsewhere to create 'new' men and women.

27. Antonio Gramsci, *op.cit..*, p281.

28. *Ibid*, p317.

29. *Ibid*, p305.

30. *Ibid*, pp287-294.

31. *Ibid*, p292.

32. Antonio Gramsci, *op.cit.*, p317. The full passage is worth considering: 'What today is called "Americanism" is to a large extent an advance criticism of old strata which will in fact be crushed by any eventual new order and which are already in the grips of a wave of social panic, dissolution and despair. It is an unconscious attempt at reaction on the part of those who are impotent to rebuild and who are emphasising the negative aspects of the revolution. But it is not from the social groups "condemned" by the new social order that reconstruction is to be expected, but from those on whom is imposed the burden of creating the material bases of the new order. It is they who "must" find for themselves an "original", and not "Americanised", system of living, to turn into "freedom" what today is "necessity" ... (B)oth the intellectual and moral reactions against the establishment of the new methods of production, and the superficial praises of Americanism, are due to the remains of old, disintegrating strata, and not to

groups whose destiny is linked to the further development of the new method'.

33. I have developed this argument more fully in 'Postcript. The People, Intellectuals, and Specialised Knowledge', in Anne Showstack Sassoon, *Gramsci's Politics, op.cit.*

34. See Antonio Gramsci, *op.cit.*, pp106-120 and Anne Showstack Sassoon, Ch. 13, in *Gramsci's Politics, op.cit.* The terms come from conservative reactions to the French Revolution and its aftermath including, indirectly, the work of Edmund Burke. The notion that things had to change in order to stay the same has been captured beautifully in Giuseppe di Lampedusa's novel, *The Leopard*, set during the Italian Risorgimento, which was made into a film by Visconti. Giuseppe di Lampedusa, *The Leopard*, Wm. Collins Sons & Company Ltd., London 1960. The incorporation of left leaders by right governments and political forces after unification was known as 'transformism'. See Antonio Gramsci, *op.cit.*, pp58, 97, 109, 128, 227.

35. Antonio Gramsci, *op.cit.*, p114.

36. *Ibid*, pp106, 109.

37. *Ibid*, pp171-2.

38. *Loc.cit.*

39. Antonio Gramsci, *op.cit.*, p173.

40. In fact, in an interview Blair gave to Martin Jacques for the *Sunday Times Magazine*, 17 July 1994, he said that at Oxford, ... 'I was very interested in political ideas. I was reading everything from Tawney and William Morris through to Gramsci and Isaac Deutscher.' Quoted in John Rentoul, *Tony Blair*, Little, Brown and Company, London 1995, pp37-38.

41. The 1997 election manifesto is explicit about the need to 'renew faith in politics'. Tony Blair, 'Britain Will Be Better with New Labour' in *New Labour. Because Britain Deserves Better*, The Labour Party, London 1997, p1.

42. Antonio Gramsci, *op.cit.*, p133. A parallel is found in Gramsci's critique of the left in the Risorgimento for not having a concrete programme of government and not understanding the primacy of the crucial concrete policy issue of that time, an agrarian reform. This exacerbated another failing of the Italian left of the period, crude anti-clericalism, *op.cit.*, pp62, 74, 78, 100-102.

43. Antonio Gramsci, *op.cit.*, pp42-3. He also writes that in the first few years of school, ' ... in addition to imparting the first "instrumental" notions of schooling – reading, writing, sums, geography, history – ought in particular to deal with an aspect of education that is now neglected – i.e. with "rights and primordial elements of a new conception of the world which challenges the conceptions that are imparted by the various traditional social environments, i.e. those conceptions which can be termed folkloristic'. *op.cit.*, p30. I discuss these points and others in the essay 'The People, Intellectuals, and Specialised Knowledge', *op.cit.*

44. There is considerable consistency of vision in Blair's speeches before the election and extensive overlaps between him and other government ministers such as Gordon Brown, and also with the perspective of the Commission on Social Justice report. See Blair, *op.cit.*; Rentoul, *op.cit.*; Commission on Social Justice, *op.cit.* These ideas are further reflected in the election manifesto, speeches after the election by many figures in the government and also in a range of policies, which are obviously, however, the product of many influences and requirements.

45. Michael Kenny, 'After the Deluge: Politics and Civil Society in the Wake of the New Right', in *Soundings*, issue 4, Autumn, 1996.

46. For a full discussion of the meaning of this term see Anne Showstack Sassoon, *Gramsci's Politics*, *op.cit.*, pp119-125.

47. I discuss this more fully in 'Back to the Future: Gramsci and the Debate in English on Civil Society' in Anne Showstack Sassoon, *Beyond Pessimism of the Intellect*, Routledge, London forthcoming. One of the important points to be derived from Gramsci about civil society is that its progressive nature is not a foregone conclusion. After all, the fascist movement arose in civil society and then tried to dominate it.

48. Stuart Hall, 'Gramsci's Relevance for the Study of Race and Ethnicity', in David Morley and Kuan-Hsing Chen, (eds), *Stuart Hall. Critical Dialogues in Cultural Studies*, Routledge, London 1996. Hall stresses that, 'Gramsci was not a "general theorist" ... .His "theoretical" writing was developed out of ... (an) organic engagement with his own society and times and was always inteded to serve, not an abstract academic purpose, but the aim of "informing political practice". ' *op.cit.*, p411. This essay is an excellent introduction to the nature of Gramsci's ideas as well as demonstrating his contemporary relevance.

49. Peter Hennessy, 'The Prospects for a Labour Government', in Giles Radice, (ed), *What Needs to Change, op.cit.*, p289.

50. Antonio Gramsci, *Prison Notebooks*, Vol. I, Columbia University Press, New York 1992, p323. Gramsci uses the metaphor of the conductor of an orchestra with regard to the legitimacy of divisions of labour within a democratic organisation of the party, but the point can be applied more broadly. See Anne Showstack Sassoon, 'The People, Intellectuals and Specialised Knowledge', *op.cit.*. The Columbia University Press edition of Gramsci's work in prison presents all versions of all of Gramsci's notes, notebook by notebook. The introduction to the first volume by Joseph A. Buttigieg, translator and editor, provides an essential discussion of Gramsci's way of working and of key features of his thought.

TOGETHER AGAIN AFTER ALL THESE YEARS:
SCIENCE, POLITICS AND THEOLOGY IN THE NEW MODERNITY

Wendy Wheeler

In the second week of September 1997, and a week after the most extraordinary, intense and insistent collective articulation of the public's voice at the death of Diana, Princess of Wales, Tony Blair addressed the Trades Union Congress at their annual conference. His theme was modernisation. The world, he said, is a radically altered place; the old ways will not do; our future does not lie in a low wage, low skills economy; *all* Britain's institutions must change. The key to all this was modernisation, partnership – from and between management and workers, unions and government – and justice. The problem with all this lies with Blair's loose definition of what it is, and isn't, to be modern.

In works of philosophy, sociology and scholarly criticism, the word 'modernity' is usually taken to refer to those processes – associated with eighteenth-century Enlightenment – which are characterised by the move from religious and monarchical societies to secular, civil society, by the move from tradition and belief to a general commitment to progress through rational reform, and by the transition from traditional agrarian societies to technological, technocratic and bureaucratic ones. Yet, from the early nineteenth century to the present day, and for all our rational, political and scientific progress, the costs of modernity, technological change, and bureaucratisation have been very great. Each step away from the bad things about premodern societies has also entailed some form of loss – for few enduring human ways of life are devoid of any merit. These include the losses of the comforts of familiar unquestioned ways of living, knowing and being known, and the unsettling of traditional relations and identities. This is not to diminish the brutishness and brevity of earlier ways of life, but it is to notice that modernisation and rationalising reform have produced their own brutalities – most noticeably, of course, in the brutalities of nineteenth-century industrial relations in which instrumental rationality produced owner/worker relations without any vestiges of earlier quasi-feudal ideas of *mutual* responsibility and obligation. Similarly, mechanisation and bureaucratisation increase efficiency, but they also dehumanise by distancing men and women from natural rhythms and organic relations – especially to their labour upon the world. Another significant loss induced by the increased development of a rationalised life-world was the loss of nonrational forms of symbolic life – religion most obviously – which have always made the harshness of mortality a little more tolerable. This has been accompanied by the gradual erosion of collective ethical commitments, expressed in religion as shared articles of faith, in favour of individualistic choices. These choices increasingly lack much in the way of shared moral ground. And this loss leads to an increased rapaciousness in the pursuit of self-interest, with considerable impact upon social relations and the natural environment – to an extent which now threatens the very future of the planet's eco-system.

Tony Blair has spoken of the importance of the underlying bases to the socialist and trade union movements: their commitment to the strength of the individual as most effectively expressed in collective commitments, voices and actions. But collective commitments are based strongly upon affective, *emotional,* identifications with the larger movement or body. By their nature, they involve strongly experienced group identifications – and these always mobilise the emotions. Margaret Thatcher's success – and, specifically, her success in weakening the power of trades unions – lay in her ability to mobilise public affect, often violently, in pursuit of political ends. No politician can afford to ignore the importance of emotional responses. Nor should they, for emotional responses are a part of what allows us to proceed rationally.[1] Blair does, of course, mobilise the emotions – everything about his rhetorical style is directed towards this end; we are meant to *believe* him; he means to carry us with him emotionally.

Yet this is, precisely, where the intellectual contradiction arises. Blair calls for a renewed 'modernity', but the idea of rationality upon which modernity has drawn is based upon a model of *individual* action and self-interest which is supposedly 'coolly' calculated and opposed to the 'hot' impulses of the heart. The forces of modernity and progress which have prevailed, in terms of the movement of modern civilisations over the past two hundred years at least, have been based on a particular understanding of what it means to think rationally. From the point of view of human beings – whose affective lives always lag behind purely rational judgements – modern rationality and rationalisations have had one fatal flaw, and that is that the account of reason embraced by the rational and utilitarian philosophers of the eighteenth century and beyond was one in which feeling could have no real part. Jeremy Bentham's *felicific calculus* – the calculation of people's behaviour on the assumption that individuals sought to maximise their own happiness – was only possible on the basis that individuals' choices were always *conscious* and *always* calculating. On this account, rationality was conscious, calculating and 'cool'. It was on this very point that John Stuart Mill's critique of Bentham rested.[2] Modernity and modernisation, rationality and rationalisation, efficiency and profit, meant that no serious account could be taken of the incalculable and the unaccountable; these latter – the stuff of the affections, of how human beings felt and feel about their daily lived experience – could not be allowed to matter or, at least, to count as *knowledge*. The model for understanding human motivations which was pursued by Bentham, and utilitarianism generally, consisted of the essentially mathematically-based idea of a calculus: Bentham's calculation of happiness. The commitment to collective voices – in which ordinary lived experience can be forcefully articulated through the affective bonds of the group – is, thus, in very many ways *inimical* to the individualising forces of modernity as they have historically played themselves out. Undoubtedly, part of the emotional pull of trade union activity lies in the dim perception that its collective human voice is being raised against the inhuman tyranny of the machine age. What happened at the Princess of Wales' funeral on 6 September 1997 was the powerful articulation of a collective voice. It *was* a demand for modernisation, but not perhaps precisely in the sense loosely used by the Prime Minister. Blair needs to think about what 'modernisation' means. If it means what it has always meant – the more or less unmediated increase in technocracy and bureaucracy – then it will not cease to be riddled by dehumanising effects. This is quite clearly *not* what people want.

HOW MOURNING BECOMES US –
MOURNING DIANA, MOURNING OURSELVES

The human process which best captures the idea of overcoming the bad things about Enlightenment modernity, whilst at the same time maintaining and developing the good ones, is the process of rebuilding self and world that occurs after traumatic, especially unexpected, loss. After John Smith's death in April 1994, the country had found itself more shocked than anyone would have imagined.[3] Not only was this a case of a 'good man who had died too soon' but, in a small prefiguring of Diana's death, in which we were again shocked at our own shock, the talk was mythic; like Chaucerian pilgrims, people spoke of travelling to Iona again the following spring. There is a series of events which all contain something of this same expression – the Hillsborough tragedy, John Smith's death, the Dunblane massacre, the 1997 General Election, Diana's death – which can only be called 'the will to mourn properly'. Each was characterised by spontaneous acts of collective will directed, as proper mourning is, by a ritualised desire to mark something deathly in order to affirm solidarity and to *change* something. All those events bore the mark of a huge will to affirm *communal* experience. All this is a *complex* articulation of a much deeper and lengthy need to mourn modernity's longer losses. The language – of pilgrimages, shrines, and saints – used in all these events was religious. It was an attempt to find affective symbolisations in a supposedly rational, secular world. The entrepreneurs, followed by the designers, know it too. Who hasn't noticed the church candles and Catholic kitsch on sale in trendy life-style shops? Who hasn't noticed the Catholic iconography appearing on fashion garments? ''There's a kind of medieval spirituality coming through,' Brigitte Appleyward, textile designer for Donna Karan, told trade magazine *Drapers Record*. 'We've got a real feeling for religious imagery, especially crosses'.[4] Designers Dolce and Gabbana, Jean Paul Gaultier, Ann Demeulemeester, Romeo Gigli, and Hussein Chalayan have all recently used religious words or iconography in their clothes designs.

It is easy to see why one should talk of grieving in relation to tragic deaths, but to speak of mourning in association with the widespread jubilation of the 1997 General Election may seem odd. And yet, what Tony Blair consistently offers the country is precisely the new selves and world which the successful mourner undertakes the labour of making. Blair's talk of a 'young country' and of 'renewal' fits perfectly with his vision of the radical renewal which mourning involves. But all this must, in itself, be understood as part of a much longer labour in the struggle to come to terms with loss, and to reinvest the spiritual desert of modernity with forms of knowledge capable of sustaining the richness of the human imagination.

We think we are modern – and indeed we are, unthinkably different from pre-modern societies – and we think that, after two hundred or so years, the great *shock of the new* which Enlightenment inaugurated must have long since been assimilated. Yet the generations, the fathers and mothers passing on little local histories, beliefs, and knowledges, which stand between us modern sophisticated selves and those deracinated souls, charted by William Cobbett at the beginning of the nineteenth century, are remarkably few.[5] Depending on your age, just five, six or seven generations with all their particular understandings of the world, stand between us and that seemingly distant time. Taking this long view, it is hardly surprising that the shocks and losses of modernity remain unassimilated even two hundred years later.

Sometime after the second world war, we gradually found a word for our vast collective confrontation with the modernity we had made. We called the state we were in – the state of trying to face our losses – postmodernity. In the 1960s, and emblematically in the 1967 'Summer of Love' when the Beatles sang 'All You Need is Love' on world-wide networked television, it took the form of a brief attempt to reaffirm – as mourners rightly will – the importance of love as a force for binding together, and the attempt to think through, and beyond, the social divisions of race, class and gender. In the 1970s and 80s it exhibited all the features of an attempted mourning which is not working – a condition which Freud called melancholia. Narcissism, bitterness, cynicism, violence and self-loving greed were the markers of our cultural life; celebrations of self-fragmentation and de-centredness were the markers of our spiritual and philosophic condition. Like all melancholics, we turned nostalgically to the past, not realising that our nostalgia was a symptom of unrepaired grief, and of a desire for an idealised community in which we could, once more, be at home. These were the first symptoms of a postmodern melancholia which *still* needs to be made into a healthy cultural mourning and a *new* modernity. If they are to seize the moment, *this* is what the new Labour government needs to do. Whilst the Prime Minister evidently has an instinctive grasp of the needs of the moment, there is, so far, no real sign that Blair and the Blairites have either an historical or a philosophical understanding of the problems inhering in the idea of modernisation. Modernisation *now* must address the bad things – the alienating and dehumanising things – about modernity. In other words, a twenty-first century modernisation must address the intellectual and emotional poverty which belonged to Enlightenment accounts of reason.

Our modern rationality is a thin and historically recent veneer upon human needs which modernity has not met. Where once we had the means to symbolise our condition, now we do not have them anything like so securely. So, it is not surprising that, when an event occurs whose features and feelings provide appropriate signs and symbols, we rush to it to cry our older and wider joys and griefs through its mouth. This was what Princess Diana's life and death was for us – a hugely appropriate affective event capable of bearing our urgent collective need to symbolise together concerns and angers which it is very hard – in a profoundly individualistic age – for a whole *people* to articulate.

Tony Blair speaks of the state of extraordinary change which we are witnessing. He talks about the effects of globalisation and the need for labour-market flexibility. But, for all his demotic responsiveness and skill, and for all his apparent understanding of the importance of authentic feeling, Blair still fails to understand that the only modernisations acceptable now are ones in which the emotional alienations produced by the 'first' modernity of the nineteenth century must be taken account of. The revolution marked is a great and continuing one. But its face is not only in globalised markets, the rise in consumer sophistication, and the need for flexibility in relation to education, training and jobs. The huge public outburst of national feeling which surrounded the Princess's death, and the initial miscalculations in response to it of the royal family, voiced the demand for another kind of flexibility. This is a flexibility of a rather wider range of human feeling and experience than that historically allowed by those cold, right little, tight little, words 'modernity' and 'rationalisation'.

Detached intellectuals remain anxious about the demotic forces displayed in the late summer of 1997. They remember the power of fascist appeals to the emotions, and the dangerous romanticisms of the nation and the *Volk*, and recoil in fear. But they should know that it is not only in artful human life that these changes are happening. In science, too, there is a change afoot. Contemporary neuroscience and artificial intelligence research are already pointing us towards an understanding of human mind and intelligence in which affect, feeling, is recognised as *integral* to human reasoning. The old divide between intellect and body is crumbling. We are on the verge of an entirely new way of thinking about human life. The appeals to feeling which have been manifested in real acts of public mourning over recent years, and in the publicly enthusiastic response to Blair's rhetoric of inclusivity, mark an epochal change in our (post)modern self-understandings.

Noting global responses to Diana's death, one BBC commentator said that, for a moment, Diana's funeral 'stopped the world'. What was happening then cannot, and should not, be ignored or written off as media hyper-inflation whipping up mass hysteria. Apparently, Diana's life – her concern about expressing feelings honestly, her evident commitment to the most unpopular end of charity work, her challenge to a fusty establishment, her desperately manipulative desire for public witness and revenge against an emotional coldness capable of pretending love in pursuit of the utilitarian self-interest of the monarchy – found an accord with millions of people. This is, undoubtedly, particularly true of women, who formed the majority of the mourners at the funeral. Of the entries written in the many books of condolence made available to the public during the days after Diana's death, the overwhelming majority were from women. One wonders how many deserted women, sitting at home alone with small children, admired – even as they wriggled at the self-exposure – the very public witness and vengeful melancholia of that show-stopping *Panorama* interview given by the Princess. We are certainly upon new ground here. We are entering upon a world trying to mourn, trying to feel, and trying to find ways of expressing things which two hundred years of rationalism and rationalisation have not done away with. Martin Jacques dubbed this national moment 'the floral revolution', a profound change, a defining moment, and the instant at which the nation demonstrated the attainment of 'emotional maturity'.

The truth which Blair's new Labour must come to understand, and which was most clearly expressed at Diana's funeral, is a truth which Blair seems – in his rhetoric – to understand quite well. That truth is that we do not *like* much of the world which modernity has bequeathed to us. This is something of which the rational, managing, side of Blairism ought to be aware. Endless acts of Blair human warmth and spontaneity on camera will quickly be perceived as empty machination if the real inhumanness of so much of our contemporary experience is not really changed. The public mood so forcibly expressed in the mourning for Diana was a vast collective demand for *change*. From the high moments of grief, and the twists and turns of public attention and anger, we can see quite precisely what it is that now revolts people; it is cynicism and greed, it is emotional coldness and cruelty, it is the kind of self-interest which is capable of treating another human being as a means instead of an end in themselves, as an object instead of a human being. The revulsion is also, one might note, a revulsion against the most despicable aspects of unconstrained capitalism. This should give the Blairites pause for thought. It hardly makes sense to make your inaugural theme in government an unproblematic call to modernity, when the nation, and perhaps a significant part of the rest of the world too (20 million people watched the funeral live – that is, in the middle of the night – in the USA), are busy rejecting some of modernity's most important features. It may have been necessary for new Labour to pursue the Tory logics of greedy self-interest and low taxation in order to get elected; yet the 'Diana' phenomenon probably indicates that, alongside a fear of being taxed more heavily, another desire – for probity, decency, and communal affirmation – also exists. Managing these 'contradictions' within a democracy means having a longer term substantive cultural analysis than anything as yet displayed by the new government. One has no sense that these deeper understandings of the present and the future are in place. The sultans of spin were effective in opposition; but in government spin and surface will just not do. There must be more in the way of intelligent long-term thinking, and more in the way of a proper political project rather than short-term responses to idle consumerist whims. There must be an attempt at the standing-back from the immediacy of the present which is necessary for long-term critical thought, and which is located in intellectual integrity rather than in the short-term response to voter 'markets'.

The Palace will survive if it changes; the British people are not particularly hostile to royalty provided it behaves as modern citizens expect it to. The quieter, but more serious, lesson may be – paradoxically since Blair catches the public mood so easily and so well – one for Downing Street. This death clarified what it is that moves people deeply now; it is clear what people want: they want a reassertion of the importance and value of the collective communal goods which eighteen years of neo-liberal self-interest under the Tories had so manifestly torn apart. If this Labour government doesn't deliver, doesn't redress the great and divisive imbalance between haves and have-nots, between insecure workers and greedy or bullying employers – between those who can buy their way, and their children's way, out of distress, and

those who cannot – and if it doesn't understand the deep, if inarticu-
late, revulsion against cynical and calculating coldness, and the depth of
yearning for decency, compassion and liberal ethical community, it too
will be as roundly punished as the royal family was in September 1997.

SCIENCE, POLITICS AND THEOLOGY:
CAPITALISM AND SPIRITUAL AWARENESS

The other speaker at the 1997 TUC Conference on the day that Tony
Blair spoke in the afternoon was, in the morning, and for the first time,
the Archbishop of Canterbury. George Carey spoke to the morality of
employers' obligations in respect of workers' rights to organise and be
recognised. Where the Prime Minister placed the bulk of his demands
for modernisation and mutuality upon the trade unions, the
Archbishop addressed the obligations of the owners and managers of
capital. Some wag said that the radical politics had been during the
morning, the sermon during the afternoon. What is evident, here again,
is the gradual breaking-down of the (always artificial) separation
between different spheres of human experience which has been one of
the driving forces of Enlightenment modernity. The eighteenth-
century Enlightenment *philosophes* believed that such a separation (the
Kantian separation between knowledge, morality and art) would
produce greater clarity and reason in human affairs. This hoped-for
benefit was always, however, only partial, and many of the effects of
modernity and modernisation were to provide rational justification for
social and economic behaviours which have proved socially injurious.

The revolutionary changes in our self-understandings – and which
were brought into such sharp *emblematic* focus by Diana's life and
death – have already gone much further than many people realise. The
'new age' which first showed itself in the 1960s has put its roots very
deep down into our culture. Now it is not only archbishops who urge
spirituality upon us; mainstream capitalist organisations are also heed-
ing both the significance and the usefulness of New Age 'spiritual'
techniques in management. Since the Second World War, systems theorists have paid attention to the 'ecological' principles of systems – principles which take account of the importance of spontaneous and
creative human initiatives, and non-organised human interactions, in
institutions and in creative institutional development.

Paul Heelas, amongst others, has documented this trend involving

increased attention to the non-calculable in human affairs and organisations, and has focussed in particular on increased attention to the
more frankly spiritual or mystical aspects of human organisation which
have been developed according to New Age principles of knowledge
since the 1980s:

> As long ago as 1984, the European Association for Humanistic
> Psychology, together with the Human Potential Research Project of the
> Department of Educational Studies of the University of Surrey, ran a
> large conference on 'Transforming Crisis'. Luminaries such as Peter
> Russell, 'one of the first people to take human potential workshops into
> corporations' according to conference material, were involved. The
> Croydon Business School, to provide a more recent illustration, has run
> a two week event, in association with the New Age Skyros Institute, on
> the subject of 'Innovative Management'. (IBM's Tom Jennings was one
> of the distinguished staff.) And Ronnie Lessem (1989), of City
> University Business School (London) has written a volume extolling the
> principles of 'metaphysical management'. Thinking of my own univer-
> sity, it will be recalled that the Centre for the Study of Management
> Learning, together with a New Age consultancy (Transform), has run a
> conference entitled 'Joining Forces: Working with Spirituality in
> Organizations'. And in the States, influential author Michael Ray is
> Professor of Creativity and Marketing at Stanford University.
> Furthermore an increasing number of articles on New Age management
> and business are appearing in academic journals. The *Journal of
> Managerial Psychology*, for example, recently ran a special issue on
> 'Spirituality in Work Organizations'.[6]

In business studies and economics, and in neuroscience and
computional logic, there is a growing awareness, too, that the spiritual
and emotional side of life is integral to accounts of human reason.

THE POSTMODERNISER'S DILEMMA

The moderniser's dilemma can be stated quite easily: it is that the
modernising impulse which is born of Enlightenment modernity is
inextricably tied up with a certain idea of rationality which has no place
for the stuff of the affections. The rationality of Enlightenment modernity has been hostile to all those aspects of human life – love, faith,

aesthetic or mystical experience, superstition – which are not subject to logic, or to empirical measurement and calculation. Most importantly, anything which is not susceptible to measurement, calculation and predictability does not, for 'properly' modern thought, count as *knowledge* at all. Today, however, and as highly emotional events over the past few years have shown, to be a moderniser – that is, to be some-one who wishes to articulate knowledge and events in ways which are in tune with the most modern of contemporary sensibilities – is to be obliged to take into account a public sensibility which is increasingly suspicious of cool rationality alone, and is increasingly interested in precisely those forms of knowledge which the true modernist does not count as knowledge at all.

The contradiction which Blair inhabits is this: he makes emotional appeals for community, inclusiveness, and 'stake holding', and his appeals meet with a widespread collective response. He wishes the country to renew itself and its political and social institutions. This call to 'mourn' by remaking political and social life also meets with a posi-tive response. But Blair's version of renewal and remaking seems *prac-tically* caught within precisely the now effectively discredited terms of the 'old modernity' in which cold rationalisation, and inhuman expec-tations of human values and modes of being, prevail. The contradiction is that the moderniser has not, it seems, *wholeheartedly* modernised. Blair speaks to the uncalculating heart, but remains *practically* caught in the machinations of the old-fashioned calculating head. The holism of the inclusive rhetoric is undermined by the instrumentalism of a political practice which involves little or no attention to the complexi-ties of affective life.

For example, in an attempt to reinvoke the ethos upon which bour-geois life has historically been founded (the psychological inwardness and self-reflectiveness of the Protestant work ethic), and from which have developed civil society, intellectual and political freedom, and scientific and technological progress, the government has undertaken to reform the welfare state, which is judged to undermine the self-suffi-ciency and proper social participation of too many citizens. One of the first moves in this reform was, however, to remove lone parent supple-ment benefit from new claimants after April 1998. Not only was this a generally emotionally illiterate move – especially where parents with children under five are concerned – but we know that good early affec-tive relations between mother and child are fundamental to later well-being. After the second world war, child psychologist D.W. Winnicott even went so far as to claim that protecting the close relationship between mother and child during infancy was essential to the preservation of democratic values.[7] What he meant was that civilised, generally peaceful, and *free* societies depend upon the capacity of individuals to enter into social relations characterised by emotional depth and sympathy. The cultivation of such individuals begins with an unimpeded maternal devotion which provides a model of reflective attention to the states of others; this is a requirement of the successful conduct of civil life in free societies. After the experience of the overbearing father-figures of fascism during the 1920s, 30s and 40s, and with the breaking down of the glue of rigid class identities after the war, the turn to the importance of maternal influences as a source of acculturation in social sympathy is unsurprising. Of course, it was also economically useful, but, nonetheless, since the war, we have increasingly believed that the special job of the mother is a job worth doing. Suggesting, by economic means, that mothers of *small* children should work is likely to increase anxiety all round. It is not that women with small children cannot, or should not, work; but the job of mothering 'well enough' is *very* hard work. Mothering as a single parent, with a job outside the home as well, is absolutely exhausting.

The cut to lone parent supplement was a piece of pure nineteenth-century utilitarian rationalism. It was utterly blind to the importance of a healthy affective life and to the implications of the latter for reasonable conduct in social relations. Unreasonable behaviour in social relations is what the Blair government is trying to amend, but this particular example of 'modernisation' would appear to demonstrate no sense at all that such rationalist instrumentalism has been, precisely, one of the major problems of modernisation since the late eighteenth century.

> The ongoing tide of research and publication around the significance of emotions and the body in rational thought processes indicates that the scientists have at last turned their minds to what has been one of modernity's most intransigent problems: its erroneous view of reason as a process which is epitomised by calculation and contaminated by affect. Added to the corresponding flow of similar literature from New Age sources, this indicates a wide-spread critique of modernity's version of rationality.

The exclusion, as sources of *knowledge* in modernity, of affective experiences has never been complete, but now a sea-change is underway. What *post*modernity is really about is the demand that *modernity* acknowledge those really human things which it excluded as knowledge. The impulse of modernity was melancholic; it inaugurated a huge loss in terms of human affective needs, but it never wholly encountered, or, in its *accounting* faced-up to, this loss. Postmodernity may, then, well be thought of as the attempt to face loss healthily. Rather than melancholia – which is a pathological response to loss characterised by denial – the postmodern can be understood as the attempt to come to terms with modernity by dealing with loss in the wholesome way which Freud called 'mourning'.[8] The moderniser's dilemma should more rightly be called the *post*moderniser's dilemma. The dilemma lies in finding ways of moving forward politically which are able, also, to take account of a growing reassessment of passion in our political and cultural lives. Blairism's emphasis on the 'new', on modernising and modernity, is right; a healthy mourning is a renewal. But what is insufficiently recognised by those managing, modernising, spin-boys of new Labour is that 'modernising' and 'modernity' *now* means *modernising modernity*. People want *renewal*, but it is not a renewal of the old modernity associated with the heartless reason and rationalisations of capitalism, the butch posturings of confrontational trade unionism or aggressive government of whatever hue.

'IT'S LIFE, JIM, BUT NOT AS WE KNOW IT: SCIENCE ON PLANET FEMALE

Writing on the public reaction to the funeral, Martin Jacques noted that the values to which Diana appealed were those, post-1960s, values of 'feelings, honesty, informality, humour, meritocracy, the personal, the admission of weakness and vulnerability, the casual, the female'.[9] One might also add, 'the spiritual and the mystical', and say that all these are the most difficult values to embody in a modern reasonable politics.

In these postmodern times, western cultures seem increasingly to be motivated by what we will have, still, to call 'feminine values'. This will frighten those many people who distrust the womanly demand to think, chat, gossip, explore complicated and incalculable things, and 'feel-think' one's way through relationships and events. Yet, according to the most recent cosmologies of mind, feel-thinking is, in fact, what human beings have always done – however much they might wish to rationalise things otherwise and call it 'being reasonable'. How should a politician – still in hock to old modernity – manifest something of the new modernity in his or her policy formulations? If the new developing cosmology of mind – in which we understand affect and the viscera to be a *part* of rational processes, not separable from them – is, to the new modernity, what physics and mathematics was to the old,[10] how can this new cosmology take *political* shape?

Blair made, very successfully, the beginnings of a new hegemony based upon assertions of the importance of community, upon a quick and effective popular touch and, in most of his speeches, and in his response to Diana's death, a willingness to appear *affected*. In doing so, he appeared in tune with the times and with the vast subterranean changes which are under way. Nevertheless, it is by no means clear that this was anything other than a general appreciation of the *Zeitgeist* without any intellectual depth to it. Certainly, the willingness to tolerate the continued marketisation and commodification of education, not to mention the cut to lone parent benefit, both suggest a failure to reflect on the nature of non-commodifiable relations of trust, and on the long-term effects of allowing market relations and imperatives to enter into, and inevitably to deform, social relations. If the dehumanising effects of unrestrained capital markets and market rationalisation are being increasingly recognised in the human sciences, and even by some capitalist organisations themselves, there is, as yet, little sense that such recognition has filtered through to the politicians. David Halpern's Nexus report on Social Capital is likely to be influential, but it is still to early to judge the outcome of research such as this is terms of government policy.[11]

NEW LABOUR, NEW POLITICS

Postmodernity is the critique of modernity; part of its symptomatology has been anti-modernity, but its better imperatives are towards a *new* modernity. The critique of Cartesian mind/body dualism, and of Enlightenment modernity's privileging of reason as calculation, and of what, in general terms, might be described as a social and historical tendency to psychical splitting[12] – are healthy. The single greatest threat to these socially healthy developments towards holistic understandings is unrestrained capitalism. Not only does it embody the worst vices of utilitarianism in regard to greed and narrow self-interest, but its relentless logic is to profit from everything and, thus, to commodify and contractualise everything. Yet, clearly, there are vast – and vastly important – areas of human experience in which value is not simply reducible to Carlyle's despised 'cash nexus'. These are the things which move and change us: the arts, education, friendship, children, and all the places where people do work not simply for financial reasons but for reasons of principle and concern.

Of course, the problem for Blair and the Blairites is that, in spite of the rhetoric, they have significantly committed themselves, politically and economically to the old, not the new. Inasmuch as they have taken on the economic philosophy of Thatcherism, they have committed themselves to nineteenth-century neo-liberal capitalism and *its* understandings of efficiency and profit. This may have been the only way to secure victory at the 1997 General Election, but it is part of the *old* world order of self-understandings, not the *new* one.

For a moderniser who sticks to the old methods, economics, and understandings of the 'first modernity', the moderniser's dilemma in this time of fundamental change is that the future will not, essentially, be simply calculating and capitalist. Or, at least, it will not be capitalism as we have known it. This is because the relatively short-termist notions of what counts as 'profit' and 'interest' will change. As Paul Heelas indicates, capitalist organisations have already begun to understand that different forms of work-place organisation – non-hierarchical sub-systems, 'spirituality' in the work-place – are more efficient and, thus, profitable; but this kind of understanding of efficiency, whilst it happily increases money profits in the short term context, *also* changes the very *idea* of what profit and efficiency really mean. Indeed, with the beginning of ideas of social and relational auditing, and the importance of social capital, the idea of profit is already beginning to change quite swiftly. Reporting on the Windsor Castle Round Table on Social and Ethical Accounting and Auditing in December 1996, Simon Zadek of the New Economics Foundation writes:

> Companies now see the need to demonstrate that they are responsible corporations. As the chairman of British Telecom, Sir Iain Vallance, stated: 'I believe that in today's society, companies not only need to operate in an ethical manner, but also need to demonstrate this publicly'. Traditional 'public relations' is not enough. The public is demanding higher ethical standards from companies. To keep the public's confidence, companies have to prove they are reaching these standards.[13]

Writing in a similar vein in *Building a Relational Society*, John Monks, General Secretary of the TUC, says:

> A job is about more than simply a formal contract between a worker and an employer. The quality of their relationship, or the 'psychological contract', as it has been called, really does matter ... It is on the quality of this relationship that the success of a business depends.[14]

Another contributor to the same collection of essays, Clive Mather of Shell International, writes:

> Inexorable forces of change have been steadily reshaping the world of business and the nature of work itself ... change which is forcing companies to rethink how to build and develop their relational bases across the stakeholder spectrum – with customers, communities and employees.

With these changes, both shorter *and* more *long-term* goals will begin to figure in the account. These changes will come, eventually, to be seen as epochal in the transformation of 'individualistic capitalism' into something we might call 'shared-profit capitalism'. Both 'shared' and 'profit' will, eventually, come to be seen in much wider terms.

If Blair's new Labour government is able to grasp the depths of the socio-cultural changes underway, it may develop a new hegemony fit for the new times. The modernisers of the New Labour project understand that something new is wanted and necessary – thus they speak of renewal – but they still 'think' modernisation in the 'old' modernity terms of efficiency as rationalisation and flexibility. They do not recognise that *post*modern renewal involves a rethinking of the basic categories and values of modernity itself. In order to become truly hegemonic, new Labour will have to demonstrate a much finer, and subtler, grasp of the present and the future. Not least – and this is politics' greatest challenge – Blair's new Labour will have to be able to *make sense*, and make *common sense*, of the strange outlines of a future they have barely yet considered.

NOTES

1. This anti-cartesian argument is now beginning to appear in many places. See A. Damasio, *Descartes' Error: Emotion, Reason and the Human Brain*, Picador, London 1995.

2. J.S. Mill, 'Bentham' in J.S. Mill and J. Bentham, *Utilitarianism and Other Essays*, A. Ryan (ed), Penguin, Harmondsworth 1987.

3. See W. Wheeler, 'Dangerous Business: Remembering Freud and a Poetics of Politics', *The Blair Agenda*, M. Perryman (ed), Lawrence and Wishart, London 1996.

4. See, for example, 'Heavenly Creatures', *Guardian Weekend* Magazine, 24 January 199, pp32-33.

5. W. Cobbett, *Rural Rides*, Penguin, Harmondsworth 1967.

6. P. Heelas, *The New Age Movement*, Blackwell, Oxford 1996, p66.

7. D.W. Winnicott, 'The Mother's Contribution to Society', in *Home Is Where We Start From*, Penguin, Harmondsworth 1990, p.124.

8. For the Freudian distinction between pathological and wholesome responses to loss, see S. Freud, 'Mourning and Melancholia?', *Pelican Freud Library 11: On Metapsychology*, Penguin, Harmondsworth 1984.

9. M. Jacques, 'The Floral Revolution', *Observer*, 7 September 1997, p15.

10. This is the claim made in G. Edelman, *Bright Air, Brilliant Fire: On the Matter of the Mind*, Penguin, Harmondsworth 1994.

11. D. Halpern, 'Social Capital, exclusion and the quality of life: Towards a causal model and policy implications', Nexus Briefing Document, 1998.

12. The sort of 'splitting' I have in mind is that described by Melanie Klein. The prototypical splitting is of the mother into 'all' good breast or 'all' bad breast. Maturity consists in the ability to contain easy and difficult things together and to tolerate the anxiety that holding together sometimes induces. See *The Selected Melanie Klein*, J. Mitchell (ed), Penguin, Harmondsworth 1986.

13. S. Zadek, 'Beyond Profit and Loss?, *Briefing*, (Spring 1997). *Briefing* is the quarterly newsletter of the Prince of Wales Business Leaders Forum and is published by The Society for International Development (SID).

14. N. Baker (ed), *Building a Relational Society: New Priorities for Public Policy*, Arena, London 1996.

WHO CARES WHO WINS?
POST-MODERNISATION AND THE
RADICALISM OF INDIFFERENCE

Timothy Bewes

The tepid, civic-minded Englishman follows his economic nose, eyes to the road, doing what the market tells him, privatising, firing, keeping down wages, telling himself we must adapt to a new era. The narky Frenchman looks ahead, sees what is coming, and says 'if that is reality, I reject it!'

George Walden, 1997

The age of bad conscience is also the age of pure cynicism.

Gilles Deleuze and Félix Guattari, 1972

In the autumn of 1997 the *Guardian* ran a report on the publication in France of a book by two physicists, Jean Bricmont of the University of Louvain and Alan Sokal of New York University, entitled *Impostures Intellectuelles*. Sokal had already published a hoax article in the humanities journal *Social Text* exposing the relativistic 'excesses' of Critical Theory. The new book, *Impostures Intellectuelles*, said the *Guardian*, elevates this attack to a new level, claiming that 'postmodern' thinkers such as Julia Kristeva, Jean Baudrillard and Jacques Lacan peddle a fraudulent, 'pseudo-scientific' discourse which displays 'a superficial erudition' by 'throwing words at the reader in a context where they have no relevance'. The article, headlined with the phrase 'Simply a load of old tosh', was sympathetic to the two physicists; along the bottom of the page quotations lifted out of context from the work of three of the philosophers under attack served to confirm their 'deliberate obscurity' and, perhaps worse, their 'verbosity'.[1]

A few weeks after the death of Princess Diana, and in the wake of a series of articles affirming the renaissance of a new 'positivity' in British cultural life, the *Guardian* piece seemed highly characteristic of the post-election mood. Fraudulence was to be rooted out from public life. New Britain was a place in which obscurity and pretension, along with bureaucracy, corruption and 'vested' interests were no longer welcome – or, more to the point, were simply out of date. Postmodern theory was presented by the article as old fashioned and anachronistic, a remnant of the academic narcissism of the 1960s, which, in encouraging students to question 'the historical and cultural situatedness of our beliefs and practices', rather than imbibe the disseminated knowledge of our accumulated cultural heritage, represents an institution mired in its own sterile orthodoxies. In the new Labour ideology of mass participation in higher education, one fully expects that the theoretical writings of French intellectuals, and everything else at the 'inefficient' – which is to say non-vocational – end of the academic spectrum, will be squeezed out altogether. Anglo-Saxon common sense is back at the centre of the intellectual agenda, a cornerstone of the resurgent British pride, along with guitar-based pop music, grilled monkfish on polenta, and a newly discovered monopoly in self-satisfied emotional honesty.

Postmodernity has been replaced by a new 'modernity' – straightforward, economically efficient, and morally sanitary. Tony Blair's *putsch* on the concept of modernity has been largely successful. Like Thatcher's rhetoric of 'choice', the new Labour claim to 'modernisation' remains almost uncontested; new Britain is seen, grudgingly or otherwise, as a more modern place than it used to be.

Detractors from this new modernity are urged in the broadsheets and elsewhere to get 'up to date'. Conservative elder statesmen like Norman Tebbit – who has lately begun rearticulating a Powellite racial agenda – as well as old Labour figures such as Tony Benn and Roy Hattersley, are dismissed by former allies as 'hopelessly out of touch'.[2] Bribery and blackmail, the corruption and compromising of public officials, is not just wrong, it is *antiquated* – almost quaintly so. There is a consensus that the Royal Family, in all their stately dignity, are a near defunct institution – defunct not *as* an institution, but on account of their *particular* aristocratic formality. The Royal Family must, as the Blairite terminology goes, 'modernise or die', meaning that they must embrace precisely those values attributed to the dead Princess if they are to survive into the next century – and these are the same values to which Tony Blair has staked such a sustained claim: sincerity, altruism, warmth and accessibility.[3]

For Blair, 'modernisation' means integration, approachability and informality, the dissolution of barriers and the forging of 'connexity', in the cute coinage of one Downing Street policy adviser.[4] Politics itself, as the representation of *competing* interests, is redundant. The new political modality is collaboration rather than antagonism, moderation rather than radicalism, and ideological flexibility rather than entrenched positions. Modernisation is a creed which transcends party politics. In place of the left-right political spectrum is a new model of politics based on the wide disparity between the extremes of Old and New Britain. Just as the terms 'left' and 'right' function as arbitrary spatial metaphors for the political positions they represent, however, so the current idea of 'New Britain' is an entirely rhetorical designation, having little or no connection with the question of its real historical progressiveness. To be a 'moderniser' means nothing more than to be a subscriber to a particular intra- (and, increasingly, inter-) party political programme.

MODERNISATION: THE REINVENTION OF POLITICS?

Raymond Williams first made clear the distinction between modernisation and modernity, pointing out that the former implies 'some local alteration or improvement of what is still, basically, an old institution or system'.[5] Andrew Rawnsley has applied a similar insight specifically to the Blair government. Modernisation, he says, is 'a way of painting go-faster stripes on what is essentially a gradualist, even conservative government'. Modernisation means not going forward, but catching up. 'In relation to the market place, it has less to do with creating a brave new future than accepting the recent past.'[6] The broad acceptance of the market place itself is essential to Blair's modernisation, and is its principal ideological focus. The old ideologies of left and right no longer hold much purchase, declaims Blair – but this by no means signifies the end of ideology *per se*.[7] The capitulation of the country, including the few remaining pockets of socialism, to the principles of market economics is a huge ideological project, for which the concept of modernisation is a powerful, far from neutral, polemical baton. Adjusting the high expectations of a new Labour government in a generally downward direction is a further ideological objective, and is one explanation for the great interest of politicians in the concept of globalisation.

Globalisation, an apparently objective and irrevocable process, the effect of drastic technological improvements in transport, communica-

tions and the movement of capital, is seen both to erode the possibilities of national state action, and to make impractical the kind of
progressive taxation that was feasible when the rich, like everybody
else, kept their money in local bank accounts. Yet like modernisation,
globalisation is a term which is inscribed with very particular ideological aims and objectives. 'There can never be "globalisation in general"',
observes Doreen Massey. 'If the world is becoming more intercon-
nected then it is doing so, and must do so, in the context of particular
power relations, and governed by particular political trajectories. What
we have now is neo-liberal, free-market, globalisation. It is most defi-
nitely, if we can still use these terms, a globalisation of "the right".'[8]

Massey's caution over terminology here is significant: what she calls
the 'discourse of inevitability' which accompanies the expansion in the
size of financial markets is reflected in the doctrine of modernisation,
which deems the concerns of the Left to be anachronistic. 'The certain
kind of capitalism we are now witnessing' writes Paul Smith in
Millennial Dreams, 'has underscored its own certainty by claiming that
its dearest dream is indeed an actually existing reality. That is to say, the
dream of the globe constituted as a single, integrated market place is
touted as if it were by now the truth.' Globalisation is entirely collu-
sive with the rarefication of politics under Tony Blair, and vice versa.
'The Enlightenment goal of domination over nature for the good of
everyone in the North has apparently now been realised in an idealised
form', continues Smith. 'Not content with simply mastering the
natural world and its resources and perfecting their exploitation, capitalism now claims dominion over even the most metaphysical components of the natural world – time and space.'[9] It is exactly this quality
of transcending the material that, for Sarah Benton, lends to Blair an
aura of something far more archaic. 'The imagery of chivalrous knights
blossoms around Blair because his leadership suggests something
mediaeval, something resonant of political authority before the era of
the nation state and civic institutions.'[10]

Like many ambitious politicians before him, Blair seeks the reinvention of politics as a sphere which exceeds the limitations of politics
itself. For theoreticians of *Realpolitik*, the ability to appear not to be a
politician has long been thought to be one of the most important of
political virtues. 'To those seeing and hearing him', writes Machiavelli,
the prince 'should appear a man of compassion, a man of good faith, a
man of integrity, a kind and a religious man. And there is nothing so
important as to seem to have this last quality.'[11] Slavoj Zizek has

described this political imperative as, precisely, an ideological tussle over concepts: 'The struggle for ideological and political hegemony is ... always the struggle for the appropriation of the terms which are "spontaneously" experienced as "apolitical", as transcending political boundaries.'[12] For the Blair government, modernisation is invested with all the demands of such an enterprise; modernisation is the central plank of an ideological programme to shift the parameters of politics 'for a thousand years',[13] out of the domain of ideology and propaganda, into the ethereal realms of theology and metaphysics.

COMPETING DIAGNOSES: SCHIZOPHRENIA V 'REFLEXIVE MODERNISATION'

That this is anything other than an ideological project is believed by no one. New Labour's insistence upon its modernity, its humanity, and its moral cleanliness imposes a schizoid mentality in the psyche of the contemporary political subject. A pragmatic mandate extended towards the new government coexists with a refusal to invest in it at the level of credibility. New Britain, we hear repeatedly, is a place where cynics have no place;[14] yet for all his rhetoric around 'cynicism', it is the incongruousness of Blair's political attempt to elevate the concerns of politics itself that has led to the growth of a fundamental, underlying incredulity towards his government. The triumph of the May 1997 election was delivered by an electorate in a state of mass psychosis, a 'schizophrenia' not unlike that which is rendered so terrifyingly in Beckett: 'She felt, as she felt so often with Murphy, spattered with words that went dead as soon as they sounded; each word obliterated, before it had time to make sense, by the word that came next; so that in the end she did not know what had been said. It was like difficult music heard for the first time.'[15] A landslide result delivered with the lowest turnout in any modern general election encapsulates what is an unprecedented level of ambivalence, even alienation, towards a new government.[16] Political discourse currently functions only in this surreal state of suspended (dis)belief, which amounts to a crisis of signification. Such a breakdown in the signifying chain has been explicitly characterised as 'schizophrenic' by the postmodern theorist Fredric Jameson, after Jacques Lacan. And for Jameson, as well as for Gilles Deleuze and Félix Guattari, this schizophrenia is a distinguishing feature of postmodern mental life.

'With the breakdown of the signifying chain,' writes Jameson, 'the schizophrenic is reduced to an experience of pure material signifiers, or in other words of a series of pure and unrelated presents in time.'[17] Schizophrenia is an experience of the radical undecidability of competing options, given the perception that no signified exists behind the various 'alternative' signifiers with which we are presented. The passage from signifier to signified is no longer negotiable. For Deleuze and Guattari, it is capitalism itself which produces a schizophrenic reaction in the minds of consumers and citizens. 'There is not a single economic or financial operation that, assuming it is translated in terms of a code, would not lay bare its own unavowable nature, that is, its intrinsic perversion or essential cynicism.'[18] In Blair's government, we encounter the unhindered operation of consumer capitalism, the dominance of a hegemony more powerful even than that which prevailed during the Thatcher years. Consumer capitalism has reached a stage of absolute consensus; Blair's doctrine of modernisation, indeed, is the final hegemonisation of this process. Under these conditions the mind of the schizophrenic, riven by the competing demands of undecidable and unfathomable alternatives, is the model for a generalised state of consciousness.

The 'modernising' argument claims that, in the current social conjuncture, both the most radical and the only possible position is one of moderation and conservatism. A pragmatic solution to the problem of alienation is proposed in which the undecidable *either/or* facing the schizophrenic is replaced by the inclusive *and* – a solution of consensus, moderation and flexibility. The implication is that the opposing terms of these concepts (dissent, radicalism, conviction) are reconceptualised so as to render them neither opposed to the primary terms, nor even incompatible with them. That consensus could provide political dynamism, that moderation might itself be a radical position, that ideological flexibility may provide a framework for a politics of conviction, however, represent the manifestation of a rupture between words and their meanings, 'a breakdown in the signifying chain' in Jameson's words. As Jonathan Meades has written, Tony Blair's rhetoric has a 'serially oxymoronic' quality; Blair is 'a man who believes in unity by inclusion, who rejects *either/or* in favour of *both/and* – rock and roll and the army; commercial excellence and human rights; *grands projets* and social housing; education for all and peanuts for teachers'.[19]

The sociologist Ulrich Beck is one of the principal theorists of this new paradigm which seeks to resolve the 'schizophrenia' of postmodernity by means of a politics of inclusion and collaboration. He writes of the year 1989 as the year of 'And', when the fall of the Berlin Wall and the Chernobyl nuclear reactor disaster combined to destabilise, for good, the left-right, 'Either-Or' model of political opposition, inaugurating an era in which doubt, hesitancy and a concern for consequences begin to function as a (long overdue) brake upon the 'arrogant' expansionism of industrial modernisation. In *Anti-Oedipus*, Deleuze and Guattari write that the most pressing question facing capitalism is that of how to bind 'the schizophrenic charges and energies into a world axiomatic that always opposes the revolutionary potential of decoded flows with new interior limits.'[20] This ideological process of 'axiomatisation' may provide one way of understanding Ulrich Beck's theory of 'reflexive modernisation'.

Reflexive modernisation mobilises a political perspective very similar to what Blair calls simply 'modernisation'. Both distance themselves, explicitly, from the politics of opposition; both also – although less distinctly in Blair's case – evince hostility to what they see as the 'apathy' and 'cynicism' of postmodernism, with its vision of an industrial democracy founded upon the 'sand of arbitrariness'.[21] In its place, a project of formulating 'new' rules for living is proposed, rules in keeping with an age of openness, flexibility and informality. Reflexive modernisation seeks the conciliation of capital, rather than the endless, apparently futile politics of opposition to it.

The theses of reflexive modernisation and postmodernism initially seem to have much in common. The replacement of alternatives by inclusiveness, for example, is sometimes taken to be a characteristic of postmodernity, rather than a solution to the problems of nihilism or relativism thrown up by postmodernity. Certainly, its theoretical justification is inseparable from the work of theorists of the postmodern such as Jean-François Lyotard, who first defined postmodernism as 'incredulity toward metanarratives'. The society of the future, writes Lyotard, 'falls less within the province of a Newtonian anthropology ... than a pragmatics of language particles. There are many different language games – a heterogeneity of elements. They only give rise to institutions in patches – local determinism.'[22] If the competing 'metanarratives' of left and right – Marxism, humanism, Christianity, fascism, the 'rationalism' of modernity – are inadequate to explain the social world and the metaphysical beliefs prevailing in the late twentieth century, perhaps the mastery of a portfolio of specific discourses directed towards heterogeneous purposes is all we can expect from the servants of public life, and from ourselves, the consumers of their products. What, in that case, distinguishes postmodernism's abjuration of the universal from the 'local determinism' advocated by the theorists of reflexive modernisation, for whom the solution to postmodern 'fragmentation' is a politics of consensus and cohesion?

One answer may be found in Lyotard. 'Where, after the metanarratives, can legitimacy reside?' he asks. 'The operativity criterion is technological; it has no relevance for judging what is true or just. Is legitimacy to be found in consensus obtained through discussion ... ? Such consensus does violence to the heterogeneity of language games. And invention is always born of dissension.' Lyotard here draws a firm distinction between the 'heterogeneity' of discourses described by postmodernity and the pragmatism of the consensus option. The attempt to develop political programmes out of the former will always end up in the collusion of the latter. 'Postmodern knowledge', he continues, 'is not simply a tool of the authorities; it refines our sensitivities to differences and reinforces our ability to tolerate the incommensurable. Its principle is not the expert's homology, but the inventor's paralogy.'[23] An institutional politics arising directly out of postmodern theory is inconceivable, therefore. What animates reflexive modernisation is a profound discomfort with, not an ability to tolerate, the incommensurable. Reflexive modernisation attempts to erase the metaphysical horror of 'postmodern knowledge' – Nietzsche's swamp of nothingness, Kierkegaard's existential sickness, Kafka's tautological nihilism – by way of a lullaby of reassurance. The 'operativity criterion' talked of by Lyotard is enacted in reflexive modernisation as a pragmatic negation of metaphysics on the grounds that its concepts – truth, justice, freedom – are undecidable, and its insights unpalatable.

Like the reflexive modernisation thesis, Blair's programme of modernisation understands postmodern 'knowledge' as a stratum of unnegotiable truths. Thus for Blair the postmodern 'incredulity toward metanarratives' is translated into metaphysical freefall. The urge to recover social cohesion originates in a sense of desperation and panic, born of the perception that the liberation of man from his 'self-incurred tutelage', in Kant's famous phrase, is at the same time a licence for roasting babies and raping grandfathers. The market economy – an apparent inevitability, after the 'erasure' of the humanist criteria of value – in turn necessitates the forcible or deliberate construction of principles based on consensus, in order to limit its own relentless, ultimately destructive logic. Reflexive modernisation, as Beck describes it, is a condition in which modernity has 'consumed and lost its other'; reflexive modernisation is a stage of modernity which takes modernisation itself as the object of its own critique, a modality which appears at the present historical juncture as an indefinite adjournment of the exhausted premises of 'industrial' modernity.

For Beck, nationalism, fascism, ethnocentrism and violence remain possible – even logically defensible – responses to 'the fundamental experience of And' – responses that the strategy of preemptive action proposed by reflexive modernisation, however, is intended to foreclose. What such responses are *not*, he says, is 'the expression or eruption of suppressed atavism continuing to be a potent force behind the facades of civilisation.'[24] Rather, they are the inevitable and comprehensible effects of an industrialisation process whose premises have imploded. In such a thesis, modern society is understood to be completely liberated from all normative values and habits. H.G. Wells's final pessimistic reference to the modern world as 'our doomed formicary', in 1945, is the defeated vision which lies behind the desperate measures proposed by the reflexive modernisation thesis.[25] That the end of the world is imminent and will happen, without immediate and universal administrative action taken to restrict irresponsible, non-officiated action, is the message of the reflexive modernisation thesis, and it is easy to see how such a vision may function ideologically to sell us an agenda of imperative and unprecedented state legislation over the details of our lives.

The implication of the theory of postmodernity, in contrast to this, is that rationality – the motor of civilisation – is retained despite the difficulty of its interpretation and application. Fascism is a *lapse* from reason, notwithstanding the claims and even the beliefs of Nazis that the Third Reich was founded upon principles of rationality. Fascism is not an excuse for giving up on reason, or abandoning its expansive principles by reformulating it as self-reflexivity; fascism, rather, is a reminder of the necessity to ceaselessly interrogate and clarify *what reason is*. Fascism is irrational, and reactionary, because it excludes that gesture towards the absolutely new which is the essence of modernity.

Postmodernity is, therefore, this element of risk within rationality. Postmodernity is inseparable from the modern project, is presupposed by it, and in some sense precedes it. The postmodern, says Lyotard, would be 'that which, in the modern, puts forward the unpresentable in presentation itself'. In his most famous formulation he makes explicit its vanguard quality:

> The postmodern artist or writer is in the position of a philosopher: the text he writes, the work he produces, are not in principle governed by preestablished rules, and they cannot be judged by a determining judgement, by applying familiar categories to the text or to the work. Those rules and categories are what the work of art itself is looking for. The artist and the writer, then, are working without rules in order to formulate the rules of what *will have been done*. Hence the fact that work and text have the characters of an *event*; hence also, they always come too late for their author, or, what amounts to the same thing, their being put into work, their realisation (*mise en oeuvre*) always begin too soon. *Post modern* would have to be understood according to the paradox of the future (*post*) anterior (*modo*).[26]

According to this thesis therefore, 'the expression or eruption of suppressed atavism continuing to be a potent force behind the facades of civilisation' would be a perfectly accurate description of nationalist, fascist, and ethnocentrist responses to the uncertainties of living in a modern age. James Joyce, Franz Kafka, Walter Benjamin and even G.W.F. Hegel are postmodern writers before/inasmuch as they are modern ones, and they embody the very antithesis of fascism. Postmodern does not succeed modernity, nor is it the irrational or unfathomable metaphysical abyss at the heart of it. Postmodern, in fact, represents the moment of risk within rationality; it is inseparable from the expansionism of modernity, and from the perception of heterogeneity which is the motivation behind the modern project. To exclude the postmodern from modernity is to try to halt the project itself in the present; it is to fetishise 'reality', the world as it is, as if it were necessarily the endpoint of historical progress. Beck's diagnosis of the 'risk society', in which industrial modernisation is perceived to have proceeded to the point of self-exhaustion, is antithetical to the modernist impulse; in the modern world, as Marshall Berman writes, 'stability can only mean entropy, slow death, while our sense of progress and growth is our only way of knowing for sure that we are alive.' Thus, 'To say that our society is falling apart is only to say that it is alive and well.'[27] It is this truth which the reflexive modernisation thesis obliterates in its panicked urge to restore a 'lost' stability.

What postmodernity retains, and what reflexive modernisation junks, is a conceptual attachment to the importance of value. What postmodern theory does is retain truth, value, subjectivity, *in all their perplexity*, at precisely the point where the reflexive modernisation thesis obliviously discards these things as intractable. When Jean Baudrillard writes of the deterioration of all moral and conceptual stability, his position – albeit a disavowed one – is that of a *moralist*, releasing his charge against a society which has allowed the values of objective culture to triumph, through a combination of inattention and bad faith on the part of intellectuals and citizens:

> Everywhere we see the same 'genesis of simulacra': the commutability of the beautiful and the ugly in fashion, of the left and right in politics, of the true and the false in every media message, the useful and the useless at the level of objects, nature and culture at every level of signification. All the great humanist criteria of value, the whole civilisation of moral, aesthetic and practical judgement are effaced in our system of images and signs. Everything becomes undecidable, the characteristic effect of the domination of the code, which everywhere rests on the principle of neutralisation, of indifference.[28]

The postmodern diagnosis is not that this process is an inevitable one, given the finite resources of the earth, and the consequent limits to the potential expansion of industrial modernisation, but that it takes place at the purely conceptual level, signifying not the 'implosion' of rationality but a lapse from its rigorous demands. This breaking up of the grand narratives, writes Lyotard,

> leads to what some authors analyse in terms of the dissolution of the social bond and the disintegration of social aggregates into a mass of individual atoms thrown into the absurdity of Brownian motion. Nothing of the kind is happening: this point of view, it seems to me, is haunted by the paradisaic representation of a lost 'organic' society.[29]

Lyotard is alluding to Baudrillard; but his comments are more applicable to the theory of reflexive modernisation, a far more *drastic* diagnosis, insofar as the ideological certainties of the period of industrial modernisation are seen by Beck to have been superseded by an irrevocable phase of ideological uncertainty, which both confirms and is fully justified by the ontological 'exhaustion' of the premises of 'simple' modernity.

CYNICISM: BLAIR'S *BÊTE NOIRE*

No politician in recent years has talked as much about cynicism as Tony Blair: he returns to the term almost obsessively. 'It's easy to be cynical about local government,' he writes in the *Guardian*, before hailing local government as 'the lifeblood of our democracy.'[30] In an interview with the *Observer*, reiterating the need for the left to 'keep faith' with the government, he says: 'It is cynical rubbish to say we are going back on our promises ... The cynics said we would never take money off the utilities to fund the welfare-to-work programme – well, we have. Before the election cynics said you will never sign the Social Chapter – well, we have.'[31] Again, writing in the *Guardian* about the 'British success story', he declares: 'Cynics might say that promoting British designers or filmmakers is modish. I say these are the new entrepreneurs, the wealth creators, and deserve our backing.'[32] In an impromptu elaboration during his speech at a pre-election conference in March 1997, Blair enjoined delegates: 'Don't let the cynics win – those people who think that it doesn't make a difference which party you vote for. The only people who benefit from cynicism are the Tories. The Tories know it makes a difference – that's why they've been in power for 18 years.'[33] And after the election, at the Labour Party conference in October, he declared that, on 1 May, it wasn't just the Tories who were defeated, but also 'cynicism', along with 'fear of change', and fear itself.[34] Clearly 'cynicism' causes the prime minister a great deal of discomfort.

'Cynicism' in this context simply means resistance to Blair's 'modernising' revolution. Accusations of cynicism represent attempts to bludgeon political detractors with the injunction to participate. As Sarah Benton has written, the future of the left is monopolised by a single party leader: 'The price of refusing our fealty is to become an exile from this new political arrangement. If we don't sign up with Blair's party, who are we, politically?'[35] Given the present reading of 'modernisation' as conservative and in essence anti-modern, the most progressive political response to new Labour in the present circumstances would be exactly what Blair calls cynicism.

The injunction to 'participate', it seems, is greater than it has ever been before. New Britain, not merely new Labour, is an ideological envelope which contains many things: the 'discourse of inevitability' called globalisation; the acceleration of consumer culture, currently on an expanded recruitment drive with the appearance of supermarket clubcard schemes, customer charters and discount 'membership' plans for consumers of the privatised utilities; the National Lottery; the Internet, with which Blair has explicitly associated himself; the international spectre of the British cultural 'Renaissance' in fashion, art, music and film. We live in a 'media-saturated and technologically-crafted culture', writes Paul Smith, the most pressing objective of which is 'the conversion of non-working time into the self-perpetuating activity of consuming that time.'[36] The structure of mass participation is being cemented into place by means of a political relationship with technology which is *fetishistic*, which invokes the new in the very process of excluding it: technology functions as the most obvious signifier of progress, standing in for it in its absence. Far from providing an expanded range of options, consumer capitalism delimits choice by rigorously circumscribing it. 'While determining consumption it excludes the untried as a risk,' write Adorno and Horkheimer of the culture industry. 'What is new about the phase of mass culture compared with the late liberal stage is the exclusion of the new. The machine rotates on the same spot.'[37] By means of the Internet, globalisation (the instantaneous, worldwide transferability of capital), and the literal *recruitment* of consumers, the culture industry takes this project to a new dimension, effectively colonising the dimensions of time and space, and institutionalising an unprecedented level of resistance to the new.

In this spiralling chain of enforced complicity, even the subjective strategy of pure indifference, says Baudrillard, is anticipated and preempted by the superior indifference of the culture industry itself.[38] In 1994 Baudrillard recommended a strategy of 'hyper-indifference' in order to be able to think; a self-conscious refusal to be seduced into the reifying process of the world by exceeding that process; a replacement of Nietzsche's will to power by Andy Warhol's will to insignificance; a flight *into* the simulacrum, as opposed to a flight from it in pursuit of a lost reality.

Perhaps it was in this spirit that the French electorate voted Lionel Jospin's Socialist-Communist coalition into power in June 1997, on a ticket of explicit anti-modernisation. 'To the rest of the world,' wrote Ian Jack, 'which has accepted globalism as an inevitability, the way things are and will be, it seemed as though its fourth-largest economy had recoiled in the face of modernity; that Fortress France was pulling up the drawbridge.'[39] Jospin's victory was the occasion for several British journalistic reflections on the extent to which the French denial of 'reality', in the form of a refusal to 'modernise', to go down the path of economic neo-liberalism, might represent a more rather than less progressive politics. On one level, wrote George Walden in *Prospect*, you could say that France is in a sulk. In the face of an apparently global consensus that the social democratic 'mess and muzziness' of the 1970s has been replaced by the 'one true faith' of market economics, France has chosen a course of stubborn resistance to modernisation. The British reaction to the French economic malaise has consequently been less than sympathetic, as Walden ventriloquises: 'Thirteen per cent unemployed? Pension entitlements beyond the state's ability to pay? Inefficient nationalised industries? My poor deluded lambs, what can you have been thinking of? Does the word 'markets' mean absolutely nothing to you? Permit us to smile down, from the pagoda of our self-righteousness, while you reap as you have sown.'[40]

On the other hand, French hostility to consumerism might be read as defiant and adventurous, a rejection of the standard model of linear, technology-driven progress for one informed by a disrupted account of historical progress, and the postmodern awareness of the co-existability of incommensurable narratives. 'The benefits of linear optimism are beginning to seem uneven' says Walden:

> Why should anyone look forward to being normalised, their culture flattened, their livelihoods thrown around like packages in a sorting office and posted God knows where? Luddite, reactionary? No, just a mildly caricatured description of what many people in and outside France are feeling. What is reactionary is to see individuals as chaff in the economic wind, or as serfs to be harried hither and thither at the push of a button in the automated marketplace. Could it be that the French are taking a stand which – however doomed – reflects a wider disgruntlement with modernity ... ?[41]

In incarcerating into its national psyche an intransigent hostility to 'modernisation', France affirms its indifference to 'the world as it is', its attachment to politics of a purer, more 'brutal' sort, and its suspicion of the modernising attempt to 'feminise', or etherealise the political. 'In France,' says Walden, 'everything is at the extremes: Le Pen is trying to monopolise patriotism, and Jospin is forced to rely on the communists, who oppose the market.'

It is tempting to see France's intransigence as an effect of the privileged relationship which France has to postmodernism, and the embodiment of a progressive political negativism. The 'incommensurability of competing discourses' spoken of by Lyotard is preserved there in the antagonistic coexistence of communism and nationalism; French mental life seems disposed to contain just the kind of schizophrenic political situation the prospect of which so horrifies the Blair government. Yet its potential as a model for resisting, say, the global economy, or the erosion of ideological certainties, is belied by Lyotard's insistence on the danger of using the 'postmodern' as the basis for a political programme, with antagonism inscribed as a founding principle. This objection must be considered with reference to the British situation.

THE PROSPECTS FOR OPPOSITION

It is a common assertion in Britain that the Blairite pursuit of openness and collaboration signals the end of politics; that, in looking to the past rather than to the future, in spurning the progressive antagonism of the classical political model for a conservative ideology of consensus, politics is retreating from politics itself. Roy Hattersley complained in the *Guardian* that Blair was effectively 'taking the politics out of politics': 'We are all pragmatists now,' he affirms sardonically. 'The rejection of the conventional rules of party politics is not an advertising gimmick. It is the Prime Minister's vision of the good government which will create the good society.'[42] Hattersley's point is that Blair has few emotional or historical links with the 'old' party, nor, consequently, with the ideological 'baggage' which takes a commitment to social equality and redistribution as an article of faith. Blair's ministerial appointments have included a number of figures from outside the party – a demonstration, in Hattersley's view, of new Labour's preference for the 'open-minded flexibility of the ideologically footloose' over the 'tribal loyalties' of the party faithful. Other critics – among them Ross McKibbin, in a succession of articles for the *London Review of Books* – have written repeatedly of the depoliticising agenda of new Labour, pointing out that for Blair, 'values' have replaced specific policy commitments in the rhetoric of leadership, while the drive to consensus has replaced the natural confrontation of an earlier, more 'political' age.[43]

This claim, insofar as it expresses a nostalgia for old and imagined forms of politics, is actually closer to being a retreat from politics than the Blairite endorsements of organic forms of social existence – community, for example – which, since they are made in the public realm, cannot be anything but political. Even Blair's apparent preference for religion over politics is, unquestionably, absolutely political, and not in the least religious. By adorning itself with the rhetoric of apoliticism, politics ensures the continuity of politics. Today, writes Zizek, 'emphasising the depoliticised "objective" economic logic against the allegedly "outdated" forms of ideological passions is *the* predominant ideological form, since ideology is always self-referential, that is, it always defines itself through a distance towards an Other dismissed and denounced as "ideological".'[44]

The implications of this are that the French intransigence is both unnecessary for the preservation of politics, and fundamentally unreliable as a guide to the options facing radical politics in Britain. Zizek points out that the cultivation of particularity, in the form of 'postmodern' racism and/or communism, such as is represented in the French 'extremism', is indissociable from the universal dimension of the world market, since it occurs as a reaction to it, is mediated by it, and takes place therefore against its background and on its terrain. Far from signalling a viable alternative to 'modernisation', the French belligerence merely confirms the fact that 'the loss of organic-substantial unity is fully consummated.'[45] The existence of Jean-Marie Le Pen's National Front, for example, is a refraction of the repressed Other of modernisation, its violent horror bringing to light 'the inherent contradiction of the liberal-democratic ideological project', and, furthermore, indicating that 'beneath the crust of its own mythology, France has already changed.'[46] France, it would be more accurate to say, has *always already* changed. While Baudrillard at times reminisces over 'a different, convulsive, contradictory world, a world with issues and passions',[47] the insight of those theorists associated with postmodernity – that a metaphysical abyss underlies the veneer of liberal democracy – is also an indication of the essential untenability of any theory of the 'end' of politics. Politics is in no danger from the Blairite attempt to 'transcend' the political. Rather, Blair's 'modernisation' signifies the continuing operation of the political at the level of the symbolic; 'modernisation' is a pure signifier, having as little to do with modernity as Thatcher's 'freedom of choice' had to do with either freedom or choice. 'Modernisation' gestures towards the end of politics and, in so doing, confirms the continuity of ideological politics.

The machine, as Adorno and Horkheimer said, rotates on the same spot. The material of new Labour modernisation – the preoccupation with cutting 'state bureaucracy', the attempt to engineer a new working relationship between parents and teachers, the enthusiastic embrace of new technology, even the proposal to 'extend the rights of royal succession to women' – represents the cultivation of differences which, in Zizek's words, 'leave the basic homogeneity of the capitalist world system intact'.[48] The abyss at the heart of new Labour is, precisely, a metaphysical absence, which is filled by nothing more profound than the global logic of capital. 'The true horror does not reside in the particular content hidden beneath the universality of global capital, but rather in the fact that capital is effectively an anonymous global machine blindly running its course, that there is effectively no particular secret agent who animates it.'[49] Yet the attempt to return to a political fullness, a perceived eroded political space, is fundamentally misguided. Such a political space has not simply been rendered untenable by globalisation; in postmodernity the 'loss' of the political, like the 'loss' of reality, has *always already* taken place – there is no question of a return, since there is no question of an origin. Politics takes place and has always taken place in the circumstances of that loss, seeking to restore that loss, but with no possibility of doing so. Thus politics labours under a peculiar imperative – that of refusing 'the world as it is'. This refusal cannot take place anywhere but in the context of the existing world. Splenetic fury, however articulate, from a position outside the existing world (the activities of the 'Unabomber', for example) is not politics; the lesson of postmodernity is that new Labour, like global capitalism, must and will produce the circumstances of its own political critique.

New Labour, notwithstanding its apolitical rhetoric, does not signify the end of politics, just as global capitalism does not signify the final homogenisation of culture, despite its ability to appropriate whatever initially parades outside it. Cultural preciosity is the always-belated urge to shut the door dividing art from commerce after the work of art has bolted; cultural preciosity can never be anything but belated. Likewise, the attempt to recuperate 'the political' is by definition a belated, antipolitical and reactionary impulse. New Labour modernisation, including the pockets of resistance to it, confirms the hegemony of global capitalism as irrevocably sundered from the perceived unity of the past; most important, however, is the recognition that this sundering has always already taken place. Derrida's *Il n'y a pas de hors-texte* – 'there is nothing outside the text' (or 'there is no outside text') – applies equally to the ideological inscriptions of new Labour and the materialistic levelling of a world inscribed within a money economy. This insight does not prohibit the possibility of oppositional politics, which is to be found precisely in the 'unconstructive' response to it. If the solitary projects of a Montana backwoodsman are politically regressive, so are the earnest exertions towards a 'positive engagement' made by the intellectual left.

A politics of opposition already exists. Schizophrenia, write Deleuze and Guattari, 'is not the identity of capitalism, but on the contrary its difference, its divergence, and its death. Monetary flows are perfectly schizophrenic realities, but they exist and function only within the immanent axiomatic that exorcises and repels this reality.'[50] New Labour provides the 'monetary flows' of global capital with an 'axiomatic' which disavows the essential hollowness with a rhetoric of consensus, inevitability, community and reflexivity. By subscribing to these myths – by the futile search for a mode of 'constructive criticism', for example – the left are complicit in the ideology of the end of politics. The abyss itself is the truth; the ambivalence of the electoral body, in the form of an underlying indifference towards the 'modernising' hegemony, is the expression of a far more profound political insight. It is here that the germ of a present and future oppositional politics is to be found; it is quite as political, and indeed ideological, as the government agenda it discards.

The widespread mistrust of Blair's rhetoric, combined with an acceptance of the 'inevitability' of globalisation; the recognition of the ideological nature of Blair's appeal to modernity, combined with the apathy and indifference characterising the predominant response to it – these are the particular inflexions given the 'schizophrenia' of the postmodern subject under new Labour. Postmodern knowledge justifies the suggestion that scepticism, radical mental dislocation and even disinterest are not merely defensible but obligatory responses to an ideological agenda primed for the enforcement of an already existing political consensus. These responses can and will provide the impetus for a progressive political intervention prepared to annihilate the present on the grounds, merely, that the present is not good enough.

I am grateful to Matt Jordan for his comments on an earlier draft of this chapter.

NOTES

1. Jon Henley, 'Euclidean, Spinozist or existentialist? Er, no. It's simply a load of old tosh', *Guardian*, 1.10.97.
2. Peter Osborne (political editor of the *Daily Express*), speaking on Medium *Wave*, BBC Radio 4, 12.10.97; Michael White, 'Hattersley and Benn are out of touch', *Guardian*, 28.7.97.
3. Colin Byrne, a former Chief Press Officer for the Labour Party, made explicit this necessity, while disavowing the phrase 'modernise or die' on behalf of the Labour Party. 'I don't think it would be as crude as picking up a telephone and saying, "Look, pull your socks up, because it's modernise or die"; but I think there are an awful lot of lessons to be learned from the way Tony Blair has reinvented the Labour Party and the Labour Government in tune with the times. And if people can't read those messages then they really are missing a trick. The message is quite clear for the Royal Family – that modernisation is not an option, it's got to happen or they risk what would have happened to the Labour Party if it had stayed stuck in *its* old traditions', *Panorama*, 'The People's Monarchy?', BBC1, 17.11.97.
4. Geoff Mulgan, *Connexity: How to Live in a Connected World*, London: Chatto & Windus, London 1997.
5. Raymond Williams, *Keywords: A Vocabulary of Culture and Society*, Fontana, London 1976, p174.
6. Andrew Rawnsley, 'Tony Blair's new Church of Modernity', *The Observer* 14.9.97.
7. Tony Blair, 'Ideological Blurring', *Prospect*, June 1996.
8. Doreen Massey, 'Editorial: Problems with Globalisation', *Soundings* Issue 7 (Autumn 1997), p8.
9. Paul Smith, *Millennial Dreams: Contemporary Culture and Capital in the North*, Verso, London 1997, pp10, 11.
10. Sarah Benton, 'Knights Against the Nightmares', *Soundings* Issue 2 (Spring 1996), p19.
11. Niccolò Machiavelli, *The Prince*, trans. George Bull, Penguin, Harmondsworth 1961, p101.
12. Slavoj Zizek, 'Multiculturalism, or, the Cultural Logic of Multinational Capitalism', *New Left Review* 225 (September/October 1997), p30.
13. This pre-millennial theme was first broached during Blair's speech at the 1996 Labour Party conference: 'A thousand days to prepare for a thousand years', he said of the period between the forthcoming election and the new millennium. 'Not just turning a page in history but writing a new book … '

14. Hugo Young, 'No place for cynics in the Blair new world', *Guardian*, 4.4.97.

15. Samuel Beckett, *Murphy*, Calder, London 1993, p27.

16. See David Denver, 'The results: how Britain voted', in Anthony Geddes and Jonathan Tonge (eds), *Labour's Landslide: The British General Election 1997*, Manchester University Press, Manchester and New York 1997. Denver points out that the decline in turnout between 1992 and 1997 was the largest recorded in the post-war period and, further, that the turnout was 'lowest of all and fell most sharply in Labour areas' (p19).

17. Fredric Jameson, 'Postmodernism, or The Cultural Logic of Late Capitalism', *New Left Review* 146 (July/August 1984), p72.

18. Gilles Deleuze and Félix Guattari, *Anti-Oedipus: Capitalism and Schizophrenia*, trans. Robert Hurley, Mark Seem, Helen R. Lane, Athlone, London 1984, p247.

19. Jonathan Meades, 'Come on down to Toni's', *The Observer* 5.10.97.

20. Gilles Deleuze and Flix Guattari, *Anti-Oedipus: Capitalism and Schizophrenia*, op. cit., p246.

21. See Ulrich Beck, *The Reinvention of Politics: Rethinking Modernity in the Global Social Order*, Polity, Cambridge 1997, p14.

22. Jean-François Lyotard, *The Postmodern Condition: A Report on Knowledge*, trans. Geoff Bennington and Brian Massumi, Manchester University Press, Manchester 1984, pxxiv.

23. *Ibid.*, pxxv.

24. Ulrich Beck, *The Reinvention of Politics*, op. cit., p6.

25. H.G. Wells, *Mind at the End of its Tether*, in *The Last Books of H.G. Wells*, The H.G. Wells Society. London 1968, p77.

26. Jean-François Lyotard, op. cit., p81.

27. Marshall Berman, *All That Is Solid Melts Into Air: The Experience of Modernity*, Verso, London 1983, p95.

28. Jean Baudrillard, *Symbolic Exchange and Death*, trans. Iain Hamilton Grant, Sage, London 1993, pp8-9.

29. Jean-Francois Lyotard, op. cit., p15.

30. Tony Blair, 'Next on the list: clean up the councils', The *Guardian*, 3.11.97.

31. *The Observer*, 23.11.97.

32. Tony Blair, 'Britain can remake it', The *Guardian* 22.7.97.

33. Nexus/Guardian conference: 'Passing the Torch', LSE 1.3.97. 'Nexus', said Blair pointedly in his opening, 'is made up of people who are free from cynicism without being naive.'

34. 'Blair calls for age of giving', The *Guardian* 1.10.97.

35. Sarah Benton, 'Knights Against the Nightmares', op. cit. p23.

36. Paul Smith, *op. cit.*, p. 201.
37. Theodor Adorno and Max Horkheimer, *Dialectic of Enlightenment*, trans. John Cumming, Verso, London 1979, p134.
38. Jean Baudrillard, *The Perfect Crime*, trans. Chris Turner, Verso, London 1996, p102.
39. Ian Jack, 'Editorial', *Granta* 59 (Autumn 1997) France, p10.
40. George Walden, 'France says no', *Prospect* Issue 23 (October 1997).
41. *Ibid.*
42. Roy Hattersley, *Guardian* 14.5.97.
43. See in particular Ross McKibbin, 'If/when Labour gets in … ', *London Review of Books*, Vol. 18 No. 4 (22.2.96).
44. Slavoj Zizek, 'Multiculturalism, or, the Cultural Logic of Multinational Capitalism', *op. cit.*, p37.
45. *Ibid.*, p. 42.
46. Ian Jack, 'Editorial', *Granta* 59, *op. cit.*, p11.
47. Jean Baudrillard, *The Perfect Crime*, *op. cit.*, p102.
48. Slavoj Zizek, 'Multiculturalism, or, the Cultural Logic of Multinational Capitalism', *op. cit.*, p46.
49. *Ibid.*, p45.
50. Gilles Deleuze and Félix Guattari, *Anti-Oedipus: Capitalism and Schizophrenia*, *op. cit.*, p246.

SECTION FIVE:
DEFINITELY, MAYBE – THE UNCERTAIN FUTURE OF POLITICS

THE DIARY OF NEW LABOUR MP STEPHEN TWIGG, AGED 31¼

Enfield Southgate has long been regarded as a safe Conservative constituency. In 1984 Michael Portillo was elected as the local MP in a by-election; Labour came a distant third with just 4000 votes. Despite a large and active local Party membership, Labour in Southgate is used to helping out our neighbouring seats when a General Election is called.

By this I mean firstly knocking on doors and asking if we can rely on the occupant's vote on Election Day. Under Millbank orders we now refer to this activity as Voter Identification. Secondly, we deliver Party leaflets, and thirdly we do both of these but in a concentrated geographical area.

1997 is no exception for Enfield Southgate's active members: most are away voter ID-ing in Edmonton, a Tory seat with a majority of just 500, which has to be won if Labour is to form a government. It would be nice for the longstanding activists to spend some time doing voter ID in Enfield Southgate for a change, but this is just not an option.

As the candidate, I have retained a small but enthusiastic team of helpers. For the first month of the campaign, we leaflet tube and rail stations, hold street stalls and put out an introductory letter from me. About a week before polling day, I am contacted by a student who has the choice of voting in Southgate or in the key Tory marginal of Leeds North East where he is studying. I have no hesitation in advising him to vote in Leeds!

It is not until the final weekend of the campaign that things really take off. A friend calls to tell me that the *Observer* has a poll putting Michael Portillo just four points ahead of me and an editorial urging

213

Liberal Democrats to vote Labour in Enfield Southgate. At our campaign meeting we agree to put out a leaflet highlighting the poll result which points out that only Labour can beat the Tories in Southgate. I spend the afternoon leafleting before joining my opponents for the one and only candidates' debate of the campaign.

Our message, hastily arranged on quickly printed leaflets, reads 'Only Labour can beat the Tories in Enfield Southgate. If you want Portillo OUT only a LABOUR vote will count!' The telephone does not stop ringing with offers of help. I am joined by TV crews from Spain and Japan. The mood generally is that we are witnessing a surge of support but that Michael Portillo will probably hold the seat.

I am blitzing the key marginal Oakwood ward when Judith Church MP joins us. She pleads with us not to tell anyone she is here because she is breaching the Party's key seat strategy. Labour Campaign strategists insist all activists must go to winnable Edmonton and are told not to waste their time on hopeless seats like mine. But the response on the doorstep is more akin to a traditional Labour stronghold than a safe Tory seat. In Oakwood, my leaflet is going down a treat. Several calls from Liberal Democrat supporters pledging their votes to Labour. A few aides to Tony Blair and Gordon Brown turn up to leaflet and tell us they don't think we will win. Judith Church is so inspired by the previous day that she turns up for more blitzing the next day.

THURSDAY 1 MAY – THE DAY OF THE GENERAL ELECTION, ENFIELD SOUTHGATE

A glorious sunny day. The Labour support is strong as always in Palmers Green, Arnos Grove and Bowes Park in the south of the constituency. These are suburban areas with a substantial Greek Cypriot community, a sizeable Turkish-speaking community and a growing Asian population.

The difference at this election is that we are now receiving support in the north of the constituency. In areas that have never been canvassed by the Labour Party, people are coming out of their front doors to take posters from us. These are affluent districts of North London – Hadley Wood, Winchmore Hill and Grange Park – as yet uncharted by the Labour Party. One man stops us and asks for a Labour poster for his Porsche.

Helpers turn up from all over the place. There is a carnival atmosphere in Palmers Green with red balloons and Labour posters everywhere. I meet a man walking down the High Street, his head barely visible over a stock of blank video-tapes still fresh in their cellophane. 'I want to savour the moment of each one of them going down, one by one, again and again and again', he says. I visit polling stations, tour the constituency with a megaphone and soak up the atmosphere. The polls close at 10 p.m. The general feeling is that we put up a brilliant fight but the Conservatives will cling on to the seat.

FRIDAY 2 MAY – THE COUNT, LEE VALLEY LEISURE CENTRE, ENFIELD

The count is nerve-racking. About two thirds of the way through it becomes clear that I am ahead. Shortly afterwards, Michael Portillo arrives smiling and says to me: 'You must be devastated!' I find out that I have won before the announcement of the results, but it does not sink in. Portillo now looks agitated and uncomfortable but acts graciously. The returning officer finally calls the candidates. 'Everybody happy?' he asks. 'Ecstatic!' says Portillo.

I am certainly stunned. I deliver an acceptance speech that I had only dreamt I would ever get to make. I thank those who voted Labour through the difficult years and the thousands of first-time voters. The thousands who switched from the Conservatives and the many Liberal Democrats who set aside their national preference and voted tactically for Labour to ensure a non-Conservative victory. I pay tribute to them all and to those people who did not vote for me and pledge to serve them just the same.

After that, I do a round of media interviews, go to our local celebration at the Grape Vine restaurant and then on to the Royal Festival Hall to join Labour's national victory party, where I am paraded shoulder high. I feel like one of the Spice Girls.

It takes some time to come down to Earth after the momentous events of 1 and 2 May. The last time Labour had won a convincing General Election victory was in 1966, the year I was born. For me, there is a special poignancy in being the first ever Labour MP for the area that I come from and was brought up in.

There are many reasons why we won seats like mine. In Southgate I benefited from the overwhelming support of the Cypriot community, a very significant swing to Labour in the Jewish community and the enthusiastic votes of young first time voters. The single overriding reason, though, was that voters felt they could trust new Labour in general and Tony Blair in particular.

WEDNESDAY 7 MAY – FIRST DAY IN PARLIAMENT

Labour MPs, long serving and newly elected, descend on Westminster. Lots of congratulations, back slapping and air kissing: this really is new Labour!

Good to see Lorna Fitzsimons, one of my best friends from National Union of Students days, who is now MP for her home town, Rochdale. There are so many Labour MPs that we have to meet at Church House because no room big enough is available in the Commons. Tony Blair addresses us.

I later decide to wander about the Commons. I was in here many times when I was a researcher, only now the police call me 'Sir' and I can go anywhere I like.

I meet a high-ranking pro-European Conservative MP in the Central Lobby. He comes up to me smiling, arms stretched out. 'Thank you so much!' he says very pointedly and puts his arms around me.

I then meet a fellow back bench Labour MP who is very much on the left of my own Party and who also comes up to congratulate me.

'I want to say congratulations for what you did.' she says. 'Thank you'.

'And that's the last nice thing I will ever say to you'. She turns on her heel and promptly walks off.

Later I find an anonymous hand-written note in my pigeon hole. It is written on House of Commons headed note paper, possibly from a Tory MP; I don't know. It reads cryptically: 'You don't know what you have done to the future of the Conservative Party and indeed of British democracy.

The sheer volume of post I have already received is overwhelming. Not only letters of support, of which there are thousands, but also hundreds of letters from constituents seeking my help. I get the impression that Enfield Southgate has being yearning for an active constituency MP for some time.

The perceived absenteeism of Michael Portillo in the constituency and his inability to take a stand on several key local issues played no small part in my victory. It is true that an appointment into government limits the time an MP can spend in his or her constituency. Michael Portillo was no exception. However, the problem was that Portillo was perceived by local people to be not the remotest bit interested in local matters.

There was also a complete meltdown in the Conservative campaigning machine in Enfield Southgate. The proposal to sell the Southgate Conservative Association building in Winchmore Hill for development as a Drive-Thru McDonalds became symbolic of the total breakdown in communication between local Tories and the people of Southgate. The Tories couldn't care less and Michael Portillo sat on the fence and did nothing.

I don't intend to make the same mistake. No matter the trappings of office, an MP is still accountable to that particular group of people who live in a proximate geographical area and who comprise his or her constituents. It is sobering to think that the Prime Minister can be thrown out by the people of Sedgefield alone, irrespective of his place on the world stage.

Portillo was not really that bad an MP. I have heard of worse. The Tories lost across the board on 1 May. Conscientious Tory MPs lost as many seats as lazy Tory MPs. Europhobes and Europhiles, wets or Thatcherites, the infamous and the unknown, they all fell under the march of new Labour.

The challenge for me in Enfield Southgate is to get those people who would have voted Liberal Democrat but who voted Labour tactically, and those Tory voters who voted Labour for the first time on 1 May, to remain principled Labour voters in 2001 or 2002.

I must answer some of my post. The first problem is that I am provided with no means whatsoever to do this simple task. There is very little you can do to change the world in this day and age if you do not have a phone or a fax at your place of work and I don't even have a desk! Still the letters and telephone messages pile up. I cannot reply to most of them. So much for wanting to be accessible to my constituents.

The powers that be tell me that I will have to wait. Obviously the interests of 70,000 constituents are second to the procedures of the Clerk to the Room Allocations Sub-Committee. On the campaign trail I had no problem communicating with the electorate. Now it is not so easy.

I had worked as a research assistant to Margaret Hodge MP, my fellow ward councillor in Islington who entered Parliament in a by-election in 1994, so I know how difficult it is for a new MP to set up a Westminster office. What I only appreciate now, is that Members *really* do not get enough assistance from the authorities at Westminster – and it is so frustrating!

First off I establish weekly surgeries. I hold four surgeries a month at public libraries dotted around the constituency. Many constituents come to see me. Usually twenty to thirty per surgery. This means that although I allocate two hours for a surgery, we frequently overrun by three hours or more.

The issues my constituents raise form a mixed bag. Planning applications, housing and school places figure highly. Immigration and asylum less so, but still account for a significant proportion of my case work. As an MP, you are aware of the trust people place in you to make a real difference to their lives. The first surgery is mobbed but hugely enjoyable. People are very happy to see their MP actually doing the surgery himself.

Next, my colleague Joan Ryan (newly elected MP for neighbouring Enfield North) and I are awarded a large room overlooking Westminster Bridge and the Thames.

I advertise in the *New Statesman* for two assistants. I offer what I consider to be a reasonable salary. I am later collared by a fellow MP who tells me I am proposing to pay my staff far too much and this is causing other researchers to demand a living wage from their employer. I tell fellow MP to mind his own business. I receive over 400 applications in one week, a considerable addition to my post-bag. I spend the day with Tim, Chair of Enfield Southgate Labour Party, interviewing twelve short-listed candidates.

I appoint Joan, an experienced House of Commons secretary who lives in Enfield Southgate, as my caseworker and Richard, a former solicitor and campaigner in the voluntary sector, as my political assistant. Together they begin the hard slog of answering the thousands of letters, running my diary, responding to emergency cases such as that of the constituent whose husband is being deported, and filing the less important letters sent to all MPs which start something like: 'It is with great pleasure that I enclose the annual report and accounts of the Allied Cement Mixers' Association'.

FRIDAY 11 JULY – YOUNG LABOUR CONFERENCE, BOURNEMOUTH.

I have been invited to speak at the Young Labour Conference in Bournemouth. I am speaking in the opening plenary alongside Gordon Brown.

Several of the 1997 new intake of Labour MPs are younger than I am. At 30, I am positively middle aged, but I accept the invitation to speak regardless and am very pleased to see a young woman from my constituency, Sarah Ward, elected as the Youth Representative on the National Executive.

When I was young, and a member of the Labour Party youth section, then known as the 'Young Socialists', you were considered right-wing and dangerous for reading the *Guardian*. Things have changed a lot since those days. Sitting at the platform, I see a young person in pin-stripes reading the *Financial Times*. A frog chorus of mobile phones and pagers chirps through my speech.

I start by saying that someone had said to me beforehand that this government will lose the trust of young people if we continue to do so-called anti youth things like implementing curfews, banning alco-pops, setting homework targets or forcing young unemployed people into welfare to work. I highlight Labour's excellent result among young voters. We are for young people's right to live without the fear of crime. We are also for young people's right to a decent education and to training and skills. Young people, like all people, deserve these rights.

I say that the experience of being an MP has convinced me that as a government we need to focus on creating opportunities for young people, and particularly young black people, who are concentrated in our inner city areas. Many, through a combination of the culture of social exclusion and racial discrimination, currently have few opportunities available to them. I also talk about young people who are so marginalised and disillusioned by what their country has to offer them that they believe they have nothing to offer society and their community.

The next step is to reach out to these young people and show them that they have a stake in the future prosperity of this country. This culture of exclusion may explain why so many young people and specifically so many young black people saw no point in voting, or even registering to vote, on 1 May.

As a younger Member of Parliament, I have a particular interest in reconnecting young people with the political process. I have never accepted the widely-held idea that these days most young people are apathetic and not interested in politics.

As General Secretary of the Fabian Society, I was involved in a research project working with young first time voters, talking to them about their attitudes and opinions. What the research showed very clearly is that young people have strong opinions. They are as concerned about education, crime, health and employment as are other age groups. They also have concerns about traditional youth issues such as the environment, drugs and higher education. What young people reject is not politics itself, but the way we do politics in this country: the style, the language and, above all, the adversarial culture.

The problem at the last election was not that so many young people did not vote Labour, but that so many young people did not vote at all. We have to connect with those who are disconnected to show them that politics can make a real difference. I close my speech by saying that if the New Deal is a practical means of showing that policies coming from the top can make a real difference to the lives of young people below, then I believe the implementation of the New Deal will not only restore some young people's faith in politicians, it will for some young people be the first time they have ever made a connection between politics and their own lives.

Waheed Ali, Chief Executive of Planet 24 and Margaret McDonagh, Campaigns Director at No.10, then give a presentation on how Labour won the youth vote. D:Ream's *Things Can Only Get Better* accompanies the presentation. Richard, my researcher, whispers he will scream if hears that bloody D:Ream record again. The morning session ends and we are played out of the conference hall by ... D:Ream's *Things Can only Get Better*.

SATURDAY 7 JULY – GAY PRIDE FESTIVAL, LONDON

I go to Pride with a bunch of my closest friends. There must have been 300,000 people on the march. For the first time I can remember the marchers cheer as we pass Downing Street. Later Chris Smith and I address the crowds assembled at the Pride festival at Clapham Common.

As an MP who is honest about his sexuality, I am expected by the lesbian and gay community to speak out on issues of concern to them.

This inevitably leads some colleagues to warn me against being pigeon-holed as 'the gay MP'. I do not worry about this. Chris Smith was able to come out without being sidelined and continues to be a credible MP on plenty of other issues. I feel a strong duty to represent the wider lesbian and gay constituency because an issue such as equal age of consent is a simple equality issue: justify yourself for being in the Labour Party if you don't believe that! Since becoming an MP I have agreed to become Patron of Body Positive and Richmond and Kingston AIDS Project. I am also Patron of the Albert Kennedy Trust, a group that helps young gay men and women who have been thrown out of their homes to find appropriate foster families.

The secret is to hit the right balance. As long as I work hard in my constituency and represent all groups who seek my time, I do not believe I have much to fear. My sexuality was never an issue on the doorsteps of Enfield Southgate, indeed people who did mention it expressed their approval of my honesty. There is a great expectation within the gay community for the Government to legislate for equality. The presence in the House of openly gay MPs, such as Ben Bradshaw and myself, has certainly heightened the expectation for change.

Some gay activists are already critical of the Government because of its policy of allowing a free vote on the age of consent. What many would like is for an equal age of consent to be government policy and whipped accordingly. Privately, this is a view with which I am not unsympathetic. However, my job as a supportive MP is to stress the importance of gaining equality through winning hearts and minds of MPs. I want to see as many MPs support equality as possible. I have always believed that achieving equality should not be the work only of Labour MPs and the Labour government. Equality should not be a one party issue and it is very important that equality is won on a cross party basis.

Much has changed since the issue was last debated. I recall that the most eloquent speech in favour of equality came from Labour's then Home Affairs spokesperson, Tony Blair. I'm glad we now have a Prime Minister and a cabinet who back sexual equality. The overwhelming majority of Labour MPs – many of whom make up the new 1997 intake – are also supportive. And of course with Chris Smith, we have the first openly gay member of the cabinet.

A commitment to equality is now one of the values of the political mainstream in this country. A politician's attitude to lesbian and gay equality is now one of those issues seen by many people, and especially by younger people, as a yardstick of how in touch that politician is with modern society. I therefore welcome the sentiments in favour of equality made by William Hague since he won the leadership of the Conservative Party: let's just hope he can bring the majority of his party with him.

TUESDAY 19 AUGUST – THE DEARING REPORT IS PUBLISHED

My background in student politics in the early 1990s means that I am very much aware of the difficulties experienced by students who are funding their way through college and university. I am therefore targeted by interviewers for comments on the Government's response to Lord Dearing's report on the future funding of higher education.

I also receive many letters from young people about to commence a course in higher education, who are genuinely concerned about their future. I believe, and have always believed, that we need to ensure that everybody – whatever his or her age or background – has access to life-long learning. I have always stressed that access to higher education should not depend upon ability to pay. The last decade has been a period of dramatic change and growth in higher education, with the number of full time students increasing by almost 70 per cent between 1989 and 1995. That was a positive change and the sort of revolution in higher education that I wanted to see when I was President of the National Union of Students from 1990-92.

However, I am also aware that this welcome growth has put a massive strain on university and college resources. And the increase in numbers has not altered the social mix of the population going into higher education – young people from poorer backgrounds are still vastly under represented in higher education.

I therefore recognise that finance for positive programmes to encourage more young people from disadvantaged backgrounds to go into higher education has got to come from somewhere. With this in mind, I don't mind admitting publicly that I see no alternative to the Government's proposal of an annual tuition fee of up to £1000, representing about a quarter of the average cost of a course and that maintenance should be funded for every student through loans. After all, no student will have to pay back a loan until after they have graduated and are earning a sufficient salary. I stress in all my correspondence and interviews on the matter that no parents will be paying more under the new system than they did under the old.

What the press wittingly or unwittingly misses is that the Government's proposals specifically exempt students from lower income families from paying the £1000 contribution to tuition fees. And those who under the old system were entitled to a maintenance grant will still be entitled to a larger loan, equivalent to the old grant plus the old student loan. In addition there will be a hardship grant available, of £250 per year.

The new era will see the expansion of access to education, among all social groups. Against this background it seems to me fair that those who benefit personally from higher education should be required to pay something towards it. The most urgent educational priority is for extra money to go into primary and early years' education. The Government and universities and colleges face a stark choice – introduce a charge for tuition or stop expanding higher education. For progressives that's no choice: expand, yes please!

Fees are in place in Germany, in the United States, in France and in Japan, and have been for a very long time. In those countries a greater percentage of young people go into higher education and of these a larger number are from lower-income backgrounds.

Also there are safeguards in this legislation to prevent future governments from raising the fee contribution. Young people would be poorly advised to choose not to go to university because of the Government's proposals. After all, graduates earn substantially more through their lifetime and have far more opportunities available to them than people who do not enjoy a university education.

FRIDAY 3 OCTOBER – THE END OF THE LABOUR PARTY CONFERENCE, BRIGHTON

One thing I do not find easy to cope with is the fact I am now being watched like a hawk. I am being followed around Party Conference by ITN for their 'And Finally' slot at the end of Friday's *News At Ten*. The idea is to film me relaxing at Conference, so I am filmed sliding down a helter-skelter. They also followed me walking down the street, in the Conference hall and at the fringes. Plus I am being filmed by the BBC for a documentary called *Class of 97*, a fly-on-the-wall documentary that is following five newly elected MPs in their first six months.

Oona King MP, who is also being filmed, is ill with tonsillitis so the BBC concentrated most of their considerable efforts on me.

I can't walk anywhere without being recognised. People who have never met me come up and say the nicest things. The problem is that I am getting nowhere fast. I have been stopped in my tracks hundreds of times each day! The publication of Brian Cathcart's book *Were You Still Up For Portillo?* this Wednesday, with a picture of yours truly on the front cover, means that those people who before just wanted to stop and congratulate me are suddenly armed with copies of the book, which they ask me to sign. Queues of well-wishers form as I sign away.

Richard shields me from people I don't want to see. He sorts out my diary, and my life generally. All week he has affected a very convincing passive smile which he uses when I am accosted by well-wishers. However after well-wisher number forty today, I think I saw his smile drop a little.

The week has been very business-like and celebratory without being triumphalist. I was called to the platform to speak in favour of the Party in Power proposals. Robin Cook introduces me to conference as 'the man who beat Portillo' which whips the delegates up to a standing ovation – more books to sign – thanks, Robin.

I am on the train home now and I just want to fade into the background and not be recognised for a few days.

FRIDAY 28 NOVEMBER – THE FOX HUNTING BILL REACHES ITS SECOND READING

I don't usually attend the House on Fridays, preferring to spend the day in the constituency. Being here I note that Fridays are rather like non-uniform days we had at school. The tradition is to turn up in country attire. Longer-serving members, especially the Tories, tend to wear country tweeds. My researcher, who resents my presence because he is used to having the office to himself, gets into the Friday feeling and is wearing trainers, jeans and an earring. I don't remember Margaret Hodge letting me dress that casually when I was a researcher.

I asked Joan to cancel all my appointments today so that I can be at Westminster to vote on the second reading of Michael Foster's Bill. The large number of letters I have received from constituents in support of Michael's Bill is astounding – more than 500 in favour. The opponents of the Bill, mainly Tories, are filibustering. Of course these tactics could not succeed if the Bill had government time. Whilst I accept that the Government has delivered on its manifesto commitment to allow a free vote on fox hunting, I would much prefer the Government to give Michael's Bill time.

Yes, I know that we have a very heavy timetable and that our key pledges on crime, education, devolution and health have priority. However, I feel that the overwhelming majority of people will not understand that the Government cannot give this Bill time, especially when we have had such a long summer recess! The electorate rightly have higher expectations of a Party elected on a platform of modernisation and reform.

I have received a letter from a Labour Party member who threatens to resign unless Michael's Bill is passed. Her point is that the free-vote pledge given by the Labour Party gave the impression that it would outlaw bloodsports. I have to defend the Government's position whilst ensuring her continuing support.

I write:

> Michael Foster MP, the sponsor of the Wild Mammals (Hunting with Dogs) Bill chose to raise the issue of hunting with hounds in his Private Members Bill when he came top of the ballot in June. After the second reading this week, the Bill will proceed to Committee and come back to the floor of the House of Commons at Report Stage. Opponents of the Bill can then use simple procedural tactics to scupper the Bill in the Commons.
>
> If the Bill does reach the House of Lords, there is a massive Conservative majority over the government, and according to all estimates a very large majority are in favour of fox hunting. The make up of the House of Lords at present is 499 Conservatives, of which 326 are hereditary peers and only 158 Labour, of which 15 are hereditary peers. The Lords controls its own time and opponents have threatened to delay all other government business.
>
> The government has one of the heaviest sets of legislative proposals since the Second World War – including legislation to reduce class sizes, action on young offenders and getting young people off welfare and into work. The Lords could devote substantial time to protracted discussion on a Bill that they can kill off anyway.
>
> I have received over 500 letters from constituents on this issue and I intend to vote in favour of Michael's Bill. I know that a majority of my colleagues will do likewise. It is to be hoped that a large majority in favour of the Bill will make opponents respect public and parliamentary

opinion, and they will not use procedural tactics to thwart the Bill. I have
every hope that Michael's bill will become law.

In a tray again piled high, I note a letter from a constituent urging me to vote against the Bill. This brings the total number of pro-hunting letters I have received from constituents to five.

Sitting at my desk waiting for the Division I write another letter.

Thank you for your letter, which I read with interest.

The Countryside Rally in Hyde Park was not a pro hunting rally although many in the pro hunt lobby would like us to think so. Very many people attended the Rally for other concerns about the future of rural life. In any case, the numbers who turned up that day are not as significant as the support of 75 per cent of the British people who back Michael Foster's Bill.

Hunting is not an integral part of the rural economy. There are very many parts of the UK which have no hunting and have not had hunting for very many years. The primary purpose of most forms of hunting with dogs is to give pleasure and enjoyment to the so-called sports participants. It is not effective management and control of certain species that may threaten the interests of farmers or others in the rural community. There are many more humane and selective solutions to the problems of pest control.

Opposition to hunting with dogs is strong in the countryside. An NOP survey found that 66 per cent of rural residents in Devon, where hunting is prevalent, approved a council ban on fox hunting and 70 per cent approved of a council ban on deer hunting. I am not persuaded either by the argument that one should not ban an activity for fear of losing jobs. As Conservative MP Ann Widdecombe argued today, the logic of such an argument is that we should not desire to end crime for fear of losing police jobs or ill health for fear of losing health workers. The number of people whose livelihoods are directly dependent on hunting is relatively small. The British Field Sports Societies Campaign for Hunting stated in an internal document dated March 1997 that currently quarry packs provide 910 full time jobs.

In any case, drag hunting – where hounds and riders follow either an artificial scent or a human runner- is a realistic replacement for those who wish to enjoy the thrill of the chase. I do not agree that hunting wild mammals with dogs is more humane and less destructive than shooting or snaring. The hunting of wild animals with dogs causes unnecessary and

226

prolonged suffering. Animals such as foxes suffer multiple bites, savaging and disembowelling before death because dogs are not capable of killing such large prey swiftly.

The hunting with hounds of foxes, hares and deer is designed to provide an unnecessarily long chase for the pleasure of the participants. Many animals are hunted to exhaustion. Foxes that escape the hounds by going to 'earth' are often later found to have died from the effects of the chase.

I believe the way a society treats its animals is indicative of the way that society treats its people. This country rightly banned cockfighting and bear baiting in the nineteenth century because it was cruel. I intend to play my part to make this country a more civilised place for people and animals to live in. That is why I also do not support battery farming or inhumane methods of slaughtering or transporting animals. That is why I will also continue to support Michael's Bill.

'Why have you done that?' my researcher asks. 'I've already done a standard letter to pro-hunters'. I am a victim of my office's efficiency, but sometimes prefer to do things my own way anyhow.

The Division Bell rings. The result? 'Ayes': 419, 'noes': 150.

Michael Foster stands outside St. Stephen's waving a stuffed toy fox.

WEDNESDAY 11 DECEMBER 1997 – VOTE TO CUT LONE PARENT BENEFIT

Debate on lone parent benefit cuts. A local Party member leaves a message urging me to vote against the Government. I shall not be doing so but feel pretty grim about the whole affair. New Labour has a responsibility to modernise the welfare state. Surely, though, we should be taking a coherent approach, not singling out one category of benefit recipient?

I stick to the line that to reverse this cut would break our pledge to stick within inherited spending limits for the first two years. Technically this is a sound argument though in practice the amount of money saved is small.

The Tories are revelling in our discomfort and division. An old Lib Dem friend chides me for my loyalism; my response is less than polite! I know that 'tough choices' are inevitable in government. I am sure that in future I shall have to vote for measures even more unpopular than this. Yet I have a deep sense that this could have been avoided. Lessons will have to be learned.

After the main vote (when forty-seven Labour MPs defy the Whip), I sit in the Chamber with my friend Judith Church and listen to the rest of the debate. Most speakers on our side are Campaign Group rebels. Judith points out that were it not for people like them we might not have been out of office for so long. Their sanctimonious attacks on the Government turn my stomach.

THURSDAY 18 DECEMBER – SOUTHGATE LABOUR PARTY GENERAL COMMITTEE

I attend the monthly meeting of the Southgate Labour Party. Most people are deeply unhappy about the benefit cut but respect my loyalty to the Government. I emphasise Harriet Harman's commitment to proper support for children and families and offer hope that the damaging effects of these cuts will be cancelled out in Gordon Brown's 1998 Budget. (As it turned out, this is exactly what happened!)

Parliament is about to break for Christmas, but the lone parent benefit cut has added a sour note to our celebration of Labour's first eight months. Nevertheless I am confident that lessons will be learnt.

WEDNESDAY 24 DECEMBER – CHRISTMAS EVE

Am absolutely exhausted. Last weekend I finally moved back to the constituency and into a flat just off Southgate Circus. Sad to leave Islington after so many enjoyable years but great to be living back in Southgate.

Moving the boxes up the stairs I tripped and fell. The result, a broken wrist now set in plaster. I spend the early hours of the morning in Accident and Emergency at the Royal Free.

The following Monday Joan is called by the *Times* Diary. They have been tipped off that I had been in Accident and Emergency. Had I received more prompt attention because I was a Labour MP and would I like to comment on NHS waiting lists? Not for the first time since 1 May, I realise that the most mundane things I do will be cause for press interest.

Tomorrow is my thirty-first birthday. I am going to spend New Year in Paris. Obvious jokes involving 'plaster' and 'Paris' have not escaped my friends.

Wednesday 18 February – the modernisation of the House of Commons Select Committee

I attend my first meeting of the Modernisation of the House of Commons Select Committee, to which I was appointed last month. The Committee, chaired by Ann Taylor MP, The Leader of the House, was set up by the Government to look at ways of modernising the procedures and practises of the House of Commons. There is plenty to do.

The committee looks at amongst other things, reforming the hours currently worked by MPs. We MPs could be more productive working a normal day. There is no need for us to start debates in the Chamber at 2.30pm causing us to hang around Westminster for votes until one or two the following morning. It is certainly unfair on Members with young children. These ridiculously inefficient working hours may explain why we've had so few women MPs in the past; and even with the progress made in 1997 fewer than one in five MPs is a woman.

I would particularly like to see better facilities provided for visitors to the Palace of Westminster. By tradition, visitors to Westminster are referred to as 'Strangers' – a dismissive term, dating back to the seventeenth century. After all, MPs are in the Chamber because these electors have put us here. The way visitors are treated is not acceptable and I am especially concerned that many older visitors have to queue outside for hours in freezing weather because no facilities are available inside. If we are to have a modern democracy, the people who elect us should not be made to feel unwelcome in their own Parliament.

We will also be trying to make Parliament a friendlier place for women and families. The fact that the Palace of Westminster has facilities for a rifle range but no crèche is symbolic of how this place is still very much a gentleman's club. With 120 women MPs in the Commons change is necessary, and things are already changing. It might seem absurd, but until the new Parliament there were no toilets for women MPs in the voting lobbies. We have only just seen the introduction of a unisex hairdresser. For the first time women MPs can have their hair cut in the Palace of Westminster, not only men! How did Barbara Castle's bouffant manage?

The facilities for new MPs could also be improved. A new MP can wait up to a month following his or her election before receiving an office. The people who lose out are the electors as it very difficult for MPs to respond to them in those crucial early weeks. However, after having been informed that I would have to wait some time for such luxuries as a desk or a telephone, I was given a coat hook in the cloak-room with a piece of pink ribbon dangling from it. The purpose? It was a ribbon from which to hang my sword! Perhaps some people carry a rapier to work each day with their brief case, but most of us, me included, do not. How ridiculous – the Palace of Westminster uses taxpayers' money to employ someone to tie pink ribbons onto 659 separate coat hooks!

The momentum for a new sort of politics is unstoppable. After the last election, two-fifths of MPs were new Members. We have a record number of women MPs, double the number of MPs from Asian and Afro Caribbean backgrounds and a significant number of young MPs. In addition, we have a Prime Minister fully committed to the modernisation of society, from Parliament down. I want to see the House of Commons become a modern and efficient working place.

My first meeting and I am delayed half an hour because the Piccadilly line has broken down yet again. Ann Taylor is fine about this but I feel like a new boy who is late for his first day at school. When we MPs have modernised the House of Commons, perhaps our newly elected mayor for London will modernise our crumbling public transport system as well?

FRIDAY 1 MAY – ONE YEAR ON CELEBRATION, WALKER'S CRICKET CLUB, SOUTHGATE

Walker's Cricket Club is the venue for an anniversary party. The event is deliberately low key – no triumphalism allowed! Chance to bring together the team that won it in '97 with other local friends, family and supporters.

It's been a good week. The Prime Minister visited Southgate on Wednesday to meet a group of local people in a Q and A session. Tony Blair went down superbly. He is such a political asset. His record in office has made the critics look pretty dim. They called him 'Phoney Tony' yet he is delivering. Perhaps the most powerful testament to his first year is the Stormont Agreement in Northern Ireland.

I first met Tony Blair in February 1992 when I was Secretary of Highbury Ward Labour Party in North Islington. I remember chatting briefly in the Blackpool-Preston train after the 1992 Labour Party conference when we both bemoaned the complacency that characterised the post-defeat conference. It sounds a bit creepish but I can say that I was very much a Blairite before it became fashionable!

Spent today visiting two primary schools in my constituency. I have now fulfilled my pledge to visit every school in Enfield Southgate in my first year as the MP. Busy advice surgery before coming up to the cricket ground. My case worker Joan is marvellous and has been such an asset to me all year in the face of the extraordinary caseload of work.

Some controversy in the *Sunday Times* a month or so ago about the usefulness of the MP's surgery, with older colleagues questioning its benefit. I do a weekly open advice session that attracts fifteen to thirty people each week. It keeps my feet firmly on the ground.

It is good to have this evening to relax and reflect on the past twelve months. I'm in the middle of a 'constituency fortnight' which has enabled me to assist the campaign for the Greater London referendum and local elections. On the doorstep there is real goodwill, both towards the Government and to me personally. I met an elderly lady yesterday who told me she had always voted Tory (even in 1997), but she was so proud of what is happening that she has switched to new Labour. A fitting testament to an amazing year.

I would like to thank my research assistant Richard Jarman who spent many late nights compiling this Diary for me and without whose valuable advice much of what happened these past twelve months would not have run so efficiently.

AT HOME IN GREEN WOOD:
THE POLITICS OF SMALL CHANGE

Nicola Baird

Few house buyers would think of Green Wood, near Birmingham, as the ideal place for a new home. It may be green belt, but the site is hemmed in by a busy dual carriageway and a quarry. Day and night cars roar down the A38 Sutton Coldfield bypass past the eastern edge of Green Wood, whilst the field next door is crossed by a row of massive electric pylons which crackle and snap in a sinister manner as you walk beneath their electro-magnetic fields. There is no running water, no mains drains and the dustmen don't come. Worse, the wood lies directly in the path of Britain's first private toll motorway, the Birmingham Northern Relief Road (BNRR), copied from pay-to-drive routes in France, Japan and the United States.

The planned 44km motorway, which will cost £400 million to build, is designed to link the M42 at Coleshill with the M6 at Cannock, allow-ing drivers who are willing to pay to bypass the notorious West Midlands congestion of the M5 and M6 between junctions 4 and 11.[1] New motorway service stations are also scheduled for Norton Canes, Saredon, Weeford and Coleshill.

The new road is to be built and run by a private consortium, Midland Expressway Ltd, over a fifty-three year concession.[2] Its construction will involve the compulsory purchase of 1536 acres. Nearly fifty suburban homes around Birmingham will be flattened; the Old Saltleians Rugby Club will lose its first-team ground and car park; part of two sites of special scientific interest (Blythe Valley and Chase Water Heath) will be lost, as will a large tranche of green belt farmland bordering car-choked Birmingham. In all 600ha will go under tarmac.[3]

After its roads review of July 1997 new Labour scrapped many of the scheduled road schemes, including the controversial Salisbury bypass and the A40 west London widening. Indeed, Minister of Transport Gavin Strang claimed the department was taking a new (almost holistic) approach by looking:

at the transport problems which lie behind proposals for road schemes and then [seeking] solutions which are environmentally sustainable. We intend to bring a fresh approach to the process of making decisions on the roads programme. We will take a strategic view and judge proposals on the criteria of accessibility, safety, economy, the environment and integration.[4]

But how honest was Strang being when it came to approving the BNRR, a road he described as 'vital'?

Two months later the *Guardian* newspaper revealed that the BNRR's success was dependent on a rather grander scheme: a plan to build Britain's biggest highway linking Manchester, Birmingham and London at a cost of £1,800 million. As environment correspondent Gerald Kells pointed out: 'It is becoming clear now that the road is far more than an isolated Birmingham bypass, and is unsustainable without massive highways' infrastructural expenditure elsewhere. Without the other schemes, the BNRR is effectively dead; traffic simply won't use the road, especially with a toll of at least £2.'[5]

HOME BASE

That's why for Paul, the BNRR is the front line against the continuing road building programme. He and three friends, outraged by the government's green light for the BNRR, built two tree houses, using reclaimed planks and old tarpaulins, in adjacent oak trees at Green Wood in October 1997. At first no one noticed, not even the commuters who race up and down the A38, but after two days, when large homemade banners had been unfurled denouncing the planned road, the Midlands press descended to find out what the protesters wanted.

After nearly a decade of protesting Paul was surprised that much of the reporting about the new camp was positive. This was partly because the Labour Party had been such vocal opponents of the BNRR until their election victory in May 1997. Indeed John Prescott had told the local *Birmingham Post*, back in 1993, that the proposed BNRR could not live up to its supporters' congestion-easing claims.[6] Then Prescott's accelerated roads review programme of July 1997 saw a dramatic about turn for the fate of the BNRR: Labour was not prepared to cancel it. Indeed Minister of Transport Gavin Strang

defended it as: 'A nationally strategic route of the first importance ...
It is up to the concessionaire to show what the private sector can do
and deliver this vital project quickly.'[7]

Suddenly new Labour was in bed with the private sector over a road
they had previously been adamantly opposed to. An angry editorial in
the *Sutton Coldfield Observer* pointed out that: 'People in the area
have fought a legal battle for years to prevent the building of this toll
road, and many felt dismayed and betrayed by the Labour government's approval of the plan.'[8]

West Midlands-based Friends of the Earth transport campaigner
Chris Crean put it more succinctly:

> People have been fighting this road for more than twelve years at all
> levels. They've mobilised the local community, they've given evidence at
> two public enquiries. This is the reason why people are so angered by
> Labour's U-turn. People felt as if they'd made the political aspect of their
> campaign successful. We've seen MP after MP voted into Westminster on
> a non-BNRR ticket, we've heard Labour's commitment not to let the
> BNRR go ahead. That's why there is a sense of betrayal and why local
> people are really angry.

Cash seems to be the problem: the Labour government is unwilling
to stop the road's construction because this will force them to compensate Midland Expresway Ltd. with a £30 million pay-off.[9] However
one opposition group, Alliance Against the BNRR, is claiming that the
Department of Environment, Transport and the Regions acted illegally
when it approved the project, because it took into account excessive
cancellation charges when approving the scheme.[10] The group has
already won the right to mount a legal challenge and seems confident
of winning as its solicitor claims it is unlawful to make a cancellation
charge agreement before a road scheme is approved or to allow it to
influence a decision to approve the scheme.[11]

MEET THE NEW BOSS, SAME AS THE OLD BOSS

The Labour government's about-turn is no surprise to anti-road
protesters. They have zero faith in the success of traditional methods of
getting views heard, such as lobbying, signing petitions or even joining
the Labour Party. The anti-roads movement is just one example of a

range of single-issue campaigns entered into by people tired of conventional political routes and planning systems which seem geared to sustaining the status quo. This doesn't mean people are becoming apolitical: instead there is a new generation of activists which believe that to get things done they must do it for themselves. That parliament is an ineffective talking shop is not a new argument: the maverick politico Tony Benn has long pointed out that every major political change has come from action outside Westminster. Think of the results of demonstrations by the Tolpuddle Martyrs, the suffragettes or even the poll tax protesters.

Over the past ten years non-parliamentary protests over activities such as road building, the arms trade and animal rights have been surprisingly successful. The Ploughshares movement saw four women smash up an Indonesian-bound BAe Hawk jet with household tools causing £1.5 million damage – but still be acquitted in court. Hunt saboteurs have highlighted the less savoury side of field sports and been rewarded with Mike Foster's private member's anti-hunt bill. Despite its eventual defeat the head of parliamentary support which has built up means that a successful bill remains a real possibility. Even middle England joined the protests at Shoreham docks helping to stop live export of animals to Europe. Surprisingly it was the normally conservative *Economist* which concluded: 'Protesting about new roads has become that rarest of British phenomena, a truly populist movement drawing supporters from all walks of life.'[12]

Initially road protests were written off as not having much to do with 'real politics', but as *Guardian* columnist George Monbiot pointed out direct activists talk about much more than roads:

> Among those swaying tree tops at Newbury, (where road protesters tried to delay construction of a bypass during the winter of 1996), discussions range from transport policy to the detention of immigrants, through alternative currencies, press ownership, animal welfare, structural adjustment in the Third World, land reform, air pollution, housing policy and the judiciary. Road building is top of today's list, but when the battle is over many activists will move on to something quite different.[13]

The new generation of activists reflect their age group's lack of interest in voting. 'For many young people, politics has become something of a dirty word. People under twenty-five are four times less likely to be registered than any other age group; less likely to vote for or join a political party, and less likely to be politically active,' reported the think tank Demos.[14] Even the Lord Chancellor, Lord Irvine, told the Law Society: 'It is increasingly well-understood that traditional political forms and structures are not attractive – or comprehensible – to the young. That may well account for the rise of direct action and greater involvement in single issue pressure groups, where the actions of the individual can be seen to have an immediate impact on the issue of concern.'[15]

Do-it-yourself solutions

The clash of green views held by anti-roads protesters, ranging from non-violent direct action – preferred by the 'fluffy greens' – to a spikier commitment to do anything – legal or illegal – to stop unwanted developments would horrify any new Labour spin doctor. Such differences though, inspire not just discussions around camp fires but an imaginative range of practical attempts at making lifestyles environmentally-sustainable. As a result Green Wood is fast becoming a model eco-village boasting tree houses, a pine-lined earth house sunk six feet into the ground for warmth, compost toilet and a magnificent tepee.

'The tepee took us two weeks to build,' explains Paul, 'because it is directly on the proposed route of the road people wouldn't normally spend so much time building. But we mind about the appearance of this camp. We want it to look good and to show that we can live in the woods.'

All the timber is collected from fallen pine in the nearby Forestry Commission's plantations planted to hide the Hanson-owned ARC Ltd's quarry. Then with the help of springier branches, nylon rope and tarpaulin, the roof can be made watertight. To prevent it taking on the gloom of a cave a number of glazed window frames have been built into the structure providing fine views into the mature woodland of oak, beech and sweet chestnut.

The giant, domed tepee has two separate wings. In one is a kitchen store house with a collection of neatly labelled units. There is a specific place for knives, matches, tea bags and rice, which makes cooking and clearing up much easier. The other wing is an information centre/office which has a low desk lined with files about multi-national companies, the BNRR and sticky-back plastic copies of press cuttings about the camp. It's very cosy. The walls are lined with pink and blue bedspreads and beach towels whilst the floor has a thick carpet, woolly bathmats and piles of cushions to get comfortable on.

Paul is at pains to explain that this is not the camp's power house. 'There is no nerve centre. No one is in charge. Some people see the person holding the mobile phone as the person in charge, but we all share jobs. There is no hierarchy.'

'This isn't a twenty-four hour protest. We want to do things differently. We're saying the woods are a nice place to live in, that's why we're here. And at the end of the day we may be the last people to enjoy them,' says Paul who has chosen a man-of-the-woods lifestyle for the past six years. 'Left wing or right wing: it's the same. I see the government as the opposition. The government could turn round the BNRR decision, but the government is controlled by multinationals.' These sentiments have been well borne out by Blair's efforts to get in bed with Murdoch's press and the Confederation of British Industry, as much as by the heavy emphasis on corporate funding for events like the Millennium Dome Experience.

'I think politicians see our counter culture as threatening,' says Paul, rolling himself a warming smoke outside the Green Wood tepee he helped build:

> We're seen as outcasts even though we're trying to make this place nice. Society doesn't like us not having jobs. But humanity's function is to be a caretaker of this planet, and that's what we're trying to do here. There are thousands of things we could protest about – like vivisection or nuclear power – but we have to do something about the BNRR, even if that's just because we live on this road's route. If we don't we may not have these woods, or the wildlife in them, any more.

It's courage like this, courage to live in the cold, to forego social security, to know that if the road isn't stopped your home – and probably all your possessions – will be trashed by bulldozers, that has helped the road protesters make such a mark on the British political scene without becoming familiar with the corridors and committee rooms of Westminster. Paul sees it as a Zen-thing. 'There is nothing I would like better than to be minding my own business strolling around the woods. But this is my home now. It's now we can try and stop this road, just by being here and getting publicity about it. I don't believe in violence at any point. You can delay a road without being nasty.'

He's right. Roads cost money; but they cost a great deal more when the schemes are delayed by protesters or the contractor decides there is a need for security guards. The police claim it cost half a million a day to evict protesters from the route of the East London M11 link road.[16]

FEELING LOCAL

'Everyone around here is against the BNRR,' says Paul, whose mum lives about ten miles away. 'There's a lot of local support for us. People come and visit and one local man helped build us two wood burning stoves.'

Even workers from ARC's nearby quarry come over for a chat and cups of tea around the fire: despite their employer evicting protesters at its massive quarry at Whatley, Somerset after they claimed it was unsustainable and would damage the historic springs at nearby Bath.[17] 'If plans to expand Whatley go ahead it will be visible from the Moon,' says Paul, in some awe. 'And the gravel they'll be extracting is what will be used to pave the new bypasses at Newbury and Fairmile which anti-roads protesters fought so hard to stop.'

It's not just the dreadlocked protesters who dislike the idea of a new six-lane motorway. 'The BNRR is a mad scheme, spoiling beautiful countryside,' Peter Quaife, a Birmingham resident told me as we drove alongside the proposed route. 'At some points it's going to be parallel to other big roads, including the A38 and the M6. The only people who want it are the contractors and the hauliers who will be willing to pay to use it.'

Families such as Sue and Gordon Craig, from Hednesford Road in Birmingham, are furious about facing the upheaval of compulsory purchase, whilst riding instructress Hazel Barnes claims she is ready to chain herself to the bulldozers to stop her twenty-one year old pony stables, and fifty-seven acres of grazing from being torn down and tarmaced.[18]

It is this same fear of being uprooted by a road that helps inspire the most dogged protesters. Four months after the first tree house was built the Green Wood camp had fifteen permanent residents, including children who clearly have fun playing with an assortment of pet dogs or bouncing around the copse on gaudy-coloured space hoppers. Most days the main task is to keep warm and delay construction. It's hard and courageous work, but as the protest builds the original group acquired many more permanent residents at the camp.

Replicated nationwide, small groups of anti-roads protesters, like the one at Green Wood, have helped publicise the lack of democracy involved when a new road gets the go-ahead. Many feel that their demonstrations helped secure a halt to the Conservative's ambitious road building programme, even if the actual brakes were applied after the 1994 review of the controversial 1989 Roads Programme (for 330 trunk roads and motorways). This enabled the Tories to save face at the same time as clawing back savings from a proposed roads budget of £2 billion a year.[19]

Yet during the early to mid-1990s, when the anti-roads protest suddenly made it on to our TV screens, armchair viewers might have thought that the protesters appeared to be experts at losing the battle. Beautiful Twyford Down in Hampshire was carved in two by the M3. The M11 link road was extended through East London, with a loss of more than 370 home after compulsory purchase by the Department of Transport. These communities tried the courts, they appealed to the EC and they approached the ombudsman, but the roads and their government supporters always triumphed, ultimately condemning the M25, Wanstead, Twyford Down, Newbury and elsewhere to become giant traffic jams and car parks. Even Swampy, the road protesters' first reluctant TV star, was dragged out of his tunnel so that the A30 Fairmile bypass could be built. And road building goes on. New Labour has agreed not just to the BNRR, but also the A13, M66, A564 Derby Southern bypass and the M2/A2.

The protesters have enjoyed important victories too, including the ancient Oxleas Wood reprieve and a halt to the eleven mile A36 Salisbury bypass which would have ruined the timeless view of this historic city, so familiar through Constable's painting of the cathedral and meadows. Less well-publicised successes included stopping the A40 Longford to M50 Gorsley 'improvement' across Gloucestershire countryside and the four-lane Norwich Inner Relief Road.

The significance of the anti-roads protesters' role was recognised by the award of the prestigious Goldman prize to Emma Must in May 1995. Awarded by the San Francisco based Goldman Environmental Foundation, and dubbed the 'green' Oscar, the prize gave Must £47,000 for her work 'galvanising a movement against the national road construction programme in England.'

Emma, then twenty-nine, had worked as a children's librarian until she became involved in the campaign to stop the M3 extension at Twyford Down. This led to her co-founding the direct action group

Road Alert. She also worked with the national alliance against new road building Alarm UK, which co-ordinated 250 protest groups fighting proposed road schemes nationwide. She spent two years organising demonstrations and a short spell in Holloway women's prison for defying injunctions to stay away from Twyford Down.

Emma saw the award as: 'Recognition for the whole spectrum of protest, from people with beads in their hair to middle-aged ladies with pleated skirts, all of whom are opposed to the roads programme.'[20] One of Emma's last pieces of work for Alarm UK was to write a short history of the roads protest. This is *Road Block*, a booklet which clearly explains how people power has wrecked the roads programme, bringing about a real change in the government's 'predict-and-provide' roads strategy. 'It looks at how the localised protests against road schemes have come together to form a vibrant, popular movement, transcending class, cultural and political barriers – a movement which has changed the course of government policy.'[21]

These days Emma works part-time at the influential national environmental transport campaign, Transport 2000, but she's rightfully proud of the anti-roads protesters' successes:

> What the protesters, both the direct activists and the grassroots campaigners, did was to bring the road programme to a halt. In 1989 there were 550 schemes, now there are very few. There were three things that caused this: it was to do with public spending cut backs at the Treasury, the fact that the Department of Environment under Gummer began to put pressure on the Department of Transport over the roads programme and because the grassroots campaigns made it clear that the public didn't want to continue down this route. So scaling down the roads programme was a soft target for the Treasury, it could do something popular and save money.

'The grassroots focus now is anti-traffic campaigns,' adds Emma. 'Very often it is people with children who are concerned about the traffic on their street and are taking action around that. Often they use imaginative stunts to lobby local councils. It's a network of people taking action for themselves which is expanding fast.' Many of these groups are members of Transport 2000's rapidly growing Streets for People network which helps local groups run campaigns, produce community newsletters or leaflets and provides advice about eye-catching stunts. Some activities, such as the human zebra crossing at

Finsbury Park in London, a weekend festival on a turf-covered rat run at Methley Terrace in Leeds or the posting of bottles of L'air de Christchurch, an explosive mix of petrol, labelled as carcinogenic, to Dorset councillors, have even helped embarrass local authorities into taking steps to improve facilities for pedestrians by curbing the car in urban areas.

And so the councils should. A recent report commissioned by the government shows that air pollution, much of it caused by vehicle exhaust fumes, kills up to 24,000 people a year.[22] Around 3500 can expect to die in road crashes: that's around 10 people a day. Another 320,000 will be injured, nearly all as a result of driver error.[23] During a car's lifetime there is a one in six chance that it will be involved in an accident which injures someone; a one in 39 chance of someone being seriously injured; and a one in 580 chance that someone will be killed.[24] Compare that with the 1:14 million chance of winning the Lottery jackpot.[25]

IN TWO MINDS

Although there are villages which continue to campaign for a bypass, such as those on the stretch of A10 near Hertford, people are expressing serious doubts about the need for more roads. The protesters' efforts have helped highlight the way total freedom for drivers is causing a deterioration in our environment. It's not just the daily clogged roads, traffic jams and no car parking spaces, it's also noise-polluted housing, accident black spots, dead bunnies, ruined countryside and global warming. For those who aren't yet convinced either by road protests or by the conclusions of the Standing Advisory Committee on Trunk Road Assessment (SACTRA) report, which showed that predict-and-provide road building was increasing traffic, one trip round the M25, the road which was built specifically to free up commuter traffic, should be enough to change their minds.[26]

For those wedded to their cars – or those with money to make – new roads are still seen as opportunities. That 'opportunity' argument is a hard one to get across, though, and it is the pointlessness of excessive road building which angers protesters. Even Lord Kennet – speaking in the House of Lords in 1996 about the impact of the Newbury bypass on the River Kennet flood plain – appealed for those with eyes to see the reality of a tarmac criss-crossed Britain:

My Lords, should not the Prime Minister witness the death throes of an impossible transport policy – hundreds of policemen, private security men and bailiffs, trying by force to evict the people who have chosen to camp in the friendly trees to protect them, and the gigantic machines waiting to uproot the trees, all in favour of juggernauts carrying nothing more important than frozen food from another country.[27]

Lest we forget, getting drivers from A to B five minutes faster does not reduce stress levels – whereas a five-minute walk in the woods which have been cut down and tarmaced might have done. Too many of us have forgotten that transport problems have been with us since the Romans invented the road – indeed Julius Caesar banned wheeled transport in Rome during the daytime in the first century BC. Yet despite the lessons of history the car has made a major impact on every aspect of our lives, wherever we live and whether we own one or not.

Protesters like Paul may not have voted on May 1. They don't have much faith in new Labour, or parliament at all for that matter, but they still have the conviction that things can only get better: as long as you are willing to do them for yourself. Altruistic personal conviction is taking its stand in Green Wood and in many other spaces and places beyond the geographical and political mainstream. But as Friends of the Earth campaigns director Tony Juniper puts it, the protesters are likely to be in for a long haul which won't begin to be measured in the time between general elections: 'When push comes to shove, short-term economic growth and pandering to the business lobby are the real priorities, and the government is prepared to sacrifice the environment for them. 'If this government wishes to maintain some green credibility, it needs to match what it says it stands for with what it decides to actually do.'[28]

NOTES

1. *Evening Mail*, 12 February 1998.
2. Department of the Environment, Transport & the Regions press notice, 28 July 1997 (638/97/98).
3. The *Guardian*, 29 July 1997.
4. Department of the Environment, Transport & the Regions press notice, 28 July 1997 (638/97/98).
5. The *Guardian*, 10 September 1997.

6. The *Guardian*, 29 July 1997.
7. Department of the Environment, Transport & the Regions press notice, 28 July 1997 (638/97/98).
8. Sutton Coldfield *Observer*, 31 October 1997.
9. The *Guardian*, 23 July 1997.
10. Sutton Coldfield *News*, 16 January 1998.
11. Sutton Coldfield *Observer*, 27 February 1998.
12. *The Economist*, 19 February 1994.
13. The *Guardian*, 7 February 1996.
14. *Freedom's Children*, Helen Wilkinson and Geoff Mulgan, Demos, London1995.
15. The *Guardian*, 29 January 1998.
16. *Times*, 30 November 1994.
17. *Times* 11 May 1994.
18. The *Guardian*, 29 July 1997.
19. *Twyford Down, roads, campaigning and environmental law*, Barbara Bryant E&FN Spon, London 1993 p304.
20. *Daily Mail*, 2 May 1995 and *Daily Telegraph*, 1 May 1995.
21. 'Road Block: how people power is wrecking the roads programme' *Alarm UK*, nd.
22. *New Scientist*, 24 January 1998, p 16.
23. Department of Transport road accident unit, figures for 1996, 1997.
24. *The Big Issue*, 22-28 September 1997.
25. Camelot, January 1998.
26. Standing Advisory Committee on Trunk Road Assessment report: *Trunk roads and the generation of traffic*, 1994.
27. *Earthmatters*, summer 1996.
28. The *Guardian* 13 August 1997.

WAR ON THE VAGUE – TOWARDS THE NEW TORIES

Michael Gove

The vision of the future which O'Brien outlines to Winston Smith in George Orwell's *Nineteen Eighty-Four* is a boot forever stamping on a human face. A better metaphor for modernity now is a Patrick Cox Wannabe pressing ever more insistently on the accelerator. Speed, not oppression, is the dynamic of today's modernity. This has been the century of the motor car and as it ends the car's power to bewitch has not diminished. The first 'modernising' ideology of the century was the Futurism of the Italian thinker and poet Filippo Marinetti.[1] The mechanical age and the motor car were agents of change which would help bury 'pastism'. Marinetti argued for 'a relentless war against pastism: archaeology, academicism, senilism, quietism' and in favour of 'anti-traditionalist nationalism' which would rid Italy of 'the ancestor worship which, far from cementing the race makes it anaemic and putrid'. Marinetti's modernising creed worshipped the motor car and so it is perhaps not such a surprise that Labour's contemporary modernisers prostrated themselves in the path of the men from Formula One.

The decision by the Government to waive a ban on tobacco advertising at the request of Bernie Ecclestone and Max Mosley is a potent metaphor for the triumph of a particular sort of modernisation within new Labour. The concession to Formula One showed one modernising strain dominant, but the pain caused to the new Labour coalition during the resolution of the affair revealed some of the strains and contradictions within the modernising project.

In the Formula One battle, one set of modernising attitudes within the new Labour ranks was defeated. The forces in retreat were those with a vision of government as moral agent, intervening in the market to influence social attitudes rather than economic outcomes, enacting legislation to promote virtue rather than extend liberty and eradicating the particular to promote the uniform.

Another bundle of modernising attitudes was victorious, specifically, a desire to privilege business expertise over other judgements, a neophilia uncritical about technology's claims and a sense of the new economic realities engendered by globalisation.

Yet, although the affair marked a victory for one set of attitudes it did not signal their permanent supremacy, only a specific episode of dominance. It did, however, reveal on a metaphorical level, the attachment to dynamism, speed, the mechanistic and engineered.

The existence of contradictory, and still contending, impulses within new Labour was emphasised by the decision to defend the Formula One concession in a manner designed to render the differences opaque. The decision was presented in traditional terms as a move to 'save British jobs'. The final line of defence to which new Labour retreated was the fortification the party had been trying to abandon – the citadel of the producer, the temple of the worker.

In this one incident, where differing forces collided, many of the distinctive features of new Labour were laid bare. The circumstances around the Government's decision, particularly the suspicion that ministers may have been influenced by the financial support they had received from Formula One, unsettled many observers.[2] Was this new administration as ethically compromised as the Tories they had replaced? It is not, however, necessary, to find moral fault in the Government's actions to level criticism. The ideological confusion exposed at the time, and underlined since, is justification enough for cynicism about new Labour. The strategic certainty and moral purpose which Mrs Thatcher enjoyed was altogether absent during the Formula One affair. It revealed an administration impressed by the dynamic but lacking a sense of direction, equipped only with a desire to remain in control. Labour is a party with a plan to re-engineer the political system, but it has no driving passion beyond power. The transformation, or modernisation, that Labour seeks to effect is about processes, not an end product. It wants to be in the driving seat but its journey has no end point, no future Utopia or recovered past to aim for. It requires no fixed compass because it wishes only, like the Formula One driver, to stay ahead of the competition – rather than to go anywhere inspiring.

OLIVER'S ARMY IS HERE TODAY

The area where the engineering impulse is strongest is in the re-making of the nation state. Labour has ambitious plans for the constitution but they are mechanistic contrivances, instruments which answer the question of how power is used, not arguments which explain why change is needed.

In so far as any analysis sustains these plans, it is a perception that existing institutions have a Conservative bias. The plans for constitutional reform reveal a desire to break down the patterns of governance which have protected traditional British liberties. They will be replaced by a network of bodies which will be staffed by professional politicians subservient to a centralised party structure. In effect, this amounts to a nationalisation of civic life by political stealth.

The adoption of a 'closed list' system of proportional representation for the European elections places the power to choose representatives with the party machine. The stripping out of hereditary peers in the second chamber reflects a wish to neuter its capacity to obstruct unwelcome legislation. Plans to change the funding of political parties to cap spending would limit the ability of dissident movements to campaign on issues, such as Europe or abortion, where an Establishment consensus might prevail. The transfer of the right to fix interest rates from accountable politicians to appointed central bankers is a bureaucratisation of one of the most intensely political questions a nation faces. It can also be seen as an attempt to prepare the ground for the transfer of economic decision making from nationally accountable politicians to a distant European clerisy. The adoption of proportional representation for Welsh and Scottish Assemblies and its consideration for the House of Commons promises to render these bodies less 'confrontational' – i.e., questioning – and will make the choice of government a matter for the political classes rather than the people.

This is all a desire to eliminate the habits and havens of dissent, particularly the interrogative, traditional House of Commons. But beyond that, there is no coherent reforming ideology discernible. Crucibles of passion will be extinguished and replaced by mechanisms for control.

There is a Cromwellian or Leninist tinge to new Labour's programme of constitutional reform. By promoting forces in the name of progress, such as Scottish nationalism, gender equality, European integration and 'fair votes' which dissolve 'reactionary' forms and processes, the ground is cleared for the installation of an even more reactionary system. It is a tactic that was pioneered by Cromwell and perfected by Lenin. The Levellers and avant-garde of today, the Charter 88 ideologues and constitution-mongers, should reflect on the fate of their forerunners after past episodes of emancipation. It is not even as though there is an ideology as compelling as the Commonwealth or Communism of yesterday to sustain the enthusiasm of the Left today.

THE FALSE PROMISE OF POLITICAL PRAGMATISM

For a Conservative to defend ideology and deprecate the pragmatic brokerage of conflicting interests might seem paradoxical. But when new Labour enthusiasts praise Tories for their pragmatism they are being disingenuous, flattering to deceive.[3] It is only when the right develops a project, actively builds a coalition and implements a strategy that the left has a worthy foe – from Joseph Chamberlain to Margaret Thatcher the left has been outmanouevred by radicalism from the right.

Political movements depend for success on a project, which firstly must be appropriate to the times, secondly be rooted in honest analysis, thirdly be resonant with the people, and, finally, needs to rest on fundamental principle. Labour had a project until 1 May 1997 which scored on all but the last of those four counts. It was a machine which could evict the Tories from office without altering their new economic settlement. The Tories, at the time, failed on all four counts. They presented no overwhelming new reason for their continuance in office, had been dishonest about the reasons for economic recovery, regarded a policy's unpopularity as evidence of their bravery in pressing ahead with the right course, and operated without an anchor of principle on questions of national survival, natural justice and private property rights. A party which was neutral on the nation's territorial integrity was incredible on the constitution, a party which abolished the right to silence was a poor opponent of the genuine damage to traditional liberties posed by rationalist and utilitarian legislation, and a party which changed leasehold rights so as to retrospectively rewrite contracts could not object in all conscience to windfall taxation.

When the Tories came to power in 1979 they had a project which responded to public weariness with corporatism. It was unsparingly honest in its analysis of past failure. And it offered economic liberation, resting on simple but durable principles of fiscal freedom and respect for the rule of law. Thatcherism was visionary in its response to the failure of the post-war settlement and inspirational in the coherence of its programme. Its enemies were as obvious as its aims, and as such it had the capacity to withstand reverses, arm its adherents with consistent answers to political problems and embed itself in hearts and minds.

New Labour, having had a project to win power, now have a different project – to keep it. Tony Blair's main ambition for the country is to give it a second term of his premiership. Along the way there are certain changes he would like to enact but, compared with the strategic certainty he brings to altering the constitution to entrench him and his allies in power, the focus in other areas is fuzzy. There are individual impulses, which have the potential to appeal; but without an organising ideology which would give them coherence Labour's particular version of modernisation is a bundle of trends and tactics not a programme capable of durable popular or intellectual inspiration.

Who, apart from the Tories, are new Labour's enemies? New Labour is undoctrinaire about whether services should be provided by the private or public sector, but what clearly intelligible criteria govern how the division should be arrived at? New Labour believes in extending the sphere of personal liberty in sexual matters but remains quite content to restrict freedom for minorities who hunt, take drugs or wish to advertise legal intoxicants. On what philosophical basis is this contradictory mix codified? No credible, let alone logical, justification is argued.

Where priorities conflict, no consistent justification guides government action. In the case of Formula One, the general rule that tobacco sponsorship of sport be banned was waived in order to protect jobs. But more jobs will be lost by a ban on fox-hunting, which the Government is prepared to allow. Why should employment considerations trump regulations designed to safeguard human health but not laws designed to safeguard animal welfare?

The more ringing the aspiration, the more insubstantial or diffuse the detail. Blair began the British Presidency of the EU in 1998 by articulating the aspiration to 'lead in Europe'.[4] But where? What is this kind of leadership that advocates joining a single currency designed by others for their purposes after they have established it? If leadership requires that we first must follow, then what quo is there for the abolition of the quid?

On welfare reform what moral purpose animates the Government? Is there a presumption that the state should do less, that its intervention is a solvent of civil ties? If not, then what should be its reach? Or should it be circumscribed by the level of spending bequeathed by a Tory Chancellor? When lone parent benefit was cut there was a clear moral justification, the ending of the privileged status hitherto enjoyed by single parents, and the affirmation of the importance of marriage. But this justification was advanced by no prominent Labour figure. Instead, the policy was either defended incoherently by Harriet Harman, as a means of helping women into work (in fact, by reducing the benefits to women who take then lose jobs, it acts as a disincentive to employment), or defended by Treasury ministers on the grounds of contingency as a simple money-saving measure. How can support for radical reform be built on intellectual dishonesty and confusion, how can a system built on moral principles be transformed without a moral case being built? It was Harold Wilson, prince of pragmatists, who recognised that 'the Labour Party is a moral crusade or it is nothing'.[5]

Without the anchor of principle, modernisation becomes mere modishness. Pressure groups which can make their clients' complaints the latest injustice or their opponent's actions the latest offence to good sense can harness the interventionist energies of an administration which has abandoned redistribution and economic equality as the means of emancipation. Thus women within the Scottish Labour Party have pressurised the Government into pledging gender equality in the Scottish parliament. The proposal requires the amendment of existing equal opportunities legislation, the twisting of due process, to promote a particular version of equality at the cost of generalised equity in current law. Jewish bodies, for impeccable motives, but with flawed logic, have secured support for plans to make holocaust denial an offence. Should that which is offensive automatically be illegal? If enough pressure is exerted then Labour seems inclined to think it should.

The International Fund for Animal Welfare and its allies in the League Against Cruel Sports helped to persuade Labour that a free vote should be granted on outlawing hunting with hounds. This zeal to ban was frustrated in the fox-hunting debate but it has found expression elsewhere. On the basis of scientific evidence, the Government outlawed beef on the bone. Yet when even more damning scientific evidence pointed to the dangers of passive smoking no action was taken. Those who consume beef on the bone risk only their own lives, and it is a risk so minuscule as to be negligible.[6] Those who smoke endanger the lives of those adjacent to them, and even though the risk is small it dwarfs that from oxtail stew.[7] The Labour minister Barbara Roche has argued that smoking in public places could not be banned because such a measure would be 'unenforceable'[8] and yet drugs laws remain in place which are mocked in minister's own homes and by millions of voters every week. What logic underlies these reflex bans and fearful flinchings from action? What conception of the citizen and his or her dignity guides the Government?

Modernisation, as currently practised, can only be understood as an attempt to ride trends, to manipulate or at best pre-empt events. By making its novelty, its rejection of traditional forms and its party's traditions, its unique selling point, new Labour has acquired for itself, as a typical marketing creation of late capitalism, built-in obsolescence. Having won power on the back of a mood that it was time for a change, new Labour is poorly positioned against the same charge in future. A party dedicated to modernity is trading in a declining stock, with a fast-approaching sell-by date.

NIXON IN CHINA AND THATCHER IN YORKSHIRE

Labour's victory in 1997 was a liberating moment for many on the left. But the sense of emancipation from an unloved government cannot be sustained by a project which constricts the passions of the left and denies its partisans the transcending vision of a better world which has driven progressives in the past. Blair's pragmatic centre-left approach has led him to be compared by critics such as Paul Foot in *The Guardian* to Ramsay MacDonald, a leader whose anxiety to appease the establishment meant he could no longer inspire his party.[9] He has been compared by others in his own party to Harold Wilson, a master tactician who squandered the opportunities his electoral talents secured. Blair himself prefers another model, William Gladstone, a moralist who harnessed a progressive majority to implement piecemeal reforms.[10]

All historical parallels are flawed. Politicians and the events they contend with are the product of contingency and accident. But history can teach lessons, for human motivation and underlying principle are durable. Those on the left should remember that Gladstone's programme eventually saw his party split. There are differences between the democratic party of today and the elite organisation of Gladstone's time, but they are unlikely to work to Blair's advantage. Habits of deference which once inhibited criticism of the leadership from the rank and file have gone. Ambition may motivate a few, but disappointed hopes are likely to move many more. The modernity which new Labour embraces is likely to see history repeat itself at an accelerated pace. Gladstone led his party away from its core principles, shattered its natural coalition and increasingly preferred alliances with politicians outside his party to nurturing critics within.

Blair's belief in his own superiority to his party, his sense that it needs him more than he it, and his willingness to dispense with it, is the hallmark of a man impatient with democracy's constraints. The most telling indication of Blair's disregard for his own party came early in his leadership. Having presided over the re-writing of Clause Four, he joked that he had a plan for the party's name. As the audience readied itself for another upheaval, he revealed, 'it's going to stay the same'.[11] He was playing with an audience who knew that his mastery was then total and his supporters could be easily enough toyed with and manipulated. The real irony of his statement lay in the subsequent decision to change the party's name in any case, if only by prefixing it with 'new'. In his speech to the party conference in 1996 Blair paid lip service to the party's household gods by praising old Labour, but only for surviving long enough to make new Labour possible.[12] Blair's impatience with his party's traditions is transparent. But Blair is not the only politician who can grow impatient.

Gratification cannot long be delayed for those on the left shut out of power for two decades. They must, soon, inevitably, tire of scraps and symbols. Will the egalitarian spirit be sustained and its expression controlled by the prospect of an end to hereditary peers and, perhaps next, fox-hunting? What in Blair's speeches to Labour Party Conferences, apart from the crumb of reforming the Lords, was thrown to a left grown ravenous over the years? What will there be in this government's programme for those who look to the bright horizon, other than the persecution of England's ermined endangered lords? Will every other instinct on the left, the desire to redistribute wealth, to manage industry, to extend the state's scope, be suppressed simply for the one dubious return of abolishing the House of Lords? Did Labour really come to power in 1997 with their most inspirational policy an assault on a class whose power was decisively broken with the passing of the Great Reform Act in 1832?

The failure to deliver promptly must lead to early disillusion. Labour ministers have been insulated from unpopularity so far by the health of an economy they inherited, but when unemployment again begins to rise, as it inevitably will, will a promise to outlaw fox-hunting keep the jobless happy?

The long shadows of past failures fall across Blair's path, portents of failure. The failure of Macdonald to stay true to his party, the failure of

Wilson to transcend the tactical, the failure of Gladstone to curb his own arrogance. These are all lessons for Blair. Yet supporters of Blair draw their own comfort from history with parallels and precepts designed to sustain their tactical decisions.

The Blairite strategy is the building of a radical 'centre' by selective betrayal. The base can be taken for granted and new support won by advancing on fronts which others cannot tackle because they have not secured their flank. The historical moment which bewitches is Nixon in China.

All the most telling examples used as precedents are episodes of betrayal. Blair himself has used the example of Nixon in China to argue that only a party trusted with a particular policy, whether the Republicans on anti-communism or Labour on health, can manage historic reforms. Other Blairites invoke De Gaulle's handling of Algeria as a reason to trust the party most closely associated with a cherished position as the best agent for abandoning it. This rhetoric of betraying the base, however, reveals the lack of any real sense of history.

Only Nixon, it is argued, could effect a rapprochement with Red China because only a cold war warrior with impeccably anti-Communist credentials could ever be trusted to deal with Beijing. It is a seductive thought, but a flawed insight into the reasons for political success.

Firstly, it is flawed because it privileges a twist in personality over consistency in ideology. If Nixon is the model, then the best leaders are those who accumulate authority in order to betray, those who secure trust on one basis only to betray it. To believe that leadership requires betrayal is to place trust in someone to do the right thing because they have been wrong for so long. It is to trust the savage over the civilised because the savage eventually sees the virtues of that which he has fought. Why should the politically mature believe in a policy – like Blair's plans to reform welfare – just because there is a romantic fitness in the apostate's advocacy of prudence?

Secondly, this line of argument is flawed because the tactical advantage secured by betrayal is never as powerful as the strategic benefit of having a leader whose policy is rooted in their being, and is the reason for their place in politics, a leader whose determination is visceral rather than contingent. Reforming the trade unions, and returning power from their counsels to Parliament, was one of the central challenges of politics from the 1950s to the 1980s. By the logic of Nixon in China it should have been a leader of the left who was best equipped to tame them, and this mistaken perspective was prevalent throughout the 1960s and 1970s. It was not, however, Harold Wilson who succeeded in taming the trade unions with his half-hearted betrayal of them when he published *In Place of Strife*. Wilson's clumsy attempt to clip their wings only poisoned relations within the labour movement and laid the ground for the Winter of Discontent. It was Margaret Thatcher who broke union power, with her legislative tenacity and resolution in the face of the miners. The correct model for fundamental reform is not Nixon in China but Thatcher in Yorkshire.

Faced with a prime minister possessed of purpose, certain of her ends, sustained by a clear philosophical framework and capable of communicating her beliefs to the public, the unions buckled. The public accepted civil strife, unemployment and austerity because they knew the direction in which they were being taken, or at the very least knew that their leader was confident of her direction and acting on her instincts.

The third flaw in the programme of abandoning one's base is the recognition that parties lose most calamitously by betraying their own followers. Labour's defeat in 1979 was the inevitable consequence of bewildering the party's base. Major's defeat in 1997 was more disastrous than it need have been because his troops were left with nothing left to fight for. Even Nixon, despite his popularity in Beijing, found his base deserted him when he needed it most, with congressional republicans under Barry Goldwater incapable of offering him the protection he sought when his enemies exploited his errors.

The attempt by Blair and his circle to appropriate Nixon for new Labour may be flawed, but it at least has a historic resonance. The pursuit of 'the centre' is, however, the political hunting of the snark. The centre, like the end of the rainbow, can only be imagined, never colonised. In so far as it can be located it is in a different position now from twenty years ago. We are all monetarists now, and genuine redistributionist egalitarians such as Sir Iain Gilmour and Roy Hattersley are now to the left of the Labour government.[13]

Voters, in so far as they pay much attention to political trigonometry, are certainly inclined to prefer 'moderates' to extremists but, more than anything, they are inclined to prefer strong to weak leaders, purpose to positioning, right and wrong as calibrators of policy, not right and left. They would not, otherwise, have chosen to support Mrs Thatcher's Tory Party rather than Roy Jenkins's SDP in the numbers they did in 1983.

The left should certainly recognise the bankruptcy of any pursuit of the centre as a project worth embracing. Not only does it starve the left of its greatest asset, passion, it also denies the historical experience of the left's greatest successes. The Bolsheviks seized power in 1917 not through delicate positioning but by the formulation of clear radical goals and determined action to ensure their consistent application. It does not require a revolutionary moment to effect such a transformation. Labour's victory in 1945 would not have been so decisive, its chance to reshape Britain so great, if the party had not been so convinced of the philosophical soundness of its principles, so determined to wrench Britain further towards collectivism. It was the promise of a new Jerusalem, and the policies which would effect huge changes, which inspired, not a pledge to give Liberals a seat on cabinet committees.

Not only would left victories have been less assured in the past if it had promised to pursue the chimera of 'the centre' but the victories would have been empty too. What use is power without principle? If politics is just a game, the manipulation of public sentiment to win office, the formulation of pragmatic responses to deal with contingencies as they arise, then what is the argument against the bureaucratisation of society? What is the use of ideas, passions, sentiment, the glue of parties and the fire that drives people? What is the defence against a society such as China knew in the middle ages, Aldous Huxley imagined in the 1930s and Brussels is building now?

DON'T BE VAGUE, WILLIAM

It falls to the Conservative Party now not only to safeguard the system of Parliamentary Government which both major parties once existed to defend but also to make the case for politics as crusade rather than calculation.

There may emerge critiques of Blair from the left which challenge all his premises, or even local resistance articulated by Liberals and Nationalists who wish to swim out of leviathan's jaws, but only the Tories have the capacity to posit an alternative modernisation of Britain, one based on the application of coherent and enduring principles to an accelerating accumulation of choice. If novelty is the essence of the Blairite modernisation then liberty, and dignity, should be the leitmotifs of the new Tories. These have the advantage of durability, transcendence even, in contrast to the built-in obsolescence of Labour's theme.

It is already clear that the aspect of the Blair government most open to populist, yet coherent, attack is its illiberalism. Alan Watkins has called it the most puritan and priggish in living memory.[14] The accumulation of petty restrictions, from meat bans to advertising controls, can help construct a coalition of opposition but also, far more importantly, provide the basis of a thoroughgoing critique. If the Tories simply seek to develop a rainbow coalition of the right then they will be defined by the constituent groups rather than their own coherent view. Instead they must seek to become the distanced defenders of the hunter and smoker, rather than their licensed lobbyists.

To properly exploit the emerging opportunities the new Tories need to champion measures which new Labour cannot enact, and the old right would have shied away from. The promise must be emancipation, both economically and socially. They must also develop a language of dignity which speaks to the affection for those parts of British life which are traditional. Labour's modishness undermines the dignity of the political process and renders its most ardent modernisers ridiculous. A belief in a Britain which does not need to be fashionable to be respected would find a ready response across the social spectrum.

Economically, the Tories need to find policies which use the market to provide a new generation with opportunities hitherto denied. The promises should be of a kind unmatchable by a Labour Party still struggling to construct a 'third way' which denies them new avenues of liberation.

The liberation of all schools by extending grant-maintained status and maximising choice, the direct ownership of health insurance and healthcare institutions, new forms of popular capitalism and, above all, lower, flatter, simpler taxation should be the building blocks.

Labour have tried to present themselves as a low-tax party, and the last government's record has helped Blair, but there are very real limits to his capacity to sustain the impression. The establishment of a 10 pence starting rate appears audacious but is minor tinkering in comparison to what the Tories could be capable of.

By removing tax-reliefs, abolishing the upper rate and establishing a single level then movement could be made towards the goal of an 'ultra-low tax economy' envisaged by Michael Portillo. In response to globalisation's pressures the education of the workforce can help establish a competitive advantage, but not as quickly as lower tax. A single, simple, rate would remove business burdens, make collection easier and avoidance scarcely worth the effort. The effect on the retention of, and capacity to attract, talent, could have a dramatic effect on revenue. The case has been made with beguiling force in the USA by Steve Forbes and only the limitations of the advocate impeded the attractiveness of the policy.[15]

A flat tax sends a simple message, of encouragement to enterprise and opposition to envy, which is truly modern as well as timelessly liberal. The inbuilt inequity of the higher rate, a concession to an egalitarianism which even forward new Labour thinkers like Philip Collins and Ian Corfield reject, will only be reformed by an administration unburdened by historic guilt.[16]

Low tax is the most easily intelligible benefit of the smaller state. It not only encourages enterprise and wealth creation, it limits the capacity of the state to interfere with the freedom of individuals by reducing its resources. The simpler the tax system, the clearer the relationship between work and reward – a relationship new Labour policy still obscures because of the interventionist and egalitarian instincts of many party members.

Socially, the terrain is more difficult. The Tories should, however, remember that their belief in the local, the particular and the communal is buttressed by an embrace of liberty. It is, as Burke, Powell and Willetts, have pointed out, the claims of the state and the centre which corrode and dissolve civil ties. Willetts, in his book *Modern Conservatism*[17] and his Social Market Foundation pamphlet *Civic Conservatism*, has argued persuasively that state intervention displaces the voluntary spirit in communities. Powell argued, in defence of the smaller state as the handmaiden of flourishing British traditions, that 'salvation lies within the grasp of the people themselves, by their unhampered pursuit of their own insights we shall forge ahead in the future just as we advanced in the past'.[18]

The removal of the state from communal life, as repentant liberals like Melanie Phillips now recognise, is the precondition of a revived civil society. Phillips has argued in *The Observer*, and in her work *All Must Have Prizes*, for the recovery of schools and hospitals from bureaucratic control and their restoration to local governance.[19] Although a liberal rather than a libertarian, Phillips has argued for private insurance and smaller central government as preconditions for the flourishing of virtue in unweeded fields. To that end the Tories should explore policies which reduce the state's reach into independent institutions, whether it is the tax take from families, the provision of childcare and education or the control of universities.

The Tories should also consider how moral principles can be supported by devolving moral choice to individuals. One of Margaret Thatcher's great successes was the removal of forces which insulated individuals and organisations from the consequences of their economic actions. Wage increases were no longer a seasonal phenomenon, like the falling of leaves, which would occur irrespective of any human intervention. They had to be earned with productivity increases or paid for by higher unemployment.

It would also be worth considering if individuals should be allowed a greater level of moral autonomy on issues such as drugs consumption. Greater honesty about the costs and consequences of a habit in which millions indulge might make government authority easier to respect in other areas. William Hague, although a social liberal in areas such as sexuality, is opposed to liberalising drugs laws. Many of his contemporaries, however, are more open-minded. His close ally Alan Duncan advocated drugs law reform in his libertarian work Saturn's Children.[20]

The Tories should never try to appeal to voters by advocating policies inimical to their instincts simply to exploit Labour's problems. Tory opposition to higher education reform was inadequate because the party preferred to side with interest groups like the National Union of Students instead of arguing for access on coherent market principles. The Tories would, however, both embarrass Labour and remain true to their principles if they supported decriminalisation. Labour would appear both anachronistic and inconsistent while the Tories could show themselves sensitive to social trends and committed to liberty. Hague may not be ready to make this most liberal of turns but consistent advocacy could yet shift his party.

IT'S COOL TO RULE BRITANNIA

As choices accumulate in the social and economic spheres of individual's lives, the attempt to regulate becomes as difficult as the effort to limit capital flows across national borders. The truly modern politician will recognise that new attempts to control are bound to be frustrated. Nowhere is that clearer than on Europe. It is an issue which, as Michael Portillo mentioned in his lecture to the 1997 Tory Party Conference, tends to crowd out debate of any other policy.[21] But the truly modern politician would certainly not support the European single currency.

Why would he or she want to take powers to hold government to account out of the hands of individual voters, and seek to stave off modernity with a new gold standard and a system of economic decision-making which is pre-democratic in composition and operation?

The two most powerful forces of the moment are the ascendancy of liberal economics and the re-emergence of popular sovereignty's challenge to elite rule. Both are contrary to the spirit of Europe at the moment. The consequences of defying both trends are now apparent in Asia. The attempt to rig the market in favour of vested interests leads to a collapse in confidence. The attempt to keep power tightly within a ruling cartel, to reduce the power of the people to throw out unpopular governments, also damages international confidence. Just as economic competition maximises benefits for all, so free political competition ensures the wisest government.

A defence of national sovereignty couched in modern terms and rooted in liberal principles, combined with a programme of economic and social emancipation, would provide the new Tories with an historic opportunity.

The nation state, although the product of the Enlightenment, is no more an anachronism than reason, democracy, free trade, scientific empiricism or any other Enlightenment product. It combines an understanding of sentiment and the social with a proven ability to hold power to account. Trans-national models of political organisation inevitably render elites less accountable. Unless power is exercised by individuals who appeal to voters in their own language and can be ejected firmly from office in a clearly intelligible way then accountability suffers.

Advocates of integration claim that global problems require larger states, but the lesson of the twentieth century, in economics and politics, is the lesson learnt painfully by the Brontosaurus millions of years ago. The small and flexible will always outlast the large and unwieldy. Power made accountable is more likely to anticipate, and outwit, challenges.

There are problems, like environmental degradation, which transcend national boundaries, but the steps required to deal with pollution can only be taken by authorities which have secured popular consent. International accords can be agreed but they can only be effectively implemented in nations where legitimacy is clear.

A modern Tory Party would also defend the nation state on the basis of dignity. The accepted traditions of the state are legitimate focuses of pride, badges of identity more enduring than the shreds and patches stitched together to make up Cool Britannia. Respect is the demand made by assertive youth, and respect can only be accorded to institutions and individuals who hold their ground instead of pandering. The defeatism of past British elites, who considered their own nation inadequate and decadent, and who wished to subsume it into Europe, can only inspire pity and contempt. Those politicians who believe in the unique genius of their people are the ones likely to be trusted by them.

To secure respect for themselves the Conservatives must demand respect for the nation and its traditions. That will require a public discourse which is demotic and direct, possessed of attitude and determined not to yield. The pompous formulations of old Tory politicians, the oblique, opaque orotundity of men like Major, was painful evidence of their own lack of core principles. They sought refuge in platitudes which recalled the style of a better age because they could not articulate a vision of the future.

A new Tory Party which believes in a strong independent nation and dignified independent individuals will not need to equivocate. Its leaders will not need pinstripes to convey authority, because their ideas will command attention.

The Tories should reject the identity politics which balkanises Britain, and make their appeal universal by developing a language of opportunity and aspiration. That language will ridicule and puncture, exploit the opportunities of a new media and ask, always, why individuals should not be allowed to exercise the maximum control over their own lives.

Personalities who exemplify the emancipating power of past Tory successes, figures from outside traditional establishment nurseries, should be in the vanguard of any Tory revival. Hague should promote Scottish meritocrats like Liam Fox[22] and Welsh street fighters like Nigel Evans[23], who have never apologised for their Toryism and fought for their beliefs in hostile territory. They are men in his own mould and will reinforce the impression he could create of the Tories as an insurgent force. The US Republicans have succeeded in identifying the Democrats with Old Corruption, the new Tories are perfectly placed to make Blair seem the conformist, the beltway bureaucrat in opposition to the liberating right. The old opposition between Court and Country should be revived with Blair as the metropolitan wire-puller and Hague speaking up for the overlooked outsiders. He could learn from the Australian premier John Howard, who made his party the vehicle for everyman, 'the strugglers', against the new establishment of Labor.

There should also be a role for politicians such as Michael Portillo and Oliver Letwin, gracious intellectuals whose backgrounds make them natural outsiders, figures whose natural dignity and attachment to liberty contrast with the constricting, restricting Blairites.

Arguing for freedom – a free nation and free individuals – would give the Tories a banner under which to fight on a battleground where the enemy has abandoned all its old standards and rallying points. In the battle between the managerial and the ideological, the ideological must triumph because it has the capacity to quicken the pulse, to stir the heart, and remind the voters why politicians pursue office; and this will make it more likely that they will win it. Without ideology, or principle, the pursuit of office is empty, a spectacle without content

NOTES

1. Filippo Marinetti in *Futurismo e fascismo* – reprinted in *Fascism – an Oxford Reader*, edited by Roger Griffin, Oxford 1995. Marinetti was the founding father of the Italian Futurist movement and, according to Griffin 'the extreme embodiment of the modernising anti-conservative thrust of Fascism'.

2. The Government's attitude to Formula One was criticised by Martin Jacques in *The Observer* 9 November, 1997, Andrew Rawnsley in *The Observer* 16 November 1997, and John Lloyd in *The Times* 14 November 1997. All three journalists were, broadly, supporters of the Blair leadership.

3. See Donald Macintyre in the *Independent*, 10 and 19 June 1997, Phillip Stephens in the *Financial Times*, 21 April 1997 and 3 December 1996, and Peter Riddell in *The Times*, 25 May 1998. Three journalists close to the Blair leadership arguing the case for pragmatism in a party which none of them support.

4. Tony Blair, 8 January 1998, speech on the British assumption of the EU Presidency.

5. Harold Wilson, 1 October 1962, speech to the Labour Party Conference.

6. MAFF scientists have confirmed the chance of contracting CJD from eating beef on the bone is 1.2 billion to one – less than the chance of being struck by lightning. Reported in the *Sunday Telegraph* on 15 February 1998.

7. The *British Medical Journal* in October 1997 argued that non-smokers living with smokers had a 25 per cent chance of contracting lung cancer, but the World Health Organisation records no definitive statistical evidence of a link. The case is unproven but the risk from passive smoking is not less than 1.2 billion to one. Reported in the *Sunday Telegraph*, 8 March 1998.

8. Barbara Roche on BBC *Any Questions?*, 13 March 1998.

9. Paul Foot in *The Guardian*, 15 December 1997. The comparison has also been made by Hugh Macpherson in *Tribune*.

10. Peter Riddell in *The Times*, 8 January 1996. Mr Blair is, of course, an admirer of Gladstone's biographer, Lord Jenkins of Hillhead.

11. Tony Blair in a speech to a Labour Party Special Conference in Westminster Central Hall on 29 April 1995.

12. Tony Blair in speech to Labour Party Conference in Blackpool, 1 October 1996.

13. The most recent statement of Iain Gilmour's admirably fixed views is in his book *Whatever Happened to the Tories ?*, Fourth Estate 1997. Roy Hattersley's weekly *Guardian* column is the best contemporary statement of straightforward re-distributionist social democracy.

14. Alan Watkins, in *The Independent*, on Sunday, 7 December 1997.

15. Michael Portillo's argument for ultra-low taxation was made at a meeting of the Conservative Political Centre at Limpley Stoke, and published in a CPC pamphlet in 1992. Steve Forbes articulated his case for the flat tax through his family magazine *Forbes* and on the stump during his bid for the republican nomination in the 1996 US Presidential election.

16. Philip Collins, a former aide to Frank Field, and Iain Corfield, a past Head of Research at the Fabians, have established a new body, The Open Society, to press for liberal values within new Labour.

17. David Willetts, *Modern Conservatism*, Penguin 1992.

18. Enoch Powell, quoted in T.E. Utley, *Enoch Powell, the Man and his Thinking*, William Kimber 1968.

19. *All Must Have Prizes*, Warner 1998, is the best guide to Phillips's thinking on issues of central concern.

20 Alan Duncan and Dominic Hobson, *Saturn's Children*, Sinclair-Stevenson 1995.

21. Michael Portillo, *The Ghost of Conservatism Past, the Spirit of Conservatism Future*, 9 October, 1997.

22. Liam Fox, MP for Woodspring since 1992, is a 37 year old frontbencher, educated in the state sector, with experience of the NHS as a GP. A talented speaker, he is destined for higher things. A supporter of Michael Howard in the first ballot of the 1997 Tory leadership election, he subsequently transferred to William Hague.

23. Nigel Evans, MP for Ribble Valley since 1992, is a 41-year-old frontbencher educated in the state sector with experience of enterprise from his family's small business. A supporter of William Hague throughout the 1997 leadership election he has an easy, demotic style.

ANXIETY AND IDENTIFICATION ON THE BRITISH LEFT

Kevin Davey

As it tries to find a third way between corporatism and *laissez faire*, new Labour will will be confronted again and again with a choice which, when it is finally made, will define the nature of its administration and the future shape of what, for want of a better phrase, I will call 'the left'.

As it endeavours to make Britain a strong and socially inclusive competitor in the world economy, Labour must answer crucial questions. Does it wish to remain a populist government with a strong executive and a cautious programme of constitutional reform and devolved responsibility, driven by the twin imperatives of maximising competitiveness and the need to secure local legitimacy for fiscal constraint? Or is it a genuinely democratic, pluralist and decentralising initiative, committed to restructuring the field of politics and capable of ceding power and not just responsibility to partners and opponents alike?

The first option may guarantee the delivery of its immediate social and economic objectives and re-election, perhaps with reduced public support, early in the new millennium. But how effectively a technocratic elite will retain the people's trust, or even its party membership, for a thoroughgoing yet parsimonious modernisation of Britain is open to question, notwithstanding Labour's skilled management of the news agenda. Nor is this mode of politics conducive to the partnerships needed for the transformations of economy and culture the government seeks. Charismatic unaccountability is the strategy of the gambler who feels that luck and the dice – one loaded with an unprecedented majority, the other with an almost unchecked executive – are both on his side.

The creation of a new kind of state, the second course of action, would multiply the spaces for political participation. It would provide the opportunity for new, and perhaps competing, regional, national and transnational political formations to take up wider social responsibilities and provide leadership in their own sectors of activity. These new political formations might result from new social identities and partnerships in civil society, from non-violent direct action and DIY movements or alliances of non-governmental organisations. This is the option of the self-denying ordinance, in which power is relinquished to others, best symbolised, if not yet enacted, by the Lords appointed to reform the House of Lords. The incorporation of the European Convention on Human Rights and legislation on Freedom of Information are tentative steps in this direction. But for elected representatives and party leaderships the acid tests of their democratic commitment will be the referendum and legislation on proportional representation in the House of Commons and relations with the Welsh and Northern Irish Assemblies, the Scottish Parliament, regional bodies and citizens newly empowered by rights legislation.

The future of British politics, and the shape of the left, is at stake in Labour's dilemma over whether to adopt the gambler's hunch or the self-denying ordinance. Put simply, by sustaining the old modes and practices of power, a centralised government which trusts to its luck is likely to give an unexpected lease of life to an old, backward-looking and oppositionalist left. The alternative, a genuine dissemination of power and decision-making, would compel participation, partnership and the final transformation or acquiescence of the left critics of new Labour.

Labour has already begun to open up new political spaces by moving towards an untried form of multi-tiered government through its cautious deepening of Britain's economic and political integration with the European Union, the introduction of a devolved United Kingdom, including new assemblies, rearrangements of local government and the introduction of regional regeneration bodies, and by agreeing to base most democratic accountabilities – with the exception, to date, of the House of Commons – on proportional voting systems.

Although the detail of these decisions may be calculated to strengthen the hold of the dominant parties in the short term, if new Labour continues on this course, over time we are likely to see the emergence of a range of popular, inclusive and egalitarian political formations – which may or may not function as parties – that are committed to modernising local and national institutions and setting limits to the operation of the market.

This non singular, polycentric force may well be called a 'left' (particularly by those who oppose it) but it is unlikely to resemble much that has traded under that name in the past. For socialists who wish to make the transition to a new political relevance, a prior transition to a new political identification and practice of politics is required. The old tools of the trade are blunt and must be laid to one side: these include nationalisation, with or without workers control; trade union and CLP steerage of decision-making; unilateral national action on tax, spending and trade; and the provision of standardised housing, education and health. There is also a need to discard sectionalism, substitution for the community and non-accountability – all of these were characteristics of many wage struggles in the 1980s, and of moribund left wing constituency parties. They were also a feature of the miner's strike and of attempts to snatch the leadership of new movements such as campaigns against racism, road building and the Criminal Justice Act.

A new sense of agency is required, plus an approach to issues that recognises the importance of pluralism, choice and partnership in the mechanisms adopted to regulate the market. That realisation is now dawning in Britain, albeit belatedly and accompanied by a great deal of doubt and anxiety. It was last prompted by the activities of the Greater London Council.[1] It is the commonsense of civil society. Politically, it is best exemplified by the government's willingness to test drive a range of innovative ideas and by the post-communist deliberation and practice of Democratic Left, a non singular networking force committed to 'a flowering of left experiments' with 'rich enough flows of communication between the different projects for there to be an overall learning process.'[2]

However, the future of the left is only partly in its own hands. Recidivism is likely to occur to the degree that new Labour plays the gambler's hunch and remains an elitist and non-participatory project, or fails in the tasks it has set itself.

THE RESIDUAL LEFT MAKES ITS TRADITIONAL WAGER

Throughout Europe, large, often communist, electoral competitors to the left of mainstream socialist and social democratic parties have disappeared. In Britain, where none was ever successfully established, what used to be called the left has been reduced and marginalised. That left was by and large a state socialist initiative, which drew on, or disputed, the Labour Party's political deployment of the resources of a sectional trade union movement and working class neighbourhood cultures.

Today this greying and residual left pines for a multiple restoration:

for the return of trade union rights, for the return to state ownership of privatised services and industries; for the return of tax and spend; for the return to Westminster of the economic discretion ceded by European treaties; and for the return of the power to define Labour Party policy to its conference.

Although each strand in the argument has its local strengths and in some cases a significant degree of public support, as a bid for hegemony it is clearly inadequate. Its supporters are the impotent Jacobin and disgruntled Jacobite fringe of contemporary politics, convinced that a tight knit group of outsiders and compromisers have taken over the leadership of the Labour movement.[3] They wish to re-occupy positions rejected by the electorate and abandoned by Neil Kinnock after the 1987 defeat. Today the never-ending battle to retain social and political authority is being fought around new ways to raise public revenues and make their spending accountable; over new forms of pooling sovereignty; and over new forms of conducting politics, guaranteeing choice and raising living standards.

The residual left is at its strongest in Scotland and Wales, where Thatcher's English nationalism had the greatest impact on manufacturing employment and public spending, Labour heartlands far from the London-based redefinition of the purpose and structures of the party engineered by Kinnock and completed by Blair. It spoke out at the Scottish Labour Party conference in Perth early in 1998, describing benefit cuts as 'economically inept, morally repugnant and spiritually bereft.' It will continue to be heard, refracted by nationalism and tongue-tied by party loyalty, in the Scottish Parliament and Welsh Assembly, where Scottish and Welsh Labour, the Scottish Nationalist Party and the trade unions have a more traditional social democratic agenda than Number Ten. But in England, and in the south-east in particular, the exigencies of the electoral battlefield have reconfigured Labour almost to the point of this left's extinction.

Traditional left formations, based on a linkage between trade unions, grassroot campaigns and Labour Party constituency branches, may undergo shortlived resurrections in England as Labour's modernising project restructures our welfare arrangements, shifting some of the burden back to the individual, in an attempt to make them sustainable; as it lays its bets almost exclusively on labour market flexibility and supply side measures intended to enhance employability as the means to increase levels of employment; and as it directs moralising, normative blasts of zeal in the direction of single parents, the unemployed, truants, teachers, trade unionists and recreational drug users, groups who are members, or the clients and children of members of its own coalition of support. The durability and likely outcomes of Labour's new strategy in office are as yet unpredictable. As Robin Blackburn has suggested, 'The rhetoric about "one nation" will return to haunt new Labour if substantial progress is not made towards reducing inequality in four or five years.'[4] A new and stable settlement cannot be assumed. This is where the old left, in and outside the Labour Party has placed its traditional bet, perhaps for the last time.[5]

Labour insiders such as the Campaign Group and supporters of the weekly newspaper *Tribune*, and seasoned outsiders such as the Socialist Workers' Party, all scent the possibility of a rearguard action against neo-liberalism and welfare reform, based on the large residue of public support for an older welfare settlement and the potential militancy of public sector workers, fuelled by resistance to erosion of democracy and the influence of the trade unions in the Labour Party. The wager of the left, both in and outside the Labour Party, is that a large consensus in favour of universal benefits, higher minimum wage, tax increases for the better off, increased employment rights and rapid improvement and resourcing of public services will not forever remain unexpressed.[6]

But this approach has a limited purchase on national politics – it may, at best, have some capacity to hustle or destabilise the Blair government, but it does not have the capacity or vision required to create an alternative hegemony, or electoral victory on new terms. There is no charmed psephological pendulum that will bring new life to this left, no invisible political or economic hand that will re-empower it in its current form.

The residual left has not only been marginalised by the Labour leadership, it has also talked itself into a corner. Its political discourse and restricted social base limit the forms of action it can endorse and initiate, frequently dissociating it from the new dynamics of British modernity: increasing civil diversity; multiracial urban youth cultures; democratisation; the proliferation of identities not registered in older political discourses; the transformation of communications and the linked mediatisation of politics; Europeanisation; the restructuring of economic sectors and workplaces as a result of globalisation with its insistent pressure for labour flexibility. Neither has this left acknowledged that power, while it may be articulated by the state and the circuits of capital, is also generated and located outside them – in culture and in representation as well as in institutions; in language and lifestyle choices as well as in the financial system and the legislature.

The themes of the Labour leadership and of the residual left are a regression from earlier attempts to articulate democracy and socialist discourses.[7] As Panitch and Leys argue, it was the Bennite left in the Labour Party in the 1970s which first saw the need to break with state socialism and Labour Party routines and create a new type of state and a different type of party.[8] The Greater London Council experimented with popular forms of planning, participatory forms of policy and decision making, and local post-Keynesian economic strategies in the 1980s.[9] Empowerment was also a touchstone of the Bennite movement, though compromised by an over emphasis on party activism. By contrast today's restorationist left has adopted a far more defensive posture, precisely because these themes have been re-articulated to the Blair agenda.

Firstly, the restorationist left has talked itself out of partnerships with agencies for democracy by claiming that national government is the motivation for electoral reform. The end of the first past the post system, they argue, will 'make possible a long term governmental alliance with the Liberal Democrats and, if possible, the Heseltine-Clarke wing of the Tory party.'[10] This left thus unmasks Tony Blair as 'a latter day Ramsey MacDonald.'[11]

Secondly, its idea of where public power should be located – in the relationship between constituency labour parties, trade unions and a subordinate government front bench – has long been discredited as unrepresentative. And this idea of power is also divorced from that held by a much changed electorate which, as Barnett argues, has voted decisively against all political forces which are identified with the old, non-European, Greater Britain, along with its pre-modern political culture and institutions and the sovereignty of the House of Commons.[12]

Thirdly, it has yet to understand the identifications generating and mobilised by nationalism and constitutional reform within the United Kingdom, nor indeed does it understand the process of identification itself.[13] And, in common with the hard left throughout Europe, Britain's residual statist left is a reluctant participant in the process of European integration.[14]

EUROPE: AN OLD TUNE IN A NEW KEY?

Acknowledging that the centre not only can, but will continue to, hold and that one nation Keynesianism has had its day, a growing number of radical intellectuals have re-articulated the themes and objectives of this residual left to larger scale regulatory possibilities offered by European integration.[15] By raising its sights one tier above Westminster, this section of the left not only makes a Keynesian and interventionist strategy more credible, it also finds new partners – similar left fragments on the continent – and receives a hearing from more traditionally social democratic, social Catholic or corporatist parties.

Blair has characterised the preferences of this hybrid residual-emergent left as a 'Eurosclerosis' that must be avoided at all costs, and replaced with a commitment to flexible labour markets, fiscal and monetary caution and welfare reform. As John Lloyd has rightly pointed out, 'Labour embraced the Union at the end of the eighties and in the first half of the nineties, but is becoming more sceptical once more because it sees the EU as too left-wing, too interventionist and obsessed with social controls.'[16] Former Labour MEPs Hugh Kerr and Ken Coates, expelled in 1997, were the first casualties in this conflict. However, it is in this space that the most substantial, and transnational, challenge to the priorities of new Labour may well be mounted. It is, after all, the arena in which its predecessor stumbled, divided and fell.

IDENTIFICATION AND ABJECTION ON THE RESIDUAL LEFT

Whatever the European prospect, at home the old left's ageing tropes imprison it in forms of thought and action that are disconnected from Britain's new social dynamics. They are difficult if not impossible to articulate with the themes of new Labour and the diverse concerns of those who currently lend it their support.

These historic tropes include:

> The vacuum on the left: the notion that as Labour moves to the right, many people do not follow it but find themselves unrepresented, providing a political base for any left brave enough to address it.[17]

> Class politics: the notion that the 'last instance' will come and economic forces, agents and interests will once again clearly determine the social and political field.

> The social evil of markets: an alertness to the non-egalitarian mechanisms and effects of the market which prompts a search for fundamentally different ways of managing production and distribution and exchange.

The need for strong intervention by the state in production, distribution and exchange: the traditional outcome of the above quest.

This discourse is common to the 15,000 residual Marxists of the Socialist Movement, the Communist Party of Britain and the *Morning Star*, the Socialist Party, the Socialist Labour Party, the national and regional Socialist Alliances, and the Socialist Worker's Party, as well as to the Campaign Group of Labour MPs and its supporters network, Labour Left Liaison, the weekly newspaper *Tribune* and the supporters of Labour Left Briefing. It even extends to significant parts of the Green Party. It unites the diverse and fissiparous bloc – including expelled EuroKeynesian Labour MEPs – which is conducting or considering electoral challenges to labour.

Like all identities, it is constructed by a process of abjection and differentiation. Abjection, in the words of the French psychoanalyst and political philosopher Julia Kristeva is 'something that disgusts you, for example, you see something rotting and you want to vomit – it is an extremely strong feeling that is at once somatic and symbolic, which is above all a revolt against an external menace from which one wants to distance oneself, but of which one has the impression that it may menace us from the inside.'[18]

Abjection is a primary distinction enabling an identification to take place. In the political identifications made by the residual Marxist left, it involves a dissociation from markets and an ambivalence about the capitalist state. Both are viewed with anxiety, at the very least, and with horror and disgust in the most extreme cases. Yet the very practice of politics brings this left into constant and intimate contact with its abjections. The regular challenge to the boundaries that constitute it usually causes anxiety and confusion, followed by the deployment of defensive tropes about fundamental economic realities and the need for planning accompanied by varying degrees of democracy.

Unable to accept the new terms of reference for political action, this left frequently abjects many aspects of political modernity itself. 'Like a deadly oil slick, Thatcherism has got everywhere,' *Red Pepper* laments.[19] *Workers Liberty* complains of 'The paralysing bureaucratisation that is creeping like black ice over politics.'[20]

The very characterisations of hard left and soft left – and their characteristic modes of politics – are based on the degree to which their language provides a carapace or permeable, flexible boundary to their identification as socialists.

An abjection of markets and the capitalist state is firmly adhered to by the hard left outside the Labour Party. For the 800-strong Socialist Party, based on expelled and refugee members of Militant, and for the Socialist Labour Party, Scargill's 1500-strong authoritarian alternative, the Labour party denuded of its state socialist aspirations and practices is nothing but a Conservative Party. This assessment is also shared by more libertarian voices: 'New Labour's economic project is little more than a variant on Thatcher's neo-liberalism,' says the editor of *Red Pepper*.[21] *Labour Left Briefing* concurs: it is 'a government which is Labour in name only.'[22]

The discourse that characterises new Labour as conservative unites the left in and outside the Labour Party. 'Everything they say of new Labour is right,' said *Briefing's* editor, of the expulsion of Ken Coates and Hugh Kerr, two Labour MEPs. 'But politics is about timing and strategy.'[23]

Tony Benn and the Campaign Group share this view of the leadership, but counsel against a breakaway. They appear prepared to endure almost any humiliation by the leadership in order to preserve the illusion that their day will come, that at some point in the future, after a shift of power in the Labour Party, the first-past-the-post electoral system will place them in control of a strong executive, which they will deploy against the operation of the market.[24]

What has kept these hopes alive? The wide alliance which mobilised against the restructuring of the Labour Party in accordance with the proposals in Partnership in Power. However, this resistance to centralisation was mounted to prevent any unrepresentative leadership, even unlikely candidates such as the Campaign Group, escaping accountability to the party mainstream. The second factor was the scale of the parliamentary protest against reductions in lone parent benefit late in 1997. This, though, was clearly more Blairite than anti-Blair in its composition. Thirdly, there was a 40 per cent vote for Socialist Campaign Group candidates in the October 1997 elections to Labour's National Executive. This, however, must be seen as a form of political insurance, a pragmatic counterbalance to an ambitious new project rather than a direct expression of support for the policies of 1983, to which the Campaign Group remains wedded.

The keepers of the state socialist flame believe that the trade unions and the defenders of welfare services will one day have nowhere else to turn. This left will therefore neither turn its back on Labour, nor risk being thrown out, before that historic vindication, a reunion which it believes is being hastened by high interest rates and the high pound, the twin harbingers of an economic downturn.

Willpower and tenacity may not be enough. As sections of this left anxiously consider jumping, they also know they may be pushed. These socialists increasingly wonder which will come first: expulsion from Labour or the opportunity for a major split. It is capable of grand illusions: 'The exclusion of the left from the Labour party would simply result in the emergence of a new party to the left of new Labour, with serious electoral support.'[25]

In England there is no evidence for this claim, neither in the electoral performance of the Socialist Labour Party (SLP) nor in the enthusiastic citation of European precedents – Die Grunen in Germany, Rifondazione Comunista in Italy, Izquierda Unida in Spain, the People's Socialist Parties of Norway and Denmark – it would like to follow.

When the SLP was founded in Britain in 1996 it invited 'all socialists and communists' to take out membership. The result was an appalling and unsuccessful bear garden of warring Stalinists, Maoists, homophobes, Trotskyists and left wing trade unionists that was bullied into quiescence or departure by an unaccountable leadership.[26] The move from Labour to the SLP was described by one bisexual convert as a move from 'the frying pan into the fire.'[27] Another disillusioned recruit described how the Lancashire Area of the National Union of Miners deployed a block vote representing 75 per cent of the total available at the party's second congress.[28] Far from indicating the possibility of a sustainable political alternative, this left is electorally insignificant, undemocratic and prey to a vicious internal culture. It has exerted no check from the left on the Labour leadership's aspirations, nor is it likely to do so.

A number of socialists, statist and libertarian, are joining the Green Party because it already has a network that can fight elections and it receives a protest vote from the left. It is regarded as a beneficiary of the alleged vacuum on the left rather than a serious political formation in its own right. Others are discussing and lobbying for another new party to be launched in this marginal space.

Hilary Wainwright, the editor of *Red Pepper*, a radical monthly which has hard and libertarian left constituents amongst its 7000 readers, has cautioned against impulsive behaviour and any green/left confrontation with the majority of state socialists who will remain, come what may, inside the Labour Party. Proportional representation is a precondition for an electoral challenge, she argues, and while this may license candidates in Scotland, Wales and in elections to the European Parliament, it also rules out any contest between the English left and Labour. 'It would be foolish if frustration with Labour led to a green/left Scargillism, arrogantly forming a political party rather than creating alliances on practical issues and building a base for moments when Labour's divisions deepen and an electoral challenge could have a serious impact.'[29]

The residual statist left defines itself through a discourse drawing on the concepts of a vacuum on the left, class politics, the evil of the market and the need for major state intervention, the latter varying greatly in its democratic nature. It polices this discourse, often fiercely, in its journals, campaigns and slogans in opposition to something it calls 'The Right', a hydra-headed figure that is acknowledged to have hard and soft faces, but whose unitary body is composed of anyone who does not share the characterisation of new Labour as Conservative.

Statements defining who is in and who is out of this left – and in particular, who is drifting to the right – use up a considerable amount of the limited resources of this fissile and unimaginative formation. The residual statist Left is fundamentally constructed as oppositionalist, and although this means it is sometimes positional rather than essen-tialist in its practice, it is still unable to act effectively in Anglo-British politics. An elite led modernisation that does not go smoothly may lead to a brief revival of its fortunes. A genuine decentralisation and empowerment would confirm its marginality and redundancy.

LEFT REALPOLITIK: REDISTRIBUTIVE STAKEHOLDING

In Britain today there is a second language of leftism based on an attempt to engage with new Labour's governmental project, but which retains some older socialist reflexes and assumptions.

The tropes of this subordinated left, which has some possibility of influence and power as Labour's project evolves and as the tensions grow within its coalition of support, include:

> stakeholding (and its figurative opposites the selfish and short termist shareholder and the trade union militant).[30]

> redistribution (and its figurative opposites, the overpaid executive, and the tax averse wage earner);

a definition of social exclusion that accepts the priority of reconnecting a small underclass to work, education, housing and health, but which does not relinquish the objective of wider ranging action against poverty;

loyalty to the party (and its figurative opposites, the irresponsible left and the splitters).

These tropes articulate the identities of established political subjects – the trade unions, the welfare professional, Labour councillors, all of whom have loyalties that compete with the government – with aspects of the Blair project. As a political discourse it constructs these subjects, redefines their problems and sets boundaries to their proper conduct and behaviour. This left knows that Labour is not a Conservative government, and cites the introduction of a minimum wage, constitutional reform and steps towards trade union recognition and EMU as evidence.

Redistributive stakeholding is the language of the cabinet left (Robin Cook and Clare Short), of Will Hutton, the TUC, *Chartist* magazine, and many of those who aspire to a modern social democracy based on European models. It is sometimes integrated with an older social democratic emphasis, such as that articulated by Roy Hattersley.

As a political identification redistributive stakeholding is positional. This left has few boundary anxieties. It tends to address real problems rather than abjectly constructed enemies, and it may, under certain conditions, come to provide the basis for a new deal between many of the existing members of Labour's coalition. However, it also risks indistinction and a long term subordination to the neo-liberal, elite driven modernising project that is the gambler's hunch. And it is not innocent of an old vice of the Labour left: putting the party before the public.

THE OLD VICE: PUTTING THE PARTY FIRST

The two lefts within the Labour Party, the subordinate and the residual, have shown little interest in the self appointed leaderships who are jostling and manoeuvring outside the party in order to benefit from the alleged vacuum on the left and their imagined exodus. Instead, where they are engaged at all, they have become preoccupied with the impact of party reorganisation on their networks and powers, displaying an old trait of the Labour left which Eric Hobsbawm once identified as 'the illusion ... that organisation can replace politics.'[31]

Since the election these lefts have been engaged in a battle against the reform of Labour Party structures, apparently believing that there is a disenfranchised non-Blairite majority in the party.[32] One of the strongest functioning left networks, Labour Reform, is focused almost exclusively on the need to replace centralised decision-making by a partnership between all elements of the party.

Joint policy committees and changes to the constitution of the National Executive Committee have indeed replaced local policy making and the potential for conference confrontations between party and government. 'This might work if the parliamentary leadership were infallible,' said Ken Livingstone. 'But it never will be and that is why the checks and balances of a democratic party are essential.'[33]

'We did not fight for one member, one vote to have it taken away by party apparatchiks or Mandelsonite fixers,' argues *Chartist*.[34] Both kinds of Labour left are likely to get involved in internal battles over the process by which policy is agreed, implemented and developed, how candidates for the London Mayor, the European and Scottish Parliaments and the Welsh Assembly will be selected and whether or not Campaign Group MPs will be allowed to stand as candidates in the next general election. Sadly, there are few signs that they have learnt how to make this relevant to the public.

There are a number of networks and forces which prioritise the democratisation of aspects of the British state, either as a freestanding priority or as the essential prelude for the pursuit of a distinct but deferred political agenda. They operate as a left in so far as they challenge the priorities, preferences or pace of the Labour leadership and organise themselves to exert pressure on the party of government. These organisations range from Scottish Labour, the Scottish National Party and Plaid Cymru through Charter 88 to Democratic Left, the Voting Reform Group and the Young Liberal Democrats.

This contemporary revival of Chartism, understanding but not foregrounding the link between our economic ills and the form of political representation, but prioritising democratic reform, offers an important positional, even prepositional form of politics. It is by nature a pluralist convergence of political subjects, and therefore a new and perhaps prefigurative mode of politics. How long it can be considered a pressure from the left is a matter for debate, for its ambiguities over social and economic issues, and its instrumental self denial, may involve an abjection of traditional left agendas.

SPEAKEASIES AND HEGEMONY

Taking Blair's Third Way as the new centre ground, Britain's lefts are constructed by four partially overlapping discourses: residual state socialism, its shrinking Marxist-Leninist shadow, redistributive stake-holding and pluralist democratisation. None is a fully coherent project or a comprehensive alternative to the Blair agenda. Some public figures – Robin Cook, Clare Short, David Blunkett, Ken Livingstone and a number of Liberal Democrats are among them – oscillate between two or more of these positions, in an uncomfortable hybrid space that may be the cause of their distinction. They could be the points around which alternative hegemonic discourses will coalesce, but they will not originate them.

So who will sustain the culture of engaged, collective (but free) thinking about practical futures essential to any feasible future left? A number of think tanks have already laid claim to the role: the Institute for Public Policy Research, Demos, the Fabian Society, Nexus and Catalyst. Most of these, though, are linked to the Labour leadership or to the redistributive stakeholding left. The same is true of the left's small stakes in print and digital media, where residual state socialism and Marxism also have holdings.

As a result it falls to self managing initiatives such as the Signs of the Times network, sustained by members of many parties and account-able to none, to prefigure and help define the new pluralist spaces, discursive and institutional, in which politics will increasingly be conducted. These networks escape the problem of parties, which are not only forced to differentiate themselves from others in a competi-tion for support but are also increasingly compelled to create unitary voices, closing debate.

These speakeasies are important because new Labour's vision, whether it goes for the gambler's hunch or the self denying ordinance, is unstable and improvised rather than hegemonic.[35] They are important as well because there is a need to re-examine the non-statist and democra-tic forms of regulation and intervention offered by utopian, co-opera-tive, guild, syndicate and market socialist traditions. Finally, they are important because the antagonistic, subordinate and democratising lefts, in their own ways, effect premature closure on the forms of thinking essential to the creation of a networked and polycentric political agency: an agency that might possibly consider itself, in a generous recognition of its fragile and compromised genealogy, to be a New Left.

NOTES

1. For an advocate's account of the GLC's break with the traditional practice of the left, see Hilary Wainwright, *Labour: A Tale of Two Parties*, Hogarth, London 1987, pp253-65 and Maureen Mackintosh and Hilary Wainwright (eds), *A Taste of Power*, Verso, London 1987. There is also a useful overview in Stewart Lansley, Sue Goss and Christian Wolmar, *Councils in Conflict: The Rise and Fall of the Municipal Left*, Macmillan, London 1989.

2. Nina Temple, 'What I mean by Left' in *New Times*, 7 June 1997, p10. See also Democratic Left, *New Times, New Labour – Arguments Towards a Democratic Left*, London 1996.

3. The Jacobins were a radical statist faction of the French revolutionary movement; they campaigned, unsuccessfully, to return the throne to the Stuart family after the Glorious Revolution of 1688.

4. Robin Blackburn, 'Reflections on Blair's Velvet Revolution', *New Left Review*, 223 May-June 1997, p11.

5. See, for example, 'Revolt Against Welfare Cuts: A Big Movement is Now Possible', *Workers' Liberty*, January 1998, p3; and 'Simple Majority Rule', *Socialist Review*, May 1998, p3.

6. Mike Marqusee, 'New Labour and its Discontents', *New Left Review*, 224 July-August 1997, pp127-42.

7. See Kevin Davey, 'Waking Up to New Times: Doubts and Dilemmas on the Left' in Mark Perryman (ed), *Altered States: Postmodernism, Politics, Culture*, Lawrence and Wishart, London 1994, pp195-217.

8. Leo Panitch and Colin Leys, *The End of Parliamentary Socialism: From New Left to New Labour*, Verso, London 1997.

9. See note 1 above.

10. 'Battle Joined Over Labour's Future', Editorial, *Socialist Action*, 2:8, Feb-Mar 1998, p3.

11. Louise Lang, 'New Labour faces New Left', *Socialist Action*, 2:8, Feb-Mar 1998, p7.

12. Anthony Barnett, *This Time: Our Constitutional Revolution*, Vintage, London 1997.

13. See Kevin Davey, *English Imaginaries*, Lawrence and Wishart, London 1998.

14. See Donald Sassoon (ed), *Looking Left: European Socialism After the Cold War*, I B Taurus, London 1997, p13.

15. This work was commenced by Tom Nairn, particularly in the essay 'The Marxist Nation: Buridan's Ass' in Tom Nairn, *The Left Against Europe?*, Penguin, London 1973, pp122-151. EuroKeynesianism also informs the

account provided by Paul Anderson and Nyta Mann, *Safety First: The Making of New Labour*, Granta Books, London 1997. For a polemical account of the emergence of new Labour written from this position, see Michael Barratt Brown and Ken Coates, *The Blair Revelation: Deliverance for Whom?*, Spokesman Books, Nottingham 1996.

16. John Lloyd, 'A Very British Lead', *New Statesman* 2 January 1998, pp10-11.

17. This has been a central trope of the British left for thirty years, from the time of the 'The Vacuum on the Left', editorial, *International Socialism* 34, Autumn 1968 right through to 'Naught's Well That Ends Welfare', editorial, *Tribune*, 19-26 December 1997, p4.

18. Julia Kristeva, quoted in Elaine Hoffman Baruch, 'Feminism and Psychoanalysis' in Ross Mitchell Guberman (ed), *Julia Kristeva: Interviews*, Columbia University Press, New York 1996, p118.

19. Hilary Wainwright, 'Inside or Out, it's time to talk', *Red Pepper*, February 1998, p5.

20. Editorial, 'The Crisis of New Labour – The End of Choice at the Ballot Box', *Workers' Liberty*, September 1997, p3.

21. Hilary Wainwright, in *Workers' Liberty*, September 1997, p9.

22. Editorial, *Labour Left Briefing*, September 1997, p3

23. Alistair Ward, 'Good Policies, Bad Tactics', *Labour Left Briefing*, February 1998, p18.

24. 'The Crisis of New Labour – The End of Choice at the Ballot Box', in *Worker's Liberty*, September 1997, p3.

25. 'Battle Joined Over Labour's Future', Editorial, *Socialist Action*, 2:8, Feb-Mar 1998, p3.

26. The best and most detailed account of the internal life of the Socialist Labour Party is Ian Dudley, 'The Socialist Labour Party: From Opportunity to Obstacle' in *What Next?*, no 7, 1998, pp-9-16.

27. Ian Driver, 'Scargill's Socialist Labour Party', *What Next?*, 6 1997, p5.

28. David Taylor, 'The Party's Over', *Labour Left Briefing*, February 1998, p19. See also Alam McArthur, 'Socialist Labour Party Severely Injured', *Workers' Liberty*, January 1998, p48.

29. Hilary Wainwright, 'Opportunities for a Creative Challenge', *Red Pepper*, December 1997, p5.

30. Will Hutton, *The State We're In*, Jonathan Cape, London 1995 and *The State to Come*, Vintage, London 1997. See also the extended exploration in Gavin Kelly, Dominic Kelly and Andrew Gamble (eds), *Stakeholder Capitalism*, Macmillan, London 1997.

31. Eric Hobsbawm, *Politics for a Rational Left*, Verso, London 1989, p34.

32. Mike Marqusee, 'New Labour and its Discontents', *New Left Review* 224 July-August 1997, p131.

33. Ken Livingstone, 'An Unequal Kind of Partnership', *New Statesman*, 29 August 1997, p12.

34. Editorial, 'Two Cheers for new Labour', *Chartist*, May-June 1998, p5.

35. As I argued in Kevin Davey, 'The Impermanence of New Labour' in Mark Perryman (ed), *The Blair Agenda*, Lawrence and Wishart, London 1996, pp76-99.

INDEX